H is for Hawk

ALSO BY HELEN MACDONALD

Shaler's Fish
Falcon

HELEN MACDONALD

H is for Hawk

JONATHAN CAPE
LONDON

Published by Jonathan Cape 2014

10

Copyright © Helen Macdonald 2014

Helen Macdonald has asserted her right under the Copyright, Designs and Patents Act 1988 to be identified as the author of this work

Letter on p.192 © Copyright Siegfried Sassoon by kind permission of the Estate of George Sassoon.
Lines from 'Consider this' by W. H. Auden copyright © 1930 by W. H. Auden, renewed. Reprinted by permission of Curtis Brown, Ltd.
Extracts from selected unpublished works by T. H. White by permission of Harry Ransom Center, The University of Texas at Austin.
Extracts from selected published works by T. H. White by permission of the Estate of T. H. White.

First published in Great Britain in 2014 by
Jonathan Cape
Random House, 20 Vauxhall Bridge Road,
London SW1V 2SA

www.vintage-books.co.uk

Addresses for companies within The Random House Group Limited can be found at:
www.randomhouse.co.uk/offices.htm

The Random House Group Limited Reg. No. 954009

A CIP catalogue record for this book is available from the British Library

ISBN 9780224097000

The Random House Group Limited supports the Forest Stewardship Council® (FSC®), the leading international forest-certification organisation. Our books carrying the FSC label are printed on FSC®-certified paper. FSC is the only forest-certification scheme supported by the leading environmental organisations, including Greenpeace. Our paper procurement policy can be found at www.randomhouse.co.uk/environment

Typeset in Sabon by Palimpsest Book Production Limited,
Falkirk, Stirlingshire

Printed and bound in Germany by GGP Media GmbH, Pößneck

To my family

Contents

H is for Hawk

PART I

I

Patience

Forty-five minutes north-east of Cambridge is a landscape I've come to love very much indeed. It's where wet fen gives way to parched sand. It's a land of twisted pine trees, burned-out cars, shotgun-peppered road signs and US Air Force bases. There are ghosts here: houses crumble inside numbered blocks of pine forestry. There are spaces built for air-delivered nukes inside grassy tumuli behind twelve-foot fences, tattoo parlours and US Air Force golf courses. In spring it's a riot of noise: constant plane traffic, gas-guns over pea fields, woodlarks and jet engines. It's called the Brecklands – the broken lands – and it's where I ended up that morning, seven years ago, in early spring, on a trip I hadn't planned at all. At five in the morning I'd been staring at a square of streetlight on the ceiling, listening to a couple of late party-leavers chatting on the pavement outside. I felt odd: overtired, overwrought, unpleasantly like my brain had been removed and my skull stuffed with something like microwaved aluminium foil, dinted, charred and shorting with sparks. *Nnngh. Must get out*, I thought, throwing back the covers. *Out!* I pulled on jeans, boots and a jumper, scalded my mouth with burned coffee, and it was only when my frozen, ancient Volkswagen and I were halfway down the A14 that I worked out where I was going, and why. Out there, beyond the foggy windscreen and white lines, was the forest. The broken forest. That's where I was headed. To see goshawks.

I knew it would be hard. Goshawks *are* hard. Have you ever seen a hawk catch a bird in your back garden? I've not, but I know it's happened. I've found evidence. Out on the patio flagstones, sometimes, tiny fragments: a little, insect-like songbird leg, with a foot clenched tight where the sinews have pulled it; or – even more gruesomely – a disarticulated beak, a house-sparrow beak top, or bottom, a little conical bead of blushed gunmetal, slightly translucent, with a few faint maxillary feathers adhering to it. But maybe you have: maybe you've glanced out of the window and seen there, on the lawn, a bloody great hawk murdering a pigeon, or a blackbird, or a magpie, and it looks the hugest, most impressive piece of wildness you've ever seen, like someone's tipped a snow leopard into your kitchen and you find it eating the cat. I've had people rush up to me in the supermarket, or in the library, and say, eyes huge, *I saw a hawk catch a bird in my back garden this morning!* And I'm just about to open my mouth and say, *Sparrowhawk!* and they say, 'I looked in the bird book. It was a *goshawk*.' But it never is; the books don't work. When it's fighting a pigeon on your lawn a hawk becomes much larger than life, and bird-book illustrations never match the memory. Here's the sparrowhawk. It's grey, with a black and white barred front, yellow eyes and a long tail. Next to it is the goshawk. This one is also grey, with a black and white barred front, yellow eyes and a long tail. You think, *Hmm*. You read the description. Sparrowhawk: twelve to sixteen inches long. Goshawk: nineteen to twenty-four inches. There. It was huge. It must be a goshawk. They look identical. Goshawks are bigger, that's all. Just bigger.

No. In real life, goshawks resemble sparrowhawks the way leopards resemble housecats. Bigger, yes. But bulkier, bloodier, deadlier, scarier and much, much harder to see. Birds of deep woodland, not gardens, they're the birdwatchers' dark grail. You might spend a week in a forest full of gosses and never see one, just traces of their presence. A sudden hush, followed by the calls of terrified woodland birds, and a sense of something moving just beyond vision. Perhaps you'll find a half-eaten pigeon sprawled in a burst of white feathers on the forest floor. Or you might be lucky: walking in a foggy ride at dawn you'll turn your head and catch a split-second glimpse of a bird hurtling past and away, huge taloned feet held loosely clenched, eyes set on a distant target. A split second that stamps the image indelibly on your brain and leaves you hungry for more. Looking for goshawks is like looking for grace: it comes, but not often, and you don't get to say when or how. But you have a slightly better chance on still, clear mornings in early spring, because that's when goshawks eschew their world under the trees to court each other in the open sky. That was what I was hoping to see.

I slammed the rusting door, and set off with my binoculars through a forest washed pewter with frost. Pieces of this place had disappeared since I was last here. I found squares of wrecked ground; clear-cut, broken acres with torn roots and drying needles strewn in the sand. Clearings. That's what I needed. Slowly my brain righted itself into spaces unused for months. For so long I'd been living in libraries and college rooms, frowning at screens, marking essays, chasing down academic references. This was a different kind of hunt. Here I was a different animal. Have you ever watched a deer walking out from cover? They step, stop, and stay, motionless, nose to the air, looking and smelling. A nervous twitch might run down their flanks. And then, reassured that all is safe, they ankle their way out of the brush to graze. That morning, I felt like the deer. Not that I was sniffing the air, or standing in fear – but like the deer, I was in the grip of very old and emotional ways of moving through a landscape, experiencing forms of attention and deportment beyond conscious control. Something inside me ordered me how and where to step without me knowing much about it. It might be a million years of evolution, it might be intuition, but on my goshawk hunt I feel tense when I'm walking or standing in sunlight, find myself unconsciously edging towards broken light, or slipping into the narrow, cold shadows along the wide breaks between pine stands. I flinch if I hear a jay calling, or a crow's rolling, angry alarum. Both of these things could mean either *Warning, human!* or *Warning, goshawk!* And that morning I was trying to find one by hiding the other. Those old ghostly intuitions that have tied sinew and soul together for millennia had taken over, were doing their thing, making me feel uncomfortable in bright sunlight, uneasy on the wrong side of a ridge, somehow required to walk over the back of a bleached rise of grasses to get to something on the other side: which turned out to be a pond. Small birds rose up in clouds from the pond's edge: chaffinches, bramblings, a flock of long-tailed tits that caught in willow branches like animated cotton buds.

The pond was a bomb crater, one of a line dropped by a German bomber over Lakenheath in the war. It was a watery anomaly, a pond in dunes, surrounded by thick tussocks of sand sedge many, many miles from the sea. I shook my head. It was odd. But then, it's very odd indeed here, and walking the forest you come across all sorts of things you don't expect. Great tracts of reindeer moss, for example: tiny stars and florets and inklings of an ancient flora growing on exhausted land. Crisp underfoot in summer, the stuff is like a patch of the arctic fallen into the world in the wrong place. Everywhere, there are bony shoulders and blades of flint. On wet mornings you can pick up shards knocked from flint cores by Neolithic craftsmen, tiny flakes of stone glowing in thin coats of cold water. This region was the centre of the flint industry in Neolithic times. And later, it became famous for rabbits farmed for meat and felt. Giant, enclosed warrens hedged by thornbanks once ranged right across the sandy landscape, giving their names to places here – Wangford Warren,

Lakenheath Warren – and eventually, the rabbits brought disaster. Their close grazing, in concert with that of sheep, reduced the short sward to a thin crust of roots over sand. Where the grazing was worst, sand blew into drifts and moved across the land. In 1688 strong south-westerly winds raised the broken ground to the sky. A vast yellow cloud obscured the sun. Tonnes of land shifted, moved, dropped. Brandon was encircled by sand; Santon Downham was engulfed, its river choked entirely. When the winds stopped, dunes stretched for miles between Brandon and Barton Mills. The area became famed for its atrociously bad travel: soft dunes, scorching in summer and infested with highwaymen at night. Our very own *Arabia deserta*. John Evelyn described them as the 'Travelling Sands' that 'so damag'd the country, rouling from place to place, like the Sands in the Deserts of Lybia, quite overwhelmed some gentlemen's whole estates'.

Here I was, standing in Evelyn's Travelling Sands. Most of the dunes are hidden by pines – the forest was planted here in the 1920s to give us timber for future wars – and the highwaymen long gone. But it still feels dangerous, half-buried, damaged. I love it because of all the places I know in England, it feels to me the wildest. It's not an untouched wilderness like a mountaintop, but a ramshackle wildness in which people and the land have conspired to strangeness. It's rich with the sense of an alternative countryside history; not just the grand, leisured dreams of landed estates, but a history of industry, forestry, disaster, commerce and work. I couldn't think of a more perfect place to find goshawks. They fit this strange Breckland landscape to perfection, because their history is just as human.

It's a fascinating story. Goshawks once bred across the British Isles. 'There are divers Sorts and Sizes of *Goshawks*,' wrote Richard Blome in 1618, 'which are different in Goodness, force and hardiness according to the several *Countries* where they are Bred; but no place affords so good as those of *Moscovy*, *Norway*, and the North of *Ireland*, especially in the County of *Tyrone*.' But the qualities of goshawks were forgotten with the advent of Land Enclosure, which limited the ability of ordinary folk to fly hawks, and the advent of accurate firearms that made shooting, rather than falconry, high fashion. Goshawks became vermin, not hunting companions. Their persecution by gamekeepers was the final straw for a goshawk population already struggling from habitat loss. By the late nineteenth century British goshawks were extinct. I have a photograph of the stuffed remains of one of the last birds to be shot; a black-and-white snapshot of a bird from a Scottish estate, draggled, stuffed and glassy-eyed. They were gone.

But in the 1960s and 1970s, falconers started a quiet, unofficial scheme to bring them back. The British Falconers' Club worked out that for the cost of importing a goshawk from the Continent for falconry, you could afford to bring in a second bird and release it. Buy one, set one free. It wasn't a hard thing to do with a bird as self-reliant and predatory as a gos. You just found a forest and opened the box. Like-minded falconers started doing this all over Britain. The hawks came from Sweden, Germany and Finland: most were huge, pale, taiga forest gosses. Some were released on purpose. Some were simply lost. They survived, found each other and bred, secretly and successfully. Today their descendants number around four hundred and fifty pairs. Elusive, spectacular, utterly at home, the fact of these British goshawks makes me happy. Their existence gives the lie to the thought that the wild is always something untouched by human hearts and hands. The wild can be human work.

It was eight thirty exactly. I was looking down at a little sprig of mahonia growing out of the turf, its oxblood leaves like buffed pigskin. I glanced up. And then I saw my goshawks. There they were. A pair, soaring above the canopy in the rapidly warming air. There was a flat, hot hand of sun on the back of my neck, but I smelt ice in my nose, seeing those goshawks soaring. I smelt ice and bracken stems and pine resin. Goshawk cocktail. They were on the soar. Goshawks in the air are a complicated grey colour. Not slate grey, nor pigeon grey. But a kind of raincloud grey, and despite their distance, I could see the big powder-puff of white undertail feathers, fanned out, with the thick, blunt tail behind it, and that superb bend and curve of the secondaries of a soaring goshawk that makes them utterly unlike sparrowhawks. And they were being mobbed by crows, and they just didn't care, like, *whatever*. A crow barrelled down on the male and he sort of raised one wing to let the crow past. Crow was not stupid, and didn't dip below the hawk for long. These goshawks weren't fully displaying: there was none of the skydiving I'd read about in books. But they were loving the space between each other, and carving it into all sorts of beautiful concentric chords and distances. A couple of flaps, and the male, the tiercel, would be above the female, and then he'd drift north of her, and then slip down, fast, like a knife-cut, a smooth calligraphic scrawl underneath her, and she'd dip a wing, and then they'd soar up again. They were above a stand of pines, right there. And then they were gone. One minute my pair of goshawks was describing lines from physics textbooks in the sky, and then nothing at all. I don't remember looking down, or away. Perhaps I blinked. Perhaps it was as simple as that. And in that tiny black gap which the brain disguises they'd dived into the wood.

I sat down, tired and content. The goshawks were gone, the sky blank. Time passed. The wavelength of the light around me shortened. The day built itself. A sparrowhawk, light as a toy of balsa-wood and doped tissue-paper, zipped past at knee-level, kiting up over a bank of brambles and away into the trees. I watched it go, lost in recollection. This memory was candescent, irresistible. The air reeked of pine resin and the pitchy vinegar of wood ants. I felt my small-girl fingers hooked through plastic chain-link and the weight of a pair of East German binoculars around my neck. I was bored. I was nine. Dad was standing next to me. We were looking for sparrowhawks. They nested nearby, and that July afternoon we were hoping for the kind of sighting they'd sometimes give us: a submarine ripple through the tops of the pines as one swept in and away; a glimpse of a yellow eye; a barred chest against moving needles, or a quick silhouette stamped black against the Surrey sky. For a while it had been exciting to stare into the darkness between the trees and the blood-orange and black where the sun slapped crazy-paving shadows across pines. But when you are nine, waiting is hard. I kicked at the base of the fence with my wellingtoned feet. Squirmed and fidgeted. Let out a sigh. Hung off the fence with my fingers. And then my dad looked at me, half exasperated, half amused, and explained something. He explained *patience*. He said it was the most important thing of all to remember, this: that when you wanted to see some-thing very badly, sometimes you had to stay still, stay in the same place, remember how much you wanted to see it, and be patient. 'When I'm at work, taking photographs for the paper,' he said, 'sometimes I've got to sit in the car for hours to get the picture I want. I can't get up to get a cup of tea or even go to the loo. I just have to be patient. If you want to see hawks you have to be patient too.' He was grave and serious, not annoyed; what he was doing was communicat-ing a grown-up Truth, but I nodded sulkily and stared at the ground. It sounded like a lecture, not advice, and I didn't understand the point of what he was trying to say.

You learn. *Today*, I thought, not nine years old and not bored, *I was patient and the hawks came*. I got up slowly, legs a little numb from so long motionless, and found I was holding a small clump of reindeer moss in one hand, a little

piece of that branching, pale green-grey lichen that can survive just about anything the world throws at it. It is patience
made manifest. Keep reindeer moss in the dark, freeze it, dry
it to a crisp, it won't die. It goes dormant and waits for things
to improve. Impressive stuff. I weighed the little twiggy
sphere in my hand. Hardly there at all. And on a sudden
impulse, I stowed this little stolen memento of the time I saw
the hawks in my inside jacket pocket and went home. I put
it on a shelf near the phone. Three weeks later, it was the
reindeer moss I was looking at when my mother called and
told me my father was dead.

2

Lost

I was about to leave the house when the phone rang. I picked it up. Hop-skippity, doorkeys in my hand. 'Hello?' A pause. My mother. She only had to say one sentence. It was this: 'I had a phone call from St Thomas' Hospital.' Then I knew. I knew that my father had died. I knew he was dead because that was the sentence she said after the pause and she used a voice I'd never heard before to say it. Dead. I was on the floor. My legs broke, buckled, and I was sitting on the carpet, phone pressed against my right ear, listening to my mother and staring at that little ball of reindeer moss on the bookshelf, impossibly light, a buoyant tangle of hard grey stems with sharp, dusty tips and quiet spaces that were air in between them and Mum was saying there was nothing they could do at the hospital, it was his heart, I think, nothing could be done, you don't have to come back tonight, don't come back, it's a long way, and it's late, and it's such a long drive and you don't need to come back – and of course this was nonsense; neither of us knew what the hell could or should be done or what this was except both of us and my brother, too, all of us were clinging to a world already gone.

I put down the phone. The keys were still in my hand. In that world already gone I was going for dinner with Christina, my Australian philosopher friend, who'd been there all along, sitting on the sofa when the phone rang. Her white face stared at me. I told her what had happened. And insisted we still go to the restaurant because we'd booked a table, of course we should go, and we did go, and we ordered, and the food came and I didn't eat it. The waiter was upset, wanted to know if anything was wrong. Well.

I think Christina told him. I can't remember her doing so, but he did something quite extraordinary. He disappeared, then reappeared at the table with an expression of anxious concern, and a double chocolate brownie with ice-cream and a sprig of mint stuck in the top, on the house, dusted with cocoa powder and icing sugar. On a black plate. I stared at it. *That is ridiculous*, I thought. Then, *What is it?* I pulled the mint out of the ice-cream, held it up, looked at its two small leaves and its tiny cut stem smeared with chocolate, and thought, *This isn't going to grow again.* Touched and bewildered that a waiter had thought that free cake and ice-cream would comfort me, I looked at the cut end of the mint. It reminded me of something. I groped for what it could be. And then I was back three days ago, back in Hampshire, out in the garden on a bright March weekend, wincing because I saw Dad had a nasty cut on his forearm. *You hurt yourself!* I said. *Oh, that*, he said, threading another spring onto the trampoline we were building for my niece. *Did that the other day. Can't remember how. On something or other. It'll be all right though. It'll be healed soon, it's healing fine.* That was when the old world leaned in, whispered farewells and was gone. I ran into the night. I had to drive back to Hampshire. I had to go *now*. Because the cut would not. It would not heal.

Here's a word. *Bereavement.* Or, *Bereaved. Bereft.* It's from the Old English *bereafian*, meaning 'to deprive of, take away, seize, rob'. Robbed. Seized. It happens to everyone. But you feel it alone. Shocking loss isn't to be shared, no matter how hard you try. 'Imagine,' I said, back then, to some friends, in an earnest attempt to explain, 'imagine your whole family is in a room. Yes, all of them. All the people you love. So then what happens is someone comes into the room and punches you all in the stomach. Each one of you. Really hard. So you're all on the floor. Right? So the thing is, you all share the same kind of pain, exactly the same, but you're too busy experiencing total agony to feel anything other than completely alone. *That's* what it's like!' I finished my little speech in triumph, convinced that I'd hit upon the *perfect* way to explain how it felt. I was puzzled by the pitying, horrified faces, because it didn't strike me at all that an example that put my friends' families in rooms and had them beaten might carry the tang of total lunacy.

I can't, even now, arrange it in the right order. The memories are like heavy blocks of glass. I can put them down in different places but they don't make a story. One day we were walking from Waterloo to the hospital under clouds. Breathing seemed an act of discipline. Mum turned to me, her face tight, and said, 'There'll be a time when all this seems like a bad dream.' His glasses, carefully folded, placed in my mum's outstretched hand. His coat. An envelope. His watch. His shoes. And when we left, clutching a plastic bag with his belongings, the clouds were still there, a frieze of motionless cumulus over the Thames flat as a matte painting on glass. At Waterloo Bridge we leant over Portland stone and looked at the water below. I smiled for the first time, then, I think, since the phone call. Partly because the water was sliding down to the sea and this simple physics still made sense when the rest of the world didn't. And partly because a decade before, Dad had invented a gloriously eccentric weekend side-project. He'd decided to photograph every single bridge over the Thames. I went with him, sometimes, on Saturday mornings, driving up into the Cotswolds. My dad had been my dad, but also my friend, and a partner in crime when it came to quests like this. From the grassy source near Cirencester we walked and explored, followed a wormy, muddy stream, trespassed

Snap, snap, her beak went. Then she turned her head to stare right at me. Locked her eyes on mine down her curved black beak, black pupils fixed. Then, right then, it occurred to me that this goshawk was bigger than me and more important. And much, much older: a dinosaur pulled from the Forest of Dean. There was a distinct, prehistoric scent to her feathers; it caught in my nose, peppery, rusty as storm-rain.

Nothing was wrong with her at all. We took her outside and let her go. She opened her wings and in a second was gone. She disappeared over a hedge slant-wise into nothing. It was as if she'd found a rent in the damp Gloucestershire air and slipped through it. That was the moment I kept replaying, over and over. That was the recurring dream. From then on, the hawk was inevitable.

3

Small worlds

I was twelve years old when I first saw a trained goshawk. *Please, please, PLEASE!* I'd begged my parents. They let me go. Drove me there, even. *We'll look after her*, the men said. They carried hawks on their fists: orange-eyed goshawks as remote and composed as statuary, with barred grey tails and breast feathers of vermiculated snow. I couldn't speak. I wanted my parents to leave. But when their car pulled away I wanted to run after it. I was terrified. Not of the hawks: of the falconers. I'd never met men like these. They wore tweed and offered me snuff. They were clubbable men with battered Range Rovers and vowels that bespoke Eton and Oxford, and I was having the first uncomfortable inklings that while I wanted to be a falconer more than anything, it was possible I might not be *entirely* like these men; that they might view me as a curiosity rather than a kindred spirit. But I pushed my fears aside in favour of silence, because it was the first time I'd ever seen falconry in the field. *I'll remember this day for ever*, I thought. *One day this will be me.*

We walked in dark winter light over fields furred with new wheat. Vast flocks of fieldfares netted the sky, turning it to something strangely like a sixteenth-century sleeve sewn with pearls. It was cold. My feet grew heavy with clay. And twenty minutes after we'd set out, it happened – the thing I expected, but for which I was entirely unprepared. A goshawk killed a pheasant. It was a short, brutal dive from an oak into a mess of wet hedge; a brief, muffled crash, sticks breaking, wings flapping, men running, and a dead bird placed reverently in a hawking bag. I stood some way off. Bit my lip. Felt emotions I hadn't names for. For a while I didn't want to look at the men and their hawks any more and my eyes slipped to the white panels of cut light in the branches behind them. Then I walked to the hedge where the hawk had made her kill. Peered inside. Deep in the muddled darkness six copper pheasant feathers glowed in a cradle of blackthorn. Reaching through the thorns I picked them free, one by one, tucked the hand that held them into my pocket, and cupped the feathers in my closed fist as if I were holding a moment tight inside itself. It was death I had seen. I wasn't sure what it had made me feel.

But there was more to that day than my first sight of death. There was something else, and it also gave me pause. As the afternoon wore on, men started disappearing from our party. One by one their hawks had decided they wanted no more of proceedings, saw no good reason to return to their handlers, and instead sat in trees staring out over acres of fading pasture and wood, fluffed and implacable. At the end of the day we left with three fewer men and three fewer hawks, the former still waiting beneath their hawks' respective branches. I knew goshawks were prone to sulk in trees: all the books had told me so. 'No matter how tame and love-able,' I'd read in Frank Illingworth's *Falcons and Falconry*, 'there are days when a goshawk displays a peculiar disposi-tion. She is jumpy, fractious, unsociable. She may develop these symptoms of passing madness during an afternoon's sport, and then the falconer is in for hours of annoyance.'

These men didn't seem annoyed; fatalistic merely. They shrugged their waxed cotton shoulders, filled and lit pipes, waved the rest of us farewell. We trudged on into the gloom. There was something of the doomed polar expedition about it all, a kind of chivalric Edwardian vibe. *No, no, you go on. I'll only slow you down.* The disposition of their hawks was peculiar. But it wasn't unsociable. It was something much stranger. It seemed that the hawks couldn't see us at all, that they'd slipped out of our world entirely and moved into another, wilder world from which humans had been utterly erased. These men knew they had vanished. Nothing could be done except wait. So we left them behind: three solitary figures staring up into trees in the winter dusk, mist thickening in the fields around them, each trusting that the world would later right itself and their hawk would return. And like the feathers in my pocket, their waiting also tugged at my faintly baffled heart.

I never forgot those silent, wayward goshawks. But when I became a falconer I never wanted to fly one. They unnerved me. They were things of death and difficulty: spooky, pale-eyed psychopaths that lived and killed in woodland thickets. Falcons were the raptors I loved: sharp-winged, bullet-heavy birds with dark eyes and an extraordinary ease in the air. I rejoiced in their aerial verve, their friendliness, their breathtaking stoops from a thousand feet, wind tearing through their wings with the sound of ripping canvas. They were as different from hawks as dogs are from cats. What's more, they seemed *better* than hawks: my books all assured me that the peregrine falcon was the finest bird on earth. 'She is noble in her nature' wrote Captain Gilbert Blaine in 1936. 'Of all living creatures she is the most perfect embodiment of power, speed and grace.' It took me years to work out that this glorification of falcons was partly down to who got to fly them. You can fly a goshawk almost anywhere, because their hunting style is a quick dash from the fist after prey at close range, but to fly falcons properly you need space: grouse moors, partridge manors, huge expanses of open farmland, things not easy to come by unless you're wealthy or well connected. 'Among the cultured peoples,' Blaine wrote, 'the use and

possession of the noble falcons were confined to the aris-
tocracy, as an exclusive right and privilege.'

Compared to those aristocratic falconers, the *austringer*, the
solitary trainer of goshawks and sparrowhawks, has had a
pretty terrible press. 'Do not house your graceless austringers
in the falconers' room,' sniped the fourteenth-century Nor-
man writer Gace de la Bigne. 'They are cursed in scripture, for
they hate company and go alone about their sport. When one
sees an ill-formed man, with great big feet and long shapeless
shanks, built like a trestle, hump-shouldered and skew-
backed, and one wants to mock him, one says, "Look, what
an austringer!"' And as the austringer, so the hawk, even in
books written six centuries later. 'One cannot feel for a goshawk the same respect and admiration that one does for a
peregrine,' Blaine explained. 'The names usually bestowed
upon her are a sufficient index to her character. Such names as
"Vampire", "Jezebel", "Swastika" or even "Mrs Glasse" aptly
fit her, but would ill become a peregrine.' Goshawks were ruf-
fians: murderous, difficult to tame, sulky, fractious and
foreign. *Bloodthirsty*, wrote nineteenth-century falconer
Major Charles Hawkins Fisher, with patent disapproval. *Vile.*
For years I was inclined to agree, because I kept having con-
versations that made me more certain than ever that I'd never
train one. 'You fly falcons?' a falconer enquired of me once. 'I
prefer goshawks. You know where you are with a gos.'

'Aren't they a pain in the arse?' I said, remembering all
those hunched forms lodged high in wintry trees.

'Not if you know the secret,' he countered, leaning closer.
There was a slight Jack Nicholson vibe to all this. I drew
back, faintly alarmed. 'It's simple. If you want a well-behaved
goshawk, you just have to do one thing. Give 'em the opportunity to kill things. Kill as much as possible. *Murder* sorts
them out.' And he grinned.

'Right,' I said. There was a pause, as if it wasn't quite the
right response. I tried again. 'Thanks.' And I was all, *Bloody*

hell! I'm sticking with falcons, thank you very much. I'd never thought I'd train a goshawk. Ever. I'd never seen anything of myself reflected in their solitudinous, murderous eyes. *Not for me*, I'd thought, many times. *Nothing like me.* But the world had changed, and so had I.

It was the end of July and I'd convinced myself that I was pretty much back to normal. But the world around me was growing very strange indeed. The light that filled my house was deep and livid, half magnolia, half rainwater. Things sat in it, dark and very still. Sometimes I felt I was living in a house at the bottom of the sea. There were imperceptible pressures. Tapping water-pipes. I'd hear myself breathing and jump at the sound. Something else was there, something standing next to me that I couldn't touch or see, a thing a fraction of a millimetre from my skin, something vastly *wrong*, making infinite the distance between me and all the familiar objects in my house. I ignored it. *I'm fine*, I told myself. *Fine.* And I walked and worked and made tea and cleaned the house and cooked and ate and wrote. But at night, as rain pricked points of orange light against the windows, I dreamed of the hawk slipping through wet air to somewhere else. I wanted to follow it.

I sat at my computer in my rain-lit study. I telephoned friends. I wrote emails. I found a hawk-breeder in Northern Ireland with one young goshawk left from that year's brood. She was ten weeks old, half Czech, one-quarter Finnish, one-quarter German, and she was, for a goshawk, small. We arranged that I should drive to Scotland to pick her up. I thought that I would like to have a small goshawk. 'Small' was the only decision I made. I didn't think for a second there was any choice in the matter of the hawk itself. The hawk had caught me. It was never the other way around.

When the rain stopped the heat began. Dogs panted flat in the black shade under the limes, and the lawns in front of the house paled and burned to hay. A damp, hot wind pushed leaves about but failed to cool anything; it was a wind that made things worse, like stirring a hot bath with your hand. Walking in it was like wading neck-deep through thick liquid. I struggled into the furnace of my car and drove to a friend's house in a village just outside the city. I wanted to talk goshawks, and there was no one better than Stuart to do it with. He is my goshawk guru. Years ago I'd hawked with him on late winter afternoons, crunched across long shadow and sugarbeet in search of wild fenland pheasants, his big old female gos sitting on his fist like a figurehead, leaning into the gilded wind. He is a splendid chap; a carpenter and ex-biker, solid and serene as a mid-ocean wave, and his partner Mandy is brilliantly generous and funny, and seeing them both was such a shot in the arm. I'd halfway forgotten how kind and warm the world could be. Stuart fired up the barbecue, and the garden filled with kids and teenagers and cigarette smoke and pointers nosing around, and ferrets rattling in their hutches, and the sky grew whiter as the afternoon went on, and the sun turned gauzy behind a spreading mat of fibrous cloud. A Spitfire banked overhead. We mopped our brows. The dogs panted, the ferrets drank from their water bottles, and Stuart slaved over his barbecue, coming back around the side of the house wiping his forehead on his arm. 'It's getting cooler!' he said, surprised. 'No, you've walked away from the barbecue!' we chorused.

I plonked myself down with a burger on a white plastic chair. And there, on a perch on the lawn, shaded by the hedge and ignoring the melee, was a perfect little peregrine, carefully preening the long, flippy barred feathers of his undercarriage. 'Half-Czech?' Stuart was saying. 'The most bloody-minded gos I ever trained was Czech. It was a *nightmare*. Are you *sure* you want to do this?' He tipped his head towards the bird on the lawn. 'You can fly that if you like,' he said. 'Want a peregrine?'

My heart skipped a beat. The falcon. There he was, an impossibly beautiful creature the colour of split flint and chalk, wings crossed sharp over his back, his dark, hooded face turned up to the sky. He was watching the Spitfire overhead with professional curiosity. I looked up at the plane. Its engine note had changed; it was throttling back, slowly descending through white air to the aviation museum where it lived. The peregrine bobbed his head, watching it too. Our gazes were exactly aligned. For a long, sinking moment, I wondered if I was making a terrible mistake.

'I'd love to,' I said stiffly, formally, the half-burger in my hand suddenly unappetising. One deep breath, then, and the words came. 'I mean, *normally* I would, I'd leap at the chance; that's an amazing offer, Stu. But I really do want this gos.' He nodded. Manfully, I finished the burger. Ketchup dripped down my arm like a wound.

There would be a goshawk. And what happened next was this: my eyes started avoiding a book that lived on the shelf by my desk. At first it was just a visual blind-spot, a tic of a blink; then something like a grain of sleep in the corner of my eye. I'd look past the place where the book was with a little flicker of discomfort I couldn't quite place. Soon I couldn't sit at my desk without knowing it was there. Second shelf down. Red cloth cover. Silver-lettered spine. *The Goshawk. By T. H. White*. I didn't want the book to be there, and I didn't want to think about why, and soon it got to the point that the bloody book was all I could see when I sat at my desk, even if it was the one thing in the room I wouldn't look at. One morning, sitting there, sun on the table, coffee to hand, computer open, unable to concentrate, I snapped: this was ridiculous. I leaned down, drew out the book and put it on the desk in front of me. It was just a book. There was nothing especially malevolent about it. It was old and stained with water, and the ends of the spine were bumped and scuffed as if it had been in many bags and boxes over the years. *Hmm*, I thought. I was interested in my emotions now. I thought about the book cautiously, ran my feelings over it the way you feel for a hurting tooth with your tongue. The dislike was palpable, but bound up with a strange kind of apprehension that needed pulling into parts, because I wasn't sure exactly what it was made of. I opened the book and began to read. *Chapter One*, it said. *Tuesday*. And then: *When I first saw him he was a round thing like a clothes basket covered in sacking*. It was a sentence from a long time ago, and it carried with it the apprehension of another self. Not the man who wrote it: me. Me, when I was eight years old.

I was a scrawny, too-tall child with ink on my fingers, binoculars around my neck, and legs covered in plasters. I was shy, pigeon-toed, knock-kneed, fantastically clumsy, hopeless at sport, and allergic to dogs and horses. But I had an obsession. Birds. Birds of prey most of all. I was sure they were the best things that had *ever* existed. My parents thought this obsession would go the way of the others: dinosaurs, ponies, volcanoes. It didn't. It worsened. When I was six I tried to sleep every night with my arms folded behind my back like wings. This didn't last long, because it is very hard to sleep with your arms folded behind your back like wings. Later, when I saw pictures of the ancient Egyptian falcon-headed god Horus, all faience and turquoise and with a perfect moustachial stripe below his wide, haunting eyes, I was stricken with a strange religious awe. *This* was my god, not the one we prayed to at school: he was an old man with a white beard and drapes. For weeks, in secret heresy, I whispered *Dear Horus* instead of *Our Father* when we recited the Lord's Prayer at school assemblies. It was a suitably formal address, I thought, having learned it from writing birthday thank-you notes. Hawk habits, hawk species, hawk scientific names; I learned them all, stuck pictures of raptors on my bedroom walls, and drew them, over and over again, on the edges of newspapers, on scraps of notepaper, on the margins of my school exercise books, as if by so doing I could conjure them into existence. I remember a teacher showing us photographs of the cave paintings at Lascaux and explaining that no one knew why prehistoric people drew these animals. I was indignant. I knew *exactly* why, but at that age was at a loss to put my intuition into words that made sense even to me.

When I discovered there was still such a thing as falconry things became less amorphously religious. I told my long-suffering parents that I was going to be a falconer when I grew up and set about learning as much as I could about this miraculous art. Dad and I hunted for falconry books on family days out, and one by one the great works came home with us, second-hand trophies in paper bags from bookshops long since gone: *Falconry* by Gilbert Blaine; *Falconry* by Freeman and Salvin; *Falcons and Falconry* by Frank Illingworth; the gloriously titled *Harting's Hints on Hawks*. All the boys' books. I read them over and over, committed great swathes of nineteenth-century prose to memory. Being in the company of these authors was like being dropped into an exclusive public school, for they were almost entirely written a long time ago by bluff, aristocratic sportsmen who dressed in tweed, shot Big Game in Africa, and had Strong Opinions. What I was doing wasn't just educating myself in the nuts and bolts of hawk-training: I was unconsciously soaking up the assumptions of an imperial elite. I lived in a world where English peregrines always outflew foreign hawks, whose landscapes were grouse moors and manor houses, where women didn't exist. These men were kindred spirits. I felt I was one of them, one of the elect.

I became the most appalling falconry bore. On wet afternoons after school my mum'd be writing up news stories for the local paper – court reports, local fêtes, planning committees – fingers hammering away on her typewriter in the dining room. There'd be a pack of Benson & Hedges on the table, a cup of tea, a shorthand notebook, and a daughter standing next to her reeling off imperfectly remembered sentences from nineteenth-century falconry books. It seemed crucial to explain to my mother that *while dog leather was the best leather for hawk-leashes, it was almost impossible to get these days.* That the problem with merlins was that they're *prone to carry their quarry*; and also did she know that *saker falcons, hailing from desert areas, are unreliable performers in English climatic conditions?* Lining up another yellow piece of copy paper, fiddling with the carbons so they didn't slip, she'd nod and agree, drag on her cigarette, and tell me how interesting it all was in tones that avoided dismissiveness with extraordinary facility. Soon I was an expert on falconry the way the carpet salesman who used to come into the bookshop where I once worked was an expert on the Greco-Persian Wars. Shy, crumpled, middle-aged, and carrying with him the air of some unspoken defeat, he rubbed his face anxiously when he ordered books at the till. He wouldn't have lasted long, I think, on a battlefield. But he knew everything about the wars, knew each battle intimately, knew exactly where the detachments of Phocian troops were stationed on high mountain paths. I knew falconry like this. When I got my first hawk, years later, I was astounded by the reality of the thing. I was the carpet salesman at the battle of Thermopylae.

It is summer 1979 and I am an eight-year-old girl in a bookshop. I'm standing under a skylight with a paperback in my hand and I am extremely puzzled. *What is an eighteenth-century story of seduction?* I had no idea. I read the words on the back cover again:

The Goshawk is the story of a concerted duel between Mr White and a great beautiful hawk during the training of the latter – the record of an intense clash of wills in which the pride and endurance of the wild raptor are worn down and broken by the almost insane willpower of the schoolmaster falconer. It is comic; it is tragic; it is all absorbing. It is strangely like some of the eighteenth-century stories of seduction.

No, still no idea. But I needed the book all the same because on the cover was a goshawk. She looked up from under her brows in truculent fury, her plumage scalloped and scaled in a riot of saffron and bronze. Her talons gripped the painted glove so tightly my fingers prickled in numb sympathy. She was beautiful; taut with antipathy; everything a child feels when angry and silenced. As soon as we were home I raced upstairs to my room, jumped onto the bed, lay on my tummy and opened the book. And I remember lying there, propped on my elbows with my feet in the air, reading the opening lines of *The Goshawk* for the very first time.

> When I first saw him he was a round thing like a clothes basket covered in sacking. But he was tumultuous and frightening, repulsive in the same way as snakes are frightening to people who do not know them.

It was unusual. It didn't sound like my other falconry books at all. The eight-year-old girl that was me read on with a frown. It wasn't *anything* like them. This was a book about falconry by a man who seemed to know nothing about it. He talked about the bird as if it were a monster and he wasn't training it properly. I was bewildered. Grown-ups were experts. They wrote books to tell you about things you didn't know; books on how to do things. Why would a grown-up write about *not* being able to do something? What's more, the book was full of things that were completely beside the point. It talked, disappointingly, of things like foxhunting and war and history. I didn't understand its references to the Holy Roman Empire and Strindberg and Mussolini and I didn't know what a pickelhaube was, and I didn't know what *any* of this was doing in a book that was supposed to be about a hawk.

Later I found a review of the book in an old British Falconers' Club journal. It was superbly terse. 'For those with an interest in the dull introspective business of manning and training a hawk, *The Goshawk* will be a well-written catalogue of most of the things one should not do,' it said. The men in tweed had spoken. I was on the right side, was allowed to dislike this grown-up and consider him a fool. It's painful to recall my relief on reading this, founded as it was on a desperate misunderstanding about the size of the world. I took comfort in the blithe superiority that is the refuge of the small. But for all that, my eight-year-old self revered the hawk in the book. Gos. Gos was real to me. Gos had steely pinions and a mad marigold eye, and hopped and flew and mantled his great wings over a fist of raw liver. He cheeped like a songbird and was terrified of cars. I liked Gos. Gos was comprehensible, even if the writer was utterly beyond understanding.

A few years ago I met a retired U2 pilot. He was tall, flinty and handsome and had just the right kind of deadly stillness you'd expect from a man who'd spent years flying at the edge of space in a dusty-black American spy plane. The geopolitical aspects of his role were truly disconcerting. But as a day job it was absurdly cool. At eighty thousand feet the world curves deep below you and the sky above is wet black ink. You're wearing a spacesuit, confined to a cockpit the size of a bathtub, piloting a machine that first flew the year James Dean died. You cannot touch the world, just record it. You have no weapons; your only defence is height. But as I talked with this man what impressed me the most weren't his deadpan tales of high adventure, the 'incidents' with Russian MiGs and so on, but his battle against boredom. The nine-hour solo missions. The twelve-hour solo missions. 'Wasn't that horrendous?' I asked. 'It could get a little lonely up there,' he replied.

But there was something about how he said it that made it sound a state still longed-for. And then he said something else. 'I used to read,' he said, unexpectedly, and with that his face changed, and his voice too: his deadpan Yeager drawl slipped, was replaced with a shy, childlike enthusiasm. '*The Once and Future King*. By T. H. White,' he said. 'Have you heard of him? He's an English writer. It's a great book. I used to take that up, read it on the way out and the way back.'

'Wow,' I said. 'Yes.' Because this story struck me as extraordinary, and it still does. Once upon a time there was a man in a spacesuit in a secret reconnaissance plane reading *The Once and Future King*, that great historical epic, that comic, tragic, romantic retelling of the Arthurian legend that tussles with questions of war and aggression, and might, and right, and the matter of what a nation is or might be.

White is not a fashionable writer. When I read English at university his name wasn't mentioned at all. But once upon a time White was very famous indeed. In 1938 he published a children's book about the boyhood of King Arthur called *The Sword in the Stone* and it made his name and his fortune. Disney snapped up the rights and turned it into an animated cartoon. White went on to write *The Once and Future King,* which covered the rest of the Arthurian story, and that in turn inspired the stage-musical and film *Camelot.* White's reworking of Arthurian legend was hugely influential: when you hear Kennedy's White House described as Camelot, that is White – Jackie Kennedy quoted lines from the musical after her husband's assassination. When you think of the wizard Merlin wearing a tall, peaked hat embroidered with stars, that is White too. And when I think of the U2 pilot up there reading a book about King Arthur, a book that had been wrenched strangely into a fairytale about American political life, I can't help but think of a line written by the poet Marianne Moore: *The cure for loneliness is solitude.* And the solitude of the pilot in the spy-plane, seeing everything, touching nothing, reading *The Once and Future King* fifty thousand feet above the clouds – that makes my heart break, just a little, because of how lonely that is, and because of some things that have happened to me, and because T. H. White was one of the loneliest men alive.

The Goshawk is the book of a young man. It was written before White's better-known works, and before he was famous. It 'would be about the efforts of a second-rate philosopher', he explained sadly, 'who lived alone in a wood, being tired of most humans in any case, to train a person who was not human, but a bird'. When I read it again, years after that first childhood encounter, I saw more in it than bad falconry. I understood why people considered it a masterpiece. For White made falconry a metaphysical battle. Like *Moby-Dick* or *The Old Man and the Sea*, *The Goshawk* was a literary encounter between animal and man that reached back to Puritan traditions of spiritual contest: salvation as a stake to be won in a contest against God. That older, wiser me decided that White's admissions of ignorance were brave rather than stupid. But I was still angry with him. First, because his hawk had suffered terribly as he tried to train it. And second, because his portrayal of falconry as a pitched battle between man and bird had hugely influenced our notions of what goshawks are and falconry is. Frankly, I hated what he had made of them. I didn't think falconry was a war, and I knew hawks weren't monsters. That small girl lying crossly on her bed was still cross.

That is what I thought as I sat there staring at the open book on my desk, four months after my father died. I read on, and as I did, there was a tiny jolt that was a realisation of why my eyes had spurned the book for weeks. I knew that part of why I was cross was that I felt, for the first time, that my urge to train a hawk was for reasons that weren't entirely my own. Partly they were his.

4

Mr White

It is 16 March 1936. On the east side of the great Palladian palace that is Stowe School, jackdaws fuss in the sweet chestnut trees, water drips from the roof of the block of rooms that used to be the stables, and inside them, Mr White, Head of English, blankets bunched up against his shins, is balancing a notebook on his knees and writing fast in a small, clear hand. He wonders if this is the most important book he's ever written. Not because it will make his fortune. But because it will save him.

He thinks he will leave. School life is unreal. All this is unreal. He has had enough. He can't bear his colleagues. He can't bear the boys any more either; en masse, he thinks, they're horrible, like haddocks. He has to get out. He'll live on his writing. His last book did well. He'll write more. He'll take a cottage in Scotland and spend his days fishing for salmon. Perhaps he'll take the barmaid with him as his wife, the dark-eyed beauty he's been courting for months, though he's only in love with her *emotionally*, so far, and he hasn't got anywhere, really, and those long hours sitting at the bar reduce him too often to hopeless drunkenness. He drinks too much. He has drunk too much, and he has been unhappy for a long time. But things are certain to change.

The notebook he writes in is grey. He's stuck a photograph of one of his grass snakes on the cover, and written ETC above it in ink. The snake is suitable because this is his dream diary, though there are other things in it too: scraps of writing, lesson plans, line drawings of sphinxes and clawed dragons rampant, and the occasional stab at self-analysis:

1) Necessity of excelling in order to be loved.
2) Failure to excel.
3) Why did I fail to excel? (Wrong attitude to what I was doing?)

But mostly the notebook records his dreams. There are dreams of women with penises, of boxes of maidenheads like fingernail parings, of hooded cobras that rear up but turn out to be harmless. There are dreams that he has forgotten his gun but can't borrow his friend's, because his friend is giving it to his wife; that he is a spy on the Hitlerists, hiding in a hole with only his cigarette poking out; that he must hide his shotgun in the boot of his mother's car to stop it being struck by lightning. And a dream in which his psychoanalyst is congratulating him on how good his dreams are.

'Bennet is the name, initials E. A.,' wrote White to Leonard Potts, his old tutor at Cambridge, who was something of a father figure. 'He is a very great man – must be, because cured cases like mine are I believe most rare, if not unique.' And then there's an assurance that is surely his wishful invention of some future self: 'I had a friend who was a sadistic homosexual, now happily married with children.' For the last year, White's craze for analysis had been in full spate: he was certain that Bennet would cure him of all of it: his homosexuality, his unhappiness, his sense of feeling unreal, his sadism, all of it; all his confusions and fears. It was all going well. He was *almost* sure he was in love with the barmaid. 'I'm so happy I hop about like a wagtail in the streets,' he told Potts, with a pride that holds within it, cupped like a small bird in the hand, his abject terror of failure.

The boys treated him with a kind of holy awe. Pacing the long corridors in grey flannels, a turtleneck sweater and gown, Mr

White looked a little like Byron. He was tall, with full lips and very pale blue eyes, a trim red moustache, and dark, unruly hair. He did all the right things: flew aeroplanes, shot, fished for salmon, hunted; and even better, all the *wrong* things: kept grass snakes in his room, rode his horse up the school steps on match days, and best of all, published racy novels under the pseudonym James Aston. When the headmaster found out he was *furious*: Mr White had to write him a letter promising never to write such filth again, said the boys, who passed copies of the novels around in agonies of delighted subterfuge. He was a startling, light-hearted, sarcastic figure. But a forbidding teacher. He never beat boys, ever, but they were terrified of his disdain. He demanded emotional sincerity. If it wasn't forthcoming, he'd cut his pupils down to size, puncturing their new-grown armour of pretension with a relish that bordered on cruelty. Even so there was something about Mr White that made him an ally of sorts; boys confided in him in a crisis, and they worshipped him for his insubordination and glamour. They knew he didn't fit, not quite, with the rest of the masters at Stowe. *Did you hear about the time he crashed his Bentley into a farmhouse and nearly died?* they whispered. And they spoke gleefully of the legendary Monday morning when Mr White arrived late and hungover, ordered the class to write an essay on the dangers of the demon drink, put his feet on his desk, and fell fast asleep.

But for all his demonstrations of bravado and skill, Mr White, Mr Terence Hanbury White, known to all as Tim after the chemists' chain Timothy Whites, was terribly afraid. He was twenty-nine years old, had been a schoolmaster at Stowe for five years and a writer for seven, but he had been afraid as long as he could remember. 'Because I am afraid of things, of being hurt, and death, I have to attempt them,' he'd explained in a book of sporting essays, *England Have My Bones*, published the previous year. He had to be brave. From the schoolroom he'd race at top speed to the aerodrome, his heart tight in his mouth, afraid of stalling, afraid of the instructor's contempt, afraid of getting into a spin from which he'd never recover, of burying himself in a wreck of crumpled wings and struts and earth. He rode with the Grafton over the muddy fields of Buckinghamshire in perpetual terror that he would fail to be brave, fail to ride well, fail to pass himself off as a gentleman, would incur the wrath of the Master of Foxhounds. And back in India, right at the beginning, where he remembered lizards and fireworks and candlelit darknesses and grown-ups in evening dress, he remembered also the terror of beatings, and arguments, and his mother's hatred of his father, and his father's hatred of her, and his drinking, and the endless, awful, violent war between them in which he was the pawn. His mother lavished attention on her dogs and her husband had them shot. She lavished attention on the boy and the boy was convinced he'd be next. 'I am told,' he wrote, 'that my father and mother were to be found wrestling with a pistol, one on either side of my cot, each claiming that he or she was going to shoot the other and himself or herself, but in any case beginning with me.' And then: 'It was not a safe kind of childhood.'

He brings the end of the fountain pen to his lips and considers what he has written.

> I pounce upon a bird with cruel talons and desperate beak. It may have been hurting me a little, but it would have hurt much more if I had let go. I held it tight and powerless to harm me, calling for somebody else to help by holding its feet. It was an English bird.

When White died of heart failure in January 1964, far from home in a cabin on the SS *Exeter* in Greece, his friends were concerned for his reputation. There were things in his journals they did not want to come to light, matters relating to his sexuality that if spoken of at all, had to be handled with rare delicacy. They needed to find a suitable biographer.

They chose Sylvia Townsend Warner, because she had corresponded with White, and he had liked her books. And for another reason: she was gay. 'You will be sympathetic to his character,' Michael Howard informed her. 'If it is a sufficiently bad character I should certainly be sympathetic to it,' she replied. She travelled to Alderney and there, walking about White's house, she found her subject. He was there, in his possessions. She wrote to her friend William Maxwell:

> His sewing basket with an unfinished hawk-hood, his litter of fishing-flies, his books, his awful ornaments presented by his hoi polloi friends, his vulgar toys bought at Cherbourg Fairs, his neat rows of books on flagellation – everything was there, defenceless as a corpse. And so was he, suspicious, morose, and determined to despair. I have never felt such an *imminent* haunt.

An imminent haunt. Her phrase gives me pause. Because that was what White was doing as I trained my hawk; he was there even as I dreamed of the vanishing gos. Haunting me. Not in the tapping-on-the-window white-sheet ghost-in-the-corridor way, but it was a haunting all the same. Ever since I'd read *The Goshawk*, I'd wondered what kind of man White was and why he had tied himself to a hawk he seemed to hate. And when I trained my own hawk a little space opened, like a window through leaves, onto this other life, in which was a man who was hurt, and a hawk who was being hurt, and I saw them both more clearly. Like White I wanted to cut loose from the world, and I shared, too, his desire to escape to the wild, a desire that can rip away all human softness and leave you stranded in a world of savage, courteous despair.

The book you are reading is my story. It is not a biography of Terence Hanbury White. But White is part of my story all the same. I have to write about him because he was there. When I trained my hawk I was having a quiet conversation, of sorts, with the deeds and works of a long-dead man who was suspicious, morose, determined to despair. A man whose life disturbed me. But a man, too, who loved nature, who found it surprising, bewitching and endlessly novel. 'A magpie flies like a frying pan!' he could write, with the joy of discovering something new in the world. And it is that joy, that childish delight in the lives of creatures other than man, that I love most in White. He was a complicated man, and an unhappy one. But he knew also that the world was full of simple miracles. 'There is a sense of creation about it,' he wrote, in wonderment, after helping a farmer deliver a mare of a foal. 'There were more horses in the field when I left it than there were when I went in.'

In *England Have My Bones* White wrote one of the saddest sentences I have ever read: 'Falling in love is a desolating experience, but not when it is with a countryside.' He could not imagine a human love returned. He had to displace his desires onto the landscape, that great, blank green field that cannot love you back, but cannot hurt you either. When, on their final meeting, he confessed to the writer David Garnett that he was a sadist, Garnett blamed White's early emotional maltreatment and years of flogging at school. 'He was an extremely tender-hearted and sensitive man,' Garnett wrote, who had 'found himself always in the dilemma of either being sincere and cruel, or false and unnatural. Whichever line he followed, he revolted the object of his love and disgusted himself.'

When White took up his position at Stowe in 1932 he was already expert at hiding who he was. For years he'd lived by the maxim Henry Green put so beautifully in his public-school memoir *Pack My Bag*: 'The safest way to avoid trouble if one may not be going to fit is to take as great a part as possible in what is going on.' To gain approval, to avoid trouble, he had to mirror what was around him: it was how he had tried to win love from his mother as a child. It was a life of perpetual disguise. After leaving Cambridge with a First in

English, White had decided to become a toff – that was the phrase he used. Snobbery 'is one of the best parlour games', he explained to Potts, with light-hearted casualness, but it was a game with the highest of stakes. He had to pass himself off as a gentleman. He took up the correct pursuits: shooting, fishing, flying and foxhunting. The latter was a perfect challenge: there were a thousand rules and protocols; it required bravery, money, social skills, horsemanship and exquisite feats of disguise. 'Can one wear topper, black coat and jacks without tops?' he anxiously enquired of his Cambridge friend Ronald McNair Scott. He was not sure about breeches. 'Mine are the right kind of buff, I think (a sort of kakhi [sic]) but perhaps the weave (or cording or whatever you call it) is too coarse or not coarse enough?' Too coarse. Not coarse enough.

He kept meticulous hunting diaries to record his progress: number of miles hacked and coverts drawn, people encountered, hedges and ditches successfully taken, thoughts on his horse's conduct, and painfully circumlocutory assessments of his own: 'I believe I did not misbehave myself, and was certainly at no time rebuked,' he wrote. Defensive, negatively couched, these are the words of a man desperate to belong. In *England Have My Bones*, he describes Buckinghamshire in a similar way – through what it is not. His county lacks outstanding qualities, beauty and historical significance, and so it avoids the attention of the world. It is safe. When White goes on to explain how Buckinghamshire 'concealed its individuality in order to preserve it' but is 'secretly exuberant in its private way' you realise that he is writing about his own character. More disguises. The mirror works both ways. The lines between the man and landscape blur. When White writes of his love for the countryside, at heart he is writing about a hope that he might be able to love himself.

But the countryside wasn't just something that was safe for White to love: it was a love that was safe to write about. It took me a long time to realise how many of our classic books on animals were by gay writers who wrote of their relationships with animals in lieu of human loves of which they could not speak. Gavin Maxwell's *Ring of Bright Water*, for example: the tale of a lonely man on the Scottish coast with an Iraqi otter on his sofa. Or the books of the BBC radio naturalist Maxwell Knight, former MI5 spymaster and closet queen. Doubly disallowed to speak openly of his allegiances, Knight wrote a book about hand-rearing a cuckoo called Goo. His obsession with this small, greedy, feathery, parasitic bird is terribly moving; it was a species made of all the hidden elements of Knight's life: subterfuge, deceit, passing oneself off as something one is not.

White is part of this poignant literary tradition. He remained alone all his life. He had a few dispiriting romances with women; nearly married one, almost proposed to another: all were very young. He was frightened of grown women. He confessed that he found their shape unpleasant and could scarcely bring himself to draw it. Much later in life he fell for the teenage son of a friend; it was his last love, hopeless and unreciprocated. But there were always animals. They populated White's life and his books. Dogs, owls, hawks, snakes, badgers, hedgehogs, even ants. And apart from his much-loved setter Brownie, whom he adored, he insisted his animals were never pets: for pets were 'almost always fatal, to oneself or to them'. They are ruined by their owners the same way that 'mothers ruin their children, choke them like ivy'. Pets meant dependency and he had a terror of it. One of the chapters in *England Have My Bones* is prefaced with a passage from Stella Benson that sheds light on why White dreamed of a hawk:

Independence – a state of being self-contained – is the only generosity, I thought, the only charity we can claim of a living creature. We must have nothing to do with another's bones; that is our only right – to have nothing to do with them. The bone must be the axis of a globe of intrusion-proof glass. One could not say, watching a hawk: 'I ought perhaps to do this for him.' Therefore, not only is he safe from me, but I am safe from him.

While still a schoolmaster he bought two Siamese cats – a breed renowned for its independence – and tried to 'train them to place no reliance or affection upon anybody but themselves'. It was what he had been trying to do himself for years. 'In vain,' he concluded, with disgust. 'Far from wandering free and independent . . . they sleep all day in the sitting room, in the intervals of mewing at me for more food.' The cats were a failure. The grass snakes he kept in his rooms were not. He kept them because 'it was impossible to impose upon them, or steal their affections'. He loved them because they were misunderstood, maligned, and 'inevitably themselves': they were versions of the self he aspired to be, just like the characters he called to life in his books: Merlyn the perfect teacher; the Wart, the orphan who was born to be king, and Sir Lancelot the ill-made knight, whose character White made his own.

Lancelot was a sadist who refrained from hurting people through his sense of honour – his Word. His Word was his promise to be gentle, and it was one of the things that made him the Best Knight in the World. 'All through his life,' White wrote of Lancelot, 'even when he was a great man with the world at his feet – he was to feel this gap: something at the bottom of his heart of which he was aware, and ashamed, but which he did not understand.' White always took great pains to be gentle precisely because he wanted to be cruel. It was why he never beat his pupils at Stowe.

And though abjuring cruelty was White's Word, animals played a curious role in keeping it. Riding out with the Old Surrey and Burstow Hunt, White recorded the first time he saw a kill with distanced fascination. The fox was dug out of a drain where it had taken refuge and thrown to the hounds.

They tore it to pieces while a circle of human onlookers 'screeched them on'. The humans, White thought, were disgusting, their cries 'tense, self-conscious, and hysterically animal'. But the hounds were not. 'The savagery of the hounds,' he wrote, 'was deep-rooted and terrible, but rang true, so that it was not horrible like that of the human.'

In this bloody scene, only one man escaped White's revulsion: the huntsman, a red-faced, grave and gentlemanly figure who stood by the hounds and blew the *mort* on his hunting horn, the formal act of parting to commemorate the death of the fox. By some strange alchemy – his closeness to the pack, his expert command of them – the huntsman was not horrible. For White it was a moral magic trick, a way out of his conundrum. By skilfully training a hunting animal, by closely associating with it, by identifying with it, you might be allowed to experience all your vital, sincere desires, even your most bloodthirsty ones, in total innocence. You could be true to yourself.

When White dreamed of the hawk his false self was cracking under strain. He felt himself 'boiling with a strange unrest'; was increasingly out to shock and appal. Colleagues remember him turning up to parties, drunkenly announcing, 'This party has no racial future. Parties should be like bird sanctuaries, people should come to them to mate.' He'd decided he hated people. He preferred animals. He was still drinking too much. He'd already turned on his former loves of foxhunting and flying. They were adulterated with death, and snobbery, and the desire to excel, and they were founded on poor motives: the fear of falling and the fear of failing. Gentility was a game he had played, but the reasons for playing it had been wrong. He was putting it aside. 'I was like that unfortunate man in Thurber who wanted a packing case in which he could conceal himself,' he wrote, 'and the solution seemed to lie in splendid isolation.' He went fishing alone in

Belmullet on the west coast of Ireland during the spring vacation. It made him more than ever certain of his course. From Belmullet he resigned his post at Stowe. 'It needed courage,' he told Potts, 'because my analyst has only got me about one quarter of the way. I don't know what my future is going to be, if I have a future.' And then, 'The barmaid is a complete write-off.'

And there was a new terror. It was war. Everyone felt it drawing closer; an almost tangible thing, acrid as sweat after nerves. 'We all stand in the shadow of a great fear,' the Oxford historian Denis Brogan had written two months earlier. 'And if the angel of death is not yet abroad in the land, we can hear the beating of his wings – and see them too, filling our old familiar sky.' White saw it too, and wrote that the war was the fault of the 'masters of men, everywhere, who subconsciously thrust others into suffering in order to advance their own powers'.

His fear of war meshed darkly with all his other fears. He'd long had nightmares of bombs and poison gas, of tunnels and flight and escape routes under the sea. The previous year he'd published *Gone to Ground*, a kind of mid-century *Decameron* in which foxhunters hiding in an underground bunker told each other stories as gas-bombs and incendiaries fell from the sky to obliterate the whole nervous, broken thing that was Civilisation. Civilisation was over. It was pointless. Modernity was bunk, and danger, and politics, and posturing, and it was going to lead to the end of everything. He needed to run. Perhaps he could escape to the past. It would be safe there. He started reading a book on falconry by Captain Gilbert Blaine.

It was there that White came across a story of a lost goshawk. 'From being on the day on which she was lost as domesticated as a household parrot,' Blaine recorded, 'she had reverted in a week to a feral state, and became thereafter a myth and legend in the neighbourhood.' For White the sentence was an epiphany. The hawk was a myth. A legend. 'There was a sentence which suddenly struck fire from the mind,' he wrote.

> The sentence was: 'She reverted to a feral state.' A longing came to my mind, then, that I should be able to do this also. The word 'feral' had a kind of magical potency which allied itself with two other words, 'ferocious' and 'free'. 'Fairy' 'Fey', 'aeriel' and other discreditable alliances ranged themselves behind the great chord of 'ferox'. To revert to a feral state! I took a farm-labourer's cottage at five shillings a week, and wrote to Germany for a goshawk.

Feral. He wanted to be free. He wanted to be ferocious. He wanted to be fey, a fairy, ferox. All those elements of himself he'd pushed away, his sexuality, his desire for cruelty, for mastery: all these were suddenly there in the figure of the hawk. White had found himself in the hawk that Blaine had lost. He clutched it tightly. It might hurt him, but he wouldn't let go. He would train it. Yes. He would teach the hawk, and he would teach himself, and he would write a book about it and teach his readers this doomed and ancient art. It was as if he were holding aloft the flag of some long-defeated country to which he staked his allegiance. He'd train his hawk in the ruins of his former life. And then when the war came, as it surely would, and everything around him crumbled into ruin and anarchy, White would fly his goshawk, eat the pheasants it caught, a survivor, a yeoman living off the land, far from the bitter, sexual confusion of the metropolis or the small wars of the schoolroom.

5

Holding tight

When you are broken, you run. But you don't always run away. Sometimes, helplessly, you run towards. My reasons weren't White's, but I was running just the same. It was a morning in early August, and I was four hundred miles from home. What I was doing felt like a drugs deal. It certainly looked like one. For minutes on end I'd paced up and down a Scottish quayside with a can of caffeinated soda in one hand, a cigarette in the other, and an envelope stuffed with £800 in twenty-pound notes in my back pocket. Over there in the car sat Christina, spectacularly impassive in a pair of aviator shades. She'd come along to keep me company, and I hoped she wasn't bored. She was probably bored. Perhaps she was asleep. I walked back to the car. It was my father's. I was driving it now, but the boot was full of things I couldn't bring myself to remove: 35mm film canisters; a crushed packet of aspirin; a newspaper with a half-finished crossword in my father's hand; a pair of winter gloves. I leaned against the bonnet, rubbed my eyes and looked out at the harbour, willing the ferry into view. A clear pool of turquoise was spreading out there over the Irish Sea; small crosses that were gulls traversed it. It seemed strange that it was day at all; both of us were wiped out from yesterday's long drive, and faintly freaked out by the hotel we'd stayed at the night before. *21st Century Hotel!* it said on a laminated paper sign by the door. When we opened it the first thing we saw was a plastic bulldog sitting on a desk, grimacing at us with the malevolent, merry belligerence of a thing from a nightmare.

In the hotel room we found a broken computer, a sink that wasn't plumbed in, and a fully functioning cooker we'd been instructed not to use under any circumstances. 'Health and Safety,' the hotelier had explained, rolling his eyes. There were, unexpectedly, two televisions, acres of brown suedette stapled to the walls, and a bathroom with a six-foot sunken bath into which Christina subsided, marvelling at the tea-tinted peat water. I collapsed into a chair, the journey running in my mind like a road-movie directed by a drug-addled auteur. Giant Irn-Bru trucks full of orange, bubblegum-flavoured fizzy Scottish soda. A raven standing in a puddle by the side of the road, wet-trousered and chisel-beaked. Motorway service station A. Motorway service station B. A sandwich. A large cup of undrinkable coffee. Endless miles. More skies. A near-accident caused by inattention on a hillside somewhere. Motorway service stations C and D. I massaged my aching right calf, blinked away the after-images, and got to making jesses.

I should have made them before, but I couldn't. Only now did the hawk seem real enough to make them necessary. Jesses are the soft leather straps that fit through the leather anklets on a trained hawk's legs. Singular, *jess*. It's a French word from the fourteenth century, back when falconry was the favourite game of the ruling elite. A little scrap of social history in the name for a strip of leather. As a child I'd cleaved to falconry's disconcertingly complex vocabulary. In my old books every part of a hawk was named: wings were *sails*, claws *pounces*, tail a *train*. Male hawks are a third smaller than the female so they are called *tiercels*, from the Latin *tertius*, for *third*. Young birds are *eyasses*, older birds *passagers*, adult-trapped birds *haggards*. Half-trained hawks fly on a long line called a *creance*. Hawks don't wipe their beaks, they *feak*. When they defecate they *mute*. When they shake themselves they *rouse*. On and on it goes in a dizzying panoply of terms of precision. The terms were precise for a reason. Knowing your falconry terminology attested to your place in society. Just as in the 1930s T. H. White worried about whether a hunting crop should be properly called a hunting whip, or a riding crop, or a riding whip, or just a crop, or a whip, so in the sixteenth century the Jesuit spy Robert Southwell was terrified he'd be found out because he kept forgetting his falconry terms. But the words weren't about social fear when I was small. They were magic words, arcane and lost. I wanted to master this world that no one knew, to be an expert in its perfect, secret language.

You can buy it all on the internet now: jesses, hoods, bells, gloves, everything. But when I began falconry, most of us made our own equipment. We'd buy swivels from deep-sea-fishing shops, leashes from ships' chandlers, beg offcuts from leather tanneries and shoe factories to make our own jesses and hoods. We adapted, we adopted, we usually didn't improve. Certainly I didn't. I spent countless hours waxing cotton thread, punching holes in my hands instead of leather in error, frowning, wiping blood away, trying again and again to cut and make and sew things that looked like the photographs in books, waiting for the glorious day when I might have a hawk of my own.

I have a suspicion that all those hours making jesses and leashes weren't just preparation games. In a scrapbook of my childhood drawings is a small pencil sketch of a kestrel sitting on a glove. The glove's just an outline, and not a good one – I was six when I drew it. The hawk has a dark eye, a long tail, and a tiny fluffy spray of feathers under its hooked beak. It is a happy kestrel, though a ghostly one; like the glove, it is strangely transparent. But one part of it has been carefully worked: its legs and taloned toes, which are larger than they ought to be, float above the glove because I had no idea how to draw toes that gripped. All the scales and talons on all the toes are delineated with enormous care, and so are the jesses around the falcon's legs. A wide black line that is the leash extends from them to a big black dot on the glove, a dot I've gone over again and again with the pencil until the paper is shined and depressed. It is an anchor point. *Here*, says the picture, *is a kestrel on my hand. It is not going away. It cannot leave.*

It's a sad picture. It reminds me of a paper by the psycho-analyst D. W. Winnicott, the one about a child obsessed with string; a boy who tied together chairs and tables, tied cush-ions to the fireplace, even, worryingly, tied string around his sister's neck. Winnicott saw this behaviour as a way of dealing with fears of abandonment by the boy's mother, who'd suf-fered bouts of depression. For the boy, the string was a kind of wordless communication, a symbolic means of joining. It was a denial of separation. *Holding tight.* Perhaps those jesses might have been unspoken attempts to hold on to something that had already flown away. I spent the first few weeks of my life in an incubator, full of tubes, under electric light, skin patched and raw, eyes clenched shut. I was the lucky one. I was tiny, but survived. I had a twin brother. He didn't. He died soon after he was born. I know almost nothing about what happened, only this: it was a tragedy that wasn't ever to be spoken of. It was a time when that's what hospitals told grieving parents to do. Move on. Forget about it. Look, you have a child! Get on with your lives. When I found out about my twin many years later, the news was surprising. But not *so* surprising. I'd always felt a part of me was missing; an old, simple absence. Could my obsession with birds, with falconry in particular, have been born of that first loss? Was that ghostly kestrel a grasped-at apprehension of my twin, its carefully drawn jesses a way of holding tight to something I didn't know I'd lost, but knew had gone? I suppose it is possible.

But now my father had died. *Hold tight.* I hadn't ever imagined that making jesses could be a symbolic act. But as

I sat there, cutting hide into long strips, soaking them in warm water, stretching them, greasing them with leather dressing, turning them this way and that in this strange room of broken objects, I knew they were more than just pieces of leather. These were the cords that would hold me to the hawk, just as they would hold the hawk to me. I picked up the craft knife and tapered the end of one jess to a point with a long, smooth cut. *There.* I was conjuring presences, doing this. Suddenly the hawk was very real. And so, in a burst of remembrance so fierce he could have been there in the room, was my father. Grey hair, glasses, blue cotton shirt, a tie slightly askew, a cup of coffee in one hand and a look of amusement on his face. He used to make me cross by calling falconry equipment by the wrong names. He'd call hoods *hats*. Creances, *bits of string*. He did it on purpose. I'd get cross and correct him, thinking he was teasing me.

And now I saw that Dad had known exactly what these things were called, but in the world of the photojournalist, the more expert you were, the less likely you were to call anything by its proper name. For him, photographs were *snaps*. Cameras simply *kit*. It wasn't ever teasing. He was paying me a compliment. Bloody fourteenth-century French vocabulary. Shit. Shit shit *shit*. It wasn't his way at all. My throat hurt. My eyes hurt too, and my heart. I cut the end of the other jess. Shaking fingers. Then I placed the two jesses side by side on the glass tabletop. They matched. *Tomorrow,* I thought, *I'm meeting a man I don't know off the Belfast ferry and I'm going to hand him this envelope full of paper in exchange for a box containing a goshawk.* It seemed the unlikeliest thing imaginable.

The goshawk I was about to collect had been bred in an aviary near Belfast. Breeding goshawks isn't for the faint-hearted. I've had friends who've tried it and shaken their heads after only one season, scratching their newly greyed hair in a sort of post-traumatic stupor. 'Never again', they say. 'Ever. Most stressful thing I've ever done.' Try it, and you discover there's a very fine line between goshawk sexual excitement and terrible, mortal violence. You have to watch your hawks constantly, monitor their behaviour, ready yourself for intervention. It's no good just putting a couple of goshawks in an aviary and leaving them to it. More often than not the female will kill her mate. So instead you house them in separate but adjoining solid-walled aviaries, with a barred hatch between the two through which the pair can see each other. As winter turns to spring they conduct their courtship, like Pyramus and Thisbe, through the gap in the wall, calling, displaying, dropping their powder-blue wings and fluffing their white undertail coverts that look for all the world like a pair of capacious marabou bloomers, and only when the female seems ready – a piece of fine judge-ment that does not admit error – do you let the male into the breeding chamber. If all goes well, they mate, lay eggs, and a new generation of home-bred goshawks, downy white chicks with bleary eyes and tiny talons, enters the world. I'd never met the breeder of my new hawk, but I knew already he was a man of steel nerves and superhuman patience.

White's hawk was taken from the wild. No one bred gos-hawks in captivity in the 1930s: there was no need to try. There were a hundred thousand wild gosses out there in European forests, and no import restrictions to speak of. Like nearly all falconers' goshawks back then, White's had come from a nest in Germany. 'A bundle of precipitous sticks and some white droppings' was how he imagined his hawk's birthplace: he'd never seen a goshawk nest. But you can see one, and there's no need to strike out into the forest to do so. There's live feed of goshawk nests, now, on the internet. One click, and you're given an up-close and personal view of the family life of this most secretive of hawks. There, in a four-inch box in low-resolution glitter, is a square of English woodland. The hissing you hear from your computer speakers is a digitised amalgam of leaves, wind and chaffinch song. You see the nest itself, a bulky concatenation of sticks pushed hard up against conifer bark and lined with sprays of green leaves. On the webcam the male goshawk appears on the nest. It's so sudden, and he's so brightly shiny white and silver-grey, that it's like watching a jumping salmon. There's something about the combination of his rapidity and the lag of the compressed image that plays tricks with your perception: you carry an impression of the bird as you watch it, and the living bird's movements palimpsest over the impression the bird has made until he fairly glows with substance. Goshawk substance. And he bows his head and calls. *Chew-chew-chew-chew-chew-chew.* Black mouth, soft smoke in the cold April morning. And then the female arrives. She's huge. She lands on the edge of the nest and it shakes. Her gnarly feet make the male's look tiny. She is like an ocean liner. A Cunard goshawk. And on each leg, as she turns, you can see the leather anklets she wears. This bird was bred in captivity somewhere, in an aviary just like the one in Northern Ireland that bred mine. She was flown by a nameless falconer, was lost, and now here she is, settling on four pale eggs, being watched on computer screens as the very type of the wild.

Time passed on the Scottish quay and brightness moved in from the sea. Then a man was walking towards us, holding two enormous cardboard boxes like a couple of oversized suitcases. Strangely alien suitcases that didn't seem to obey the laws of physics, because as he walked they moved unpredictably, in concert neither with his steps nor with gravity. *Whatever is in them is moving*, I thought with a little thump of my heart. He set the boxes down, ran his hand through his hair. 'I'm meeting another falconer here in a bit. He's having the younger bird. Yours is the older. Bigger too,' he said. 'So.' He ran his hand through his hair again, exposing a long talon scratch across his wrist, angry at its edges and scurfed with dried blood. 'We'll check the ring numbers against the Article 10s,' he explained, pulling a sheaf of yellow paper from the rucksack and unfolding two of the official forms that accompany captive-bred rare birds throughout their lives. 'Don't want you going home with the wrong bird.'

We noted the numbers. We stared down at the boxes, at their parcel-tape handles, their doors of thin plywood and hinges of carefully tied string. Then he knelt on the concrete, untied a hinge on the smaller box and squinted into its dark interior. A sudden *thump* of feathered shoulders and the box shook as if someone had punched it, hard, from within. 'She's got her hood off,' he said, and frowned. That light, leather hood was to keep the hawk from fearful sights. Like us.

Another hinge untied. Concentration. Infinite caution. Daylight irrigating the box. Scratching talons, another thump. And another. *Thump.* The air turned syrupy, slow, flecked with dust. The last few seconds before a battle. And with the last bow pulled free, he reached inside, and amidst a whirring, chaotic clatter of wings and feet and talons and a high-pitched twittering and it's all happening at once, the man pulls an enormous, *enormous* hawk out of the box and in a strange coincidence of world and deed a great flood of sunlight drenches us and everything is brilliance and fury. The hawk's wings, barred and beating, the sharp fingers of her dark-tipped primaries cutting the air, her feathers raised like the scattered quills of a fretful porpentine. Two enormous eyes. My heart jumps sideways. She is a conjuring trick. A reptile. A fallen angel. A griffon from the pages of an illuminated bestiary. Something bright and distant, like gold falling through water. A broken marionette of wings, legs and light-splashed feathers. She is wearing jesses, and the man holds them. For one awful, long moment she is hanging head-downward, wings open, like a turkey in a butcher's shop, only her head is turned right-way-up and she is seeing more than she has ever seen before in her whole short life. Her world was an aviary no larger than a living room. Then it was a box. But now it is this; and she can see *everything*: the point-source glitter on the waves, a diving cormorant a hundred yards out; pigment flakes under wax on the lines of parked cars; far hills and the heather on them and miles and miles of sky where the sun spreads on dust and water and illegible things moving in it that are white scraps of gulls. Everything startling and new-stamped on her entirely astonished brain.

Through all this the man was perfectly calm. He gathered up the hawk in one practised movement, folding her wings, anchoring her broad feathered back against his chest, gripping her scaled yellow legs in one hand. 'Let's get that hood back on,' he said tautly. There was concern in his face. It was born of care. This hawk had been hatched in an incubator, had broken from a frail bluish eggshell into a humid perspex box, and for the first few days of her life this man had fed her with scraps of meat held in a pair of tweezers, waiting patiently for the lumpen, fluffy chick to notice the food and eat, her new neck wobbling with the effort of keeping her head in the air. All at once I loved this man, and fiercely. I grabbed the hood from the box and turned to the hawk. Her beak was open, her hackles raised; her wild eyes were the colour of sun on white paper, and they stared because the whole world had fallen into them at once. *One, two, three.* I tucked the hood over her head. There was a brief intimation of a thin, angular skull under her feathers, of an alien brain fizzing and fusing with terror, then I drew the braces closed. We checked the ring numbers against the form.

It was the wrong bird. This was the younger one. The smaller one. This was not my hawk.

Oh.

So we put her back and opened the other box, which was meant to hold the larger, older bird. And dear God, it did. Everything about this second hawk was different. She came out like a Victorian melodrama: a sort of madwoman in the attack. She was smokier and darker and much, much bigger, and instead of twittering, she wailed; great, awful gouts of sound like a thing in pain, and the sound was unbearable. *This is my hawk*, I was telling myself and it was all I could do to breathe. She too was bareheaded, and I grabbed the hood from the box as before. But as I brought it up to her face I looked into her eyes and saw something blank and crazy in her stare. Some madness from a distant country. I didn't recognise her. *This isn't my hawk.* The hood was on, the ring numbers checked, the bird back in the box, the yellow form folded, the money exchanged, and all I could think was, *But this isn't my hawk.* Slow panic. I knew what I had to say, and it was a monstrous breach of etiquette. 'This is really awkward,' I began. 'But I really liked the first one. Do you think there's any chance I could take that one instead . . . ?' I tailed off. His eyebrows were raised. I started again, saying stupider things: 'I'm sure the other falconer would like the larger bird? She's more beautiful than the first one, isn't she? I know this is out of order, but I . . . Could I? Would it be all right, do you think?' And on and on, a desperate, crazy barrage of incoherent appeals.

I'm sure nothing I said persuaded him more than the look on my face as I said it. A tall, white-faced woman with wind-wrecked hair and exhausted eyes was pleading with him on a quayside, hands held out as if she were in a seaside production of *Medea*. Looking at me he must have sensed that my stuttered request wasn't a simple one. That there was something behind it that was very important. There was a moment of total silence.

'All right,' he said. And then, because he didn't see me believe him, 'Yes. Yes, I'm sure that'll be OK.'

6

The box of stars

'Hiding to nothing!' my old friend Martin Jones had said, and he'd raised both hands in the air in a gesture half of supplication, half exasperation. 'It's like banging your head against a wall. Don't do it. It'll drive you mad.' I kept thinking of what he'd said as I drove. Clutch, into fourth gear. Roundabout. Change down. Fierce acceleration. Slight resentment. I didn't want to think of all the things the men had told me. 'It'll drive you mad. Leave goshawks to the goshawk boys. Get something more sensible.'

I knew training this hawk would be hard. Goshawks are famously difficult to tame. To *man*, in falconry parlance. You can man a merlin in a few days. I once flew a Harris Hawk free after four. But gosses are nervous, highly-strung birds and it takes a long time to convince them you're not the enemy. Nervousness, of course, isn't quite the right word: it's simply that they have jacked-up nervous systems in which nerve pathways from the eyes and ears to the motor neurons that control their muscles have only minor links with associated neurons in the brain. Goshawks are nervous because they live life ten times faster than we do, and they react to stimuli literally without thinking. 'Of all Hawks,' wrote seventeenth-century falconer Richard Blome, 'she is doubtless the most Shie and Coy both towards the Men and Dogs, requiring more the Courtship of a Mistress than the Authority of a Master, being apt to remember any unkind and rough usage; but being gently handled, will become very tractable, and kind to her keeper.' Well, kindness it would be, and kindness we shall hope for.

Kindness and love. I remember thinking idly as I drove about that fierce burst of love I'd felt on the quayside for a man who held a bird terrified by a world it couldn't comprehend. It took me miles of gentle puzzling before I worked out that the love was about my father and me. For weeks after he died, I'd sat in front of the television watching the British television drama *Tinker Tailor Soldier Spy* over and over again; hours of grainy 1970s 16mm cinefilm, soft and black on an old VHS tape. I'd curled up mentally in its dark interiors, its Whitehall offices and gentlemen's clubs. It was a story of espionage and betrayal that fitted together like a watch, and it was glacially slow and beautiful. But it was also a story about a boy called Jumbo, a boarder at a second-rate prep school in the Quantock Hills. Jumbo was one of life's losers. Plump, short-sighted, asthmatic, he suffered from a terrible sense of uselessness and all the guilt of a broken home. When a new French master arrived – a hunchbacked, piratical chap called Prideaux – Jumbo took him as an ally. Someone who understood. 'You're a good watcher,' Prideaux said. 'I'll tell you that for nothing, old boy. Us singles always are.' What Jumbo didn't know, couldn't know, was that Prideaux had been a spy, and Prideaux' hurt back was a Russian bullet, and that there were other hurts, too, for Prideaux had been betrayed by his friend and former lover. Jumbo's world was too small to encompass such things, but he sensed that his teacher had lost some great friend all the same, and took it upon himself to stand in for that friend until he returned. He had found a use for himself. Watching the video I loved Prideaux, and his prep-school landscape – with hills buried in mist and rooks querulous in elms, rugger matches and white breath from the mouths of boys on fields on winter mornings – became the setting for a whole series of grief-spurred dreams that spring.

What happens to the mind after bereavement makes no sense until later. Even as I watched I'd half-realised Prideaux was a figure I'd picked out for a father. But what I should have realised, too, on those northern roads, is that what the mind does after losing one's father isn't just to pick new fathers from the world, but pick new selves to love them with. Back in those first few weeks, small and desperate, I'd chosen to be Jumbo. And on that Scottish quayside, just for a moment, without knowing why, I'd chosen to be the hawk. And I drove and drove, and the roads slipped by and the sky annealed into slews of the hardest white and blue.

I started to fret. The box was far too quiet. I pulled gloomily into the next motorway services. Christina ran off to buy ice-cream and I squinted into one of the airholes punched in the box's cardboard sides. After hours of top-lit tarmac my vision was in ruins. I couldn't see anything at all, and I didn't really want to, because of course the hawk was dead. And then, all at once, *my God*, the box was full of stars.

A long time ago I'd seen a suitcase in an art gallery, a small brown leather suitcase lying on its side on a white table. It was the most mundane object imaginable, and faintly sad, as if someone had put it down on their way somewhere and forgotten to pick it up. The artist had cut a small round hole through the leather. *Look inside*, said a pasted label, and with the faint embarrassment of being required to participate in a work of art, I leaned and put my eye to the hole. Started in surprise. Looked again. And there I was, a king of infinite space, dizzy, exhilarated, looking into a deep starfield that stretched into infinity. It was cleverly done; the artist had stuck two acid-spotted mirrors to the top and bottom of the case and lit them with a parade of tiny bulbs. The reflections of the spots and holes in the glass and the bright points of light turned the interior of that suitcase into a bright, cold universe that went on for ever.

Crouched over the car's back seat and lost in the memory of the suitcase I stared at a field of stars in darkness. Slowly it resolved into specks of feather-dust, little pieces of the crumbled keratin that protects growing feathers, loosed from the hawk's young plumage and lit by a shaft of stray sunlight from a crack in the top of the box. Eyes and brain fell into place, and now I could see a dull shine of half-light on one lemon-yellow, taloned foot. Dim feathers, shivering with apprehension. The hawk knew she was being watched. I shivered too. 'She's OK?' asked Christina, back and biting into a Solero. 'Fine,' I said. 'Absolutely fine.' Engine on. We pulled away. Hawks have been traded for centuries, I chided myself. Of *course* she was alive. Seven hours is nothing. Think of the seventeenth-century falcon traders who brought wild hawks to the French court from as far away as India. Think of the Fifth Earl of Bedford importing falcons from Nova Scotia and New England; rows of perched hawks in wooden ships, hooded and still, and the lowing of cattle that were carried as cargo on those ships to feed them. And as we drove onward, I thought of White's goshawk, of how much worse its journey had been than this: first from its nest to a German falconer; then by aeroplane to England, then by train from Croydon to a falconer called Nesbitt in Shropshire; then to a different falconer in Scotland as part of a swap that didn't seem to come off, for the hawk was returned to Nesbitt. A few days' reprieve in an airy loft, and it was back on a train, this time to Buckingham, a small, red-brick market town five miles from Stowe. And that is where White picked it up. How many miles? I reckon that's about fifteen hundred or so, over many days. I'm not altogether sure how the hawk survived.

Small souls, sent far from safety. In the opening pages of *The Goshawk*, White describes the awful journey of his fledgling hawk: torn from its nest, stuffed in a basket, and sent to a strange land to receive an education. He asks us to imagine what it was like, to put ourselves in the hawk's bewildered, infant mind; to experience the heat and noise, confusion and terror that was its journey to his door. 'It must have been like death,' he wrote, 'the thing which we can never know beforehand.'

What we see in the lives of animals are lessons we've learned from the world. A while ago, in a yellow tin chest in a college library, I found some photographs of White as a toddler. They're silvered prints of a dusty Karachi landscape; a jandi tree, long shadows, a clear sky. In the first the boy sits on a donkey looking at the camera. He wears a loose shalwar kameez and a child's sun hat, and his small round face has no interest in the donkey except for the fact that he is sitting on it. His mother stands behind him in impeccable Edwardian whites, looking beautiful and bored. In the second photograph the boy runs towards the camera over parched earth. He is running as fast as he can: his stubby arms are blurred as they swing, and the expression on his face, half-terror, half-delight, is something I've never seen on any other child. It is triumph that he has ridden the donkey, but relief that it is over. It is a face in desperate need of safety, with certain knowledge that there is none.

There was none. His parents' marriage was ill-starred from the first. Constance Aston had been nearly thirty when her mother's jibes about the cost of keeping her became unbearable. 'I'll marry the next man who asks me,' she snapped. The man was Garrick White, a District Commissioner of Police in Bombay. The newly-weds travelled to India, and as soon as Terence was born, Constance refused to sleep with her husband any more. He took to drink and the marriage toppled into violence. Five years later, the family came back to England to live for a while with Constance's parents in the south-coast resort of St Leonards-on-Sea. When they returned to India they left the boy behind. It was an abandonment, but it was also a reprieve from fear. *All that time was too beautiful for these words*, was how White described his St Leonards life in a faintly fictionalised autobiographical fragment that in places breaks into his own, childish voice, the voice of a small boy desperate for attention and already desirous of transformation into other, safer selves: *Look at me, Ruth, I am a pirate chief! Look, I am an aeroplane! Look, I am a polar bear! Look! Look! Look!* There were puss-moth caterpillars, a tortoise, a storeroom with chocolate and sugar in jars, and endless games with his cousins.

But it could not go on for ever. 'They took us away from that life,' he wrote, shortly, 'and sent us to schools.' The idyll was over, the child pitched back into a life of fear and violence. His Cheltenham housemaster was a 'sadistic middle-aged bachelor with a gloomy suffused face' and the prefects were his acolytes. They used to beat the younger boys after evening prayers. Every day the boy prayed, 'Please, God, don't let me be beaten tonight.' He usually was. 'I knew in a dumb way it was a sexual outrage,' he later mused, 'though I could not have phrased that charge.' No wonder he felt so deeply for the hawk. The boy had been torn from the only place he'd ever felt was home and sent away to be educated in a world of exacting bureaucratic cruelty. It was a betrayal that marked White for ever. And it would also mark his hawk.

Ferox. Fairy. Free. Tim White sits at his kitchen table and fills his fountain pen from a bottle of green ink that stands on the oilskin tablecloth. The ink is a mischievous thing, a small, fierce thing. He is writing of his new life with a colour that is the ink of – what does Havelock Ellis call it? The favourite ink of inverts. The hawk arrives tomorrow. Soon there will be three souls in the house: himself, his dog, his hawk. The thought thrills him. He loves this house. He calls it his workman's cottage, his badger's sett, his refuge. Outside, light and leaf-shadows move on the high grey gables. It is not a grand house – the water comes from a well and there is an earth-closet in the garden – but he thinks it is a beautiful one. And yes, it is rented, costs him five shillings a week, but it is the first time he has ever lived in a place of his own. He is making it his. He's varnished the ceilings, painted everything bright. Red glossy paint. Blue Robiallac. On the mantelpiece, birds' wings. A spill-jar. Patterned wallpaper. A mirror. Books everywhere. He's spent £66 on deep-pile carpets, bought a winged brocade armchair and laid in a stock of Madeira. Upstairs he's transformed the guest bedroom into a fairy-tale room of secret, romantic exuberance: mirrors and gilt, blue bed-linen and a golden bedspread, surrounded by candles. Still, he can't bring himself to sleep in it. The camp bed in the other room with the brown curtains will suffice. And the hawk will live in the barn outside, and they will both call this place home.

The Victorian terrace loomed and swayed in the summer dusk. I walked to my door, box in my arms. I don't remember opening the box that night. What I remember is my bare feet treading on carpet and the weight of the hawk on my fist. Her shape, long and haunted, and the hitch of her nervous shoulders as she stepped backwards onto the shadow of the bowperch on my living-room floor. I remember thinking of the passage in *The Sword in the Stone* where a falconer took a goshawk back onto his own fist, 'reassuming him like a lame man putting on his accustomed wooden leg, after it had been lost'. Yes, holding the hawk for the first time felt like that. Exactly like that. Mutely I crawled up the stairs and fell into bed. The hawk was here, the journey was over.

That night I dreamed of my father. It wasn't the usual dream of a family reunited. In the dream I'm searching for something in a house, an empty house with pale squares on the walls where pictures should be. I can't find what I am looking for. I open an upstairs door onto a room that is not like the others. Three white walls run with water and the far wall is gone. No wall at all: just air, falling into the pale violet of a city evening. Below me is a bombsite. Tons of bricks and rubble, rosebay willowherb blooming in drifts between broken rafters and spars that are ruined chairs and the shadows between all these things are thickening to night. But they are not what I am looking at. Because standing on top of the tallest pile of bricks is a small boy with sandy hair. His face is turned away, but I recognise him immediately, and not just because he's wearing the same short trousers and lumpy grey jacket in a photograph in our family album. It is my father.

As soon as I see him I know where I am. This is Shepherd's Bush, where he'd run wild as a boy, clambering over bombsites with his friends, collecting things, salvaging them, hiding, watching. 'We used to bomb bricks with bombs made of bricks,' he'd told me once. 'There wasn't much else to play with.' And then the boy turns, looks up at me standing in the ruined house, and I know he is going to say something. But there are no words. Instead, he points with one arm. Points *up*. I look. There's an aeroplane up there, thousands of feet above us, so high its fuselage and wings are still lit by the setting sun. There's no engine noise, no sound, nothing moving anywhere else. Just this small point of light crossing the sky until it passes over and is lost in the shadow of the world. And I look down again, and the boy that was my father is gone.

7

Invisibility

Prrt. Prrt. Prrt. One interrogatory note over and over again, like a telephone call from a bird deep in leaves. That's what pulled me from sleep. The noise came from a chaffinch in the lime tree outside my window, and I lay watching the day grow bright listening to the sound move about in the tree behind the glass. It was a *rain call*, a beautiful name for a noise like an unanswered question. No one knows why chaffinches make it, but the name comes from an old tradition that it portends bad weather.

In the 1950s, in a small research station in Madingley a few miles north of where I lay, a scientist called Thorpe experimented on chaffinches to try to understand how they learned to sing. He reared young finches in total isolation in soundproofed cages, and listened, fascinated, to the rudimentary songs his broken birds produced. There was a short window of time, he found, in which the isolated chicks needed to hear the elaborate trills of adult song, and if that window was missed, they could never quite manage to produce it themselves. He tried exposing his isolated fledglings to looped tapes of the songs of other species: could they be persuaded to sing like tree pipits? It was a groundbreaking piece of research into developmental learning, but it was also a science soaked deep in Cold War anxieties. The questions Thorpe was asking were those of a post-war West obsessed with identity and frightened of brainwashing. How do you learn who you are? Can your allegiances be changed? Can you be trusted? What makes you a chaffinch? Where do you come from? Thorpe discovered that wild chaffinches from different places had different dialects. I listened carefully to the bird outside. Yes, its song was different from the song of Surrey chaffinches I'd learned as a child. It was thinner, less complicated; seemed to cut off before it was properly finished. I thought I would like to hear Surrey chaffinches again. I thought of sad birds in soundproofed cages, and how your earliest experiences teach you who you are. I thought of the house from my dream. I thought of home. And then, with a slow, luxuriant thrill, I realised that everything was different about the house I was in. It was the hawk. I shut my eyes. The hawk had filled the house with wildness as a bowl of lilies fills a house with scent. It was about to begin.

In the half-light through the drawn curtains she sits on her perch, relaxed, hooded, extraordinary. Formidable talons, wicked, curved black beak, sleek, *café-au-lait* front streaked thickly with cocoa-coloured teardrops, looking for all the world like some cappuccino samurai. 'Hello hawk,' I whisper, and at the sound she draws her feathers tight in alarm. 'Hush,' I tell myself, and the hawk. *Hush*. Then I put on my falconer's glove, step forward and take her up onto my fist, untying the falconer's knot that secures her leash to the perch.

She bates. *Bating*. A 'headlong dive of rage and terror, by which a leashed hawk leaps from the fist in a wild bid for freedom'. That's how White described it in *The Goshawk*. The falconer's duty, he explained, 'is to lift the hawk back to the fist with his other hand in gentleness and patience'. I lift her back onto my fist with gentleness and patience. Her feet grip the glove convulsively. *This perch is moving*. I feel her mind grappling with novelty. *But still it is the only thing I understand. I shall hold it tight*. I persuade her to step onto a perch on a modified set of scales. Hawks have a flying weight, just as boxers have a fighting weight. A hawk that's too fat, or *high*, has little interest in flying, and won't return to the falconer's call. Hawks too low are awful things: spare, unhappy, lacking the energy to fly with fire and style. Taking the hawk back onto my fist I feel for her breastbone with the bare fingers of my other hand. She is plump, her skin hot under her feathers, and through my fingertips I feel the beating of her nervous heart. I shiver. Draw my hand back. Superstition. I can't bear to feel that flickering sign of life, can't help but suspect that my attention might somehow make it stop.

In the front room I sit, tuck a piece of raw steak into the glove under her scaly feet, and wait. One minute, two. Three. And I take the hood from her head.

Two wide, wild eyes stare at me for a fraction of a second, and then they are gone. Before the hawk can work out what the hell is happening she is trying to fly away as fast as possible. Brought up short by her jesses she twitters in high-pitched distress as the realisation of her hateful circumstances strikes. She can't get away. I lift her back onto the glove. Under her feathers is sinew, and bone, and that fast-beating heart. She bates again. And again. I *hate* this. In these first few minutes there's nothing you can do but accept that you are terrifying the hawk when it is the very opposite of everything you desire. After three more bates my heart is beating like a fitting beast, but she's back on the glove, beak open, eyes blazing. And then there is a long moment of extraordinary intensity.

The goshawk is staring at me in mortal terror, and I can feel the silences between both our heartbeats coincide. Her eyes are luminous, silver in the gloom. Her beak is open. She breathes hot hawk breath in my face. It smells of pepper and musk and burned stone. Her feathers are half-raised and her wings half-open, and her scaled yellow toes and curved black talons grip the glove tightly. It feels like I'm holding a flaming torch. I can feel the heat of her fear on my face. She stares. She stares and stares. Seconds slow and tick past. Her wings are dropped low; she crouches, ready for flight. I don't look at her. I mustn't. What I am doing is concentrating very hard on the process of *not being there*.

Here's one thing I know from years of training hawks: one of the things you must learn to do is become invisible. It's what you do when a fresh hawk sits on your left fist with food beneath her feet, in a state of savage, defensive fear. Hawks aren't social animals like dogs or horses; they understand neither coercion nor punishment. The only way to tame them is through positive reinforcement with gifts of food. You want the hawk to eat the food you hold – it's the first step in reclaiming her that will end with you being hunting partners. But the space between the fear and the food is a vast, vast gulf, and you have to cross it together. I thought, once, that you did it by being infinitely patient. But no: it is more than that. You must become invisible. Imagine: you're in a darkened room. You are sitting with a hawk on your fist. She is as immobile, as tense and sprung as a catapult at full stretch. Underneath her huge, thorny feet is a chunk of raw steak. You're trying to get her to look at the steak, not at you, because you know – though you haven't looked – that her eyes are fixed in horror at your profile. All you can hear is the wet *click, click, click* of her blinking.

To cross this space between fear and food, and to somehow make possible an eventual concord between your currently paralysed, immobile minds, you need – very urgently – not to be there. You empty your mind and become very still. You think of exactly nothing at all. The hawk becomes a strange, hollow concept, as flat as a snapshot or a schematic drawing, but at the same time, as pertinent to your future as an angry high court judge. Your gloved fist squeezes the meat a fraction, and you feel the tiny imbalance of weight and you see out of the very corner of your vision that she's looked down at it. And so, remaining invisible, you make the food the only thing in the room apart from the hawk; you're not there at all. And what you hope is that she'll start eating, and you can very, very slowly make yourself visible. Even if you don't move a muscle, and just relax into a more normal frame of mind, the hawk *knows*. It's extraordinary. It takes a long time to be yourself, in the presence of a new hawk.

But I didn't have to learn how to do this. I was already an expert. It was a trick I'd learned early in my life; a small, slightly fearful girl, obsessed with birds, who loved to disappear. Like Jumbo in *Tinker Tailor Soldier Spy*, I was a watcher. I had always been a watcher. When I was a child I'd climb the hill behind my house and crawl into my favourite den under a rhododendron bush, wriggling down on my tummy under overhanging leaves like a tiny sniper. And in this secret foxhole, nose an inch from the ground, breathing crushed bracken and acid soil, I'd look down on the world below, basking in the fierce calm that comes from being invisible but seeing everything. Watching, not doing. Seeking safety in not being seen. It's a habit you can fall into, willing yourself into invisibility. And it doesn't serve you well in life. Believe me it doesn't. Not with people and loves and hearts and homes and work. But for the first few days with a new hawk, making yourself disappear is the greatest skill in the world.

The confidence with which I sat there with the hawk was absolute. *I know how to do this*, I thought. *I am good, at least, at this. I know all the steps to this dance.* First the hawk will feed on my gloved fist. Then as the days pass she'll grow tamer, partly because I am keeping her indoors and constantly in my presence, just as fifteenth-century falconers had done. Soon she will step to my fist for food, and later she will jump to it. We'll go for long walks to accustom her to cars and dogs and people. And then she'll fly to me when I call her, first on a line, the creance, and then free. And then.

And then. I'd instructed my friends to leave me alone. I'd filled the freezer with hawk food and unplugged the phone.

Now I was a hermit with a hawk in a darkened room with books on three walls, a faded Afghan rug, and a sofa of stained yellow velvet. A mirror hung over the boarded-up fireplace, and a Shell poster from the 1930s on the wall above me was reflected backwards and watery in the old glass. YOU CAN BE SURE OF SHELL, it said, along with a scumble of stormclouds and a part of the Dorset coast. There was an old television, a mint-green vinyl cloth on the floor with the hawk's perch on it, and a pair of deep green curtains printed with flowers that shut out the world. The goal was to be motionless, the mind empty, the heart full of hope. But as the minutes stretched I had to move, just slightly: angle my foot to stop it sleeping; wrinkle my nose if it itched, and each time I did so I felt the hawk flinch in fear. But I also saw from the corner of my eye that she was pulling herself up incrementally from that sprung-to-fly crouch. Her stance was more upright. There was a little less fear in the room.

The old falconers called the manning of a hawk like this *watching*. It was a reassuringly familiar state of mind, meditative and careful and grave. For the first time in months my life had a purpose. I was waiting for the moment from which all else follows: the hawk lowering her head and beginning to feed. That was all I wanted. That was all there was. Waiting. Watching. Sitting with the hawk felt as if I were holding my breath for hours with no effort. No rise, no fall, just my heart beating and I could feel it, in my fingertips, that little clipping throb of blood that – because it was the only thing I could sense moving – didn't feel part of myself at all. As if it was another person's heart, or something else living inside me. Something with a flat, reptilian head, two heavy, down-dropped wings. Shadowed, thrush-streaked sides. There was a greenish cast to the light in the room, dark and cool and faintly submarine. Outside life went on, hot and distant. Shadows passed behind the curtains that were shoppers and students and bicycles and dogs. Vague, person-shaped shades making sounds like tin-can telephones, burred and incomprehensible. The *slap, slap* of walking feet. The hissing buzz of another bicycle. Long minutes passed. A piece of down dislodged from the hawk's covert-feathers drifted slowly to the carpet at my feet. A tiny star, barely any quill to it, just a muss of soft white plumes. I looked at it for a long time. I'd not looked at an object like this, with such searching attention with my mind elsewhere, since that reindeer moss, on the day the phone call came.

White-knuckle jobs, Dad used to call them: it was Fleet Street slang for the dangerous assignments. Leaning out of a helicopter with a camera in one hand and the other gripping the door-frame because the safety harness had snapped. Or looking through a fish-eye lens from the top of Salisbury Cathedral, standing on a frail iron rung hammered into stone four hundred feet in the sky. 'White-knuckle jobs? I get through them by looking through the camera,' he said. 'I bring it up like this' – and he mimed holding it to his eye. 'Look through the viewfinder. Stops you being involved. Stops you being scared.' You no longer possess a body to fall or fail: all that exists is a square of finely ground glass and the world seen through it, and a whole mass of technical decisions in your head about exposure and depth of field and getting the shot you hope for.

Sitting there with the hawk in that darkened room I felt safer than I'd done for months. Partly because I had a purpose. But also because I'd closed the door on the world outside. Now I could think of my father. I began to consider how he had coped with difficulty. Putting a lens between himself and the world was a defence against more than physical danger: it shielded him from other things he had to photograph: awful things, tragic things; accidents, train crashes, the aftermath of city bombs. He'd worried that this survival strategy had become a habit. 'I see the world through a lens,' he said once, a little sadly, as if the camera were always there, stopping him getting involved, something between him and the life that other people had.

The chaffinch was calling again. *How you learn what you are*. Had I learned to be a watcher from my father? Was it a kind of childhood mimicking of his professional strategy for dealing with difficulty? I kicked the thought around for a while, and then I kicked it away. *No*, I thought. *No*. It was more *I can't think that* than *It's not true*. All those thousands upon thousands of photographs my father had taken. Think of them instead. Each one a record, a testament, a bulwark against forgetting, against nothingness, against death. Look, *this happened*. A thing happened, and now it will never unhappen. Here it is, in the photograph: a baby putting its tiny hand in the wrinkled palm of an octogenarian. A fox running across a woodland path and a man raising a gun to shoot it. A car wreck. A plane crash. A comet smeared across the morning sky. A prime minister wiping his brow. The Beatles, sitting at a café table on the Champs-Elysées on a cold January day in 1964, John Lennon's pale face under the brim of his fisherman's cap. All these things had happened, and my father had committed them to a memory that wasn't just his own, but the world's. My father's life wasn't about disappearance. His was a life that worked against it.

He'd come home from work strangely disheartened one winter evening. We asked him what was wrong. 'Did you see the sky today?' he said. He'd been walking through a London park on his way back from a press-call. It was deserted but for a small boy playing by a frozen boating lake. 'I said, "Look up, look at that. Remember you saw that. You'll never see it again."' Above them both was a vast tracery of ice-rings and sun-dogs in a wintry, hazy sky. A 22° halo, a circumzenithal arc and an upper tangent arc, the sun's light refracting and cutting the heavens into a complicated geometry of ice and air and fire. But the boy didn't seem interested at all. Dad was baffled. 'Maybe he thought you were one of those strange men,' we sniggered, rolling our eyes, and he looked embarrassed and faintly cross. But he was so very sad about the boy who didn't see.

Now that Dad was gone I was starting to see how mortality was bound up in things like that cold, arc-lit sky. How the world is full of signs and wonders that come, and go, and if you are lucky you might see them. Once, twice. Perhaps never again. The albums on my mother's shelves are full of family photographs. But also other things. A starling with a crooked beak. A day of hoarfrost and smoke. A cherry tree thick with blossom. Thunderclouds, lightning strikes, comets and eclipses: celestial events terrifying in their blind distances but reassuring you, too, that the world is for ever, though you are only a blink in its course.

Henri Cartier-Bresson called the taking of a good photograph a *decisive moment*. 'Your eye must see a composition or an expression that life itself offers you, and you must know with intuition when to click the camera,' he said. 'The Moment! Once you miss it, it is gone for ever.' I thought of one of these moments as I sat there waiting for the hawk to eat from my hand. It was a black-and-white photograph my father had taken many years ago of an elderly street-cleaner with a white goatee beard, wrinkled socks and down-at-heel shoes. Crumpled work trousers, work gloves, a woollen beret. The camera is low, on the pavement: Dad must have crouched in the road to take it. The man is bending down, his besom of birch twigs propped against his side. He has taken off one of his gloves, and between the thumb and first finger of his bare right hand he is offering a crumb of bread to a sparrow on the kerbstone. The sparrow is caught mid-hop at exactly at the moment it takes the crumb from his fingers. And the expression on the man's face is suffused with joy. He is wearing the face of an angel.

* * *

Time passed. Hawks gorge themselves in the wild and can spend days without food. I knew the hawk would not eat from my hand today. She was scared, she wasn't hungry; the world was an insult. Both of us needed a break. I popped the hood back over her head. *There.* Fleeting panic, nerves afire, and then she relaxed because the day had turned to night and I had disappeared. The terror had gone. *Hood-winked.* It was an ancient piece of trickery and an excusable one: the darkness would give her space to set her frayed nerves to rights. As would it mine. On her perch, she slept. I slept too, wrapped in a duvet dragged over the sofa. Later, when I picked her up again, the mood in the room had changed. She had done this before; was no longer entirely certain I was a monster. She bated, once, towards the floor, but it was a bate to the floor, not away from me in blind terror. I lifted her back onto the glove. We sat some more. Then, instead of fixing her gaze on me in horror, she began to examine her surroundings. New things. Shelves, walls, floor: she inspected them all carefully with small, sideways movements of her head. Hawk parallax, judging perfect distances. She observed the ceiling as far as it would go, the lines of the bookshelves beneath it, cocked her head to consider the strip of messy tassels along the edge of the rug. Then came a decisive moment. It was not the one I was hoping for, but it was thrilling all the same. Regarding the room with simple curiosity, she turned her head and saw me. And jumped. Jumped exactly like a human in surprise. I felt the scratch of her talons and her shock, too, cold and electric. That was the moment. Until a minute ago I was so terrifying I was all that existed. But then she had forgotten me. Only for a fraction of a second, but it was enough. The forgetting was delightful because it was a sign that the hawk was starting to accept me. But there was a deeper, darker thrill. It was that I had been forgotten.

8

The Rembrandt interior

White loosed his young male goshawk in the barn that first night and in the early hours, at five minutes past three, it stepped onto his fist and fed. It was hungry, familiar with humans, willing already to come to the falconer for food. It was a state that my hawk had not yet reached and would not reach for days. If White had only known what he was doing, Gos could have been flying free in a week. But he didn't know what he was doing. He didn't understand that a hawk in training must be kept a little hungry, for only through gifts of food will a wild bird begin to see you as a benevolent figure and not an affront to all existence.

White was petrified. On his hawk's tail were strange pale transverse stripes, as if someone had drawn a razor blade across the quills. He knew what they were: hunger-traces caused by lack of food as the feathers grew; weaknesses that made them liable to break. Guilt and blame. He worried that it was his fault the hawk was damaged. He wanted to stop these hunger-traces, make up for whatever early lack had scarred his hawk and made its feathers weak. So he fed it. He fed it as much as he possibly could. He didn't know that because those feathers were now full-grown there was no danger of making the traces worse. He gave the hawk so much food that the hawk couldn't eat it, bear the sight of it, and here is White, the terrified austringer, stroking the hawk's breast-feathers with a split rabbit skull showing all the rabbit's spilled brains in desperate attempts to get it to eat, when the hawk doesn't want to eat because it is full. *Love me*, he is saying. *Please. I can make it up to you, make it better. Fix you. Please eat.* But a fat, stuffed goshawk doesn't want anything other than to be left alone, to disappear into that half-world of no-humans, replete and contented, eyes half-closed, one foot tucked up into soft feathers, to digest its food and sleep. Over the coming days and weeks, White tries different food, better food, trying to tempt the hawk to eat more that it can bear. He is wheedling, desperate, certain that his patience will triumph. And of course at some point the hawk becomes half-hungry enough to eat, and White stuffs it with food, convinced that all will now be well. And then the hawk hates him, and the strange cycle begins again. 'Days of attack and counter-attack,' was how White described it; 'a kind of sweeping to and fro across disputed battle fields.' There is a nightmarish logic to White's time with the hawk: the logic of a sadist who half-hates his hawk because he hates himself, who wants to hurt it because he loves it, but will not, and insists that it eats so that it will love him. And these twisted logics were met with the simple logic of a wild, fat goshawk that considers this man the most inimical thing on earth.

'I had only just escaped from humanity,' White wrote, 'and the poor gos had only just been caught by it.' But he hadn't escaped, not quite. When you read *The Goshawk* you're given to understand that his cottage was miles from anywhere, a remote outpost deep in a wood half a mile from the nearest road. But the cottage was on the Stowe estate; it had been built on one of the old roads laid out as carriage routes to the great house centuries before. They were called the Ridings, and one ran in a shifting river of grass straight past White's cottage, over the crest of a sheep-cropped hill and down to the doors of the school. The house was rustic, yes: it had an earth-closet and a well, and when White stood with his hawk in the barn he could still see where a Victorian gamekeeper had written of vanished bags of game in pencil on the back of the door. *Phesant*, it said. *Harn*. But remote it was not. There was his house, not quite in a wood, sitting on the old and open road to Stowe, like a promise not quite kept, and White in it, like a dog who sits at the very end of his chain, or the sad divorcee who moves out of their partner's house to live at the bottom of the road. For all his joy in freedom, the schoolmaster had not escaped the bounds of the school, and he'd not escaped schoolmastering either.

In Blaine's book White read that falconry was the art of control over the wildest and proudest of living creatures, and that to train them the falconer must battle their defiance and rebellious attitude. The training of a hawk mirrored the education of the public schoolboy. In both, a wild and unruly subject was shaped and moulded, made civilised; was taught good manners and obedience. But the methods were different, and this gave White much pleasure. 'I had been a schoolmaster for so long,' he wrote, 'in which profession the standard way of meeting a difficult situation was by punishment. It was nice after this to discover a profession of education where punishment was treated as ridiculous.'

It was the perfect kind of education, he decided, for him and for the hawk. He would call his book *The Austringer*, and in its pages he and his readers would take a 'patient excursion into the fields and back into the past'. That excursion wasn't just back into an imagined English past; it was also a journey back into his own. White had 'dropped out of the curious adult heterosexual competition', had become again 'a monastic boy'. In those long hours of psychoanalysis with Bennet, White had learned that going back in time was a way of fixing things; uncovering past traumas, revisiting them and defusing their power. Now he was going back in time with the hawk. He'd already empathised with the fledgling in the

basket, had seen the hawk as himself. Now he was unconsciously re-enacting his childhood – with the hawk standing
in for himself as a boy, and the grown-up White playing the
role of an enlightened teacher who could not, would not,
must not beat or hurt the child in his care.

He considers falconry the most glorious of mysteries. He has
no one to teach him and two books to learn from, not count-
ing the description in the *Encyclopaedia Britannica,* which
he has almost by heart. There is Blaine's *Falconry,* published
the previous year, and *Coursing and Falconry* by Gerald
Lascelles, from 1892. But the book White cleaves to is much
older; it was published in 1619. Called *An Approved Treatise of Hawkes and Hawking*, it is all about goshawks, and it
was written by Edmund Bert, Gentleman. White didn't yet
possess a copy of his own, for it was a rare volume; but he'd
read it. Perhaps he'd read the copy kept at the Cambridge
University Library. Perhaps it was the very same copy I'd
pored over as a student. As White was seduced by Bert's book,
so was I. It is bloody marvellous. Bert is the seventeenth-
century counterpart of some of the blunter Yorkshire goshawkers of my acquaintance on whom something of the
hawk's character has rubbed off. Accomplished, cantanker-
ous, with a bracing wit, he never fails to arrogate himself,
tell us how perfectly his hawks behave: craning on tiptoe to
pick marrow from his fingertips, they are happy to travel
with him wherever he goes. When away from home, Bert
boasts, he'd put his hawk on 'a velvet stoole, in a dining-
chamber or parlour, as the place was whereunto I went, for
I would have my Hawke as much in my eye as could be.
Perhaps I should see the Lady or Mistress of the house look
discontentedly thereat,' he deadpans, 'but so well have I been
acquainted with my hawk's good disposition that I have
promised if my hawk should make a mute in the room, I
would lick it up with my tongue.'

Edmund Bert haunted White as he trained his hawk, just as White haunted me. But it was a different kind of haunting. 'I had a sort of schoolgirlish "pash" for that serious old man who lived three hundred years ago,' he privately confessed. He wanted to impress Bert. He was in love with him. Dizzied by medievalist imaginings, in love with a falconer three hundred years dead, he had decided to ignore the teachings of Blaine, for the most part, and train his hawk the old-fashioned way.

> The old hawk masters had invented a means of taming them which offered no visible cruelty, and whose secret cruelty had to be born [sic] by the trainer as well as by the bird. They kept the bird awake. Not by nudging it or by any mechanical means, but by walking about with their pupil on their fist and staying awake themselves. The hawk was 'watched', was deprived of sleep by a sleepless man, for a space of two, three, or as much as nine nights together.

White wilfully misunderstood Bert's methods. The seventeenth-century austringer would have had any number of friends and attendants to take over while he slept. But White was desirous of a rite of passage. A proper knight's vigil. And he needed to do it alone, man against man, as it were. Watching his hawk would be a privation, an ordeal, a test of his Word. He would not be cruel. But he would conquer both the hawk and himself in one fell swoop. 'Man against bird,' he wrote, 'with God as an umpire, they had sat each other out for three thousand years.' In this long vigil – White had six hours' sleep in six days – the effects of extreme tiredness took their toll. Again and again, delirious from lack of sleep, sitting in the kitchen or standing in the lamplit barn, he lifted the fat and frightened hawk onto his fist, reciting it passages from *Hamlet*, *Macbeth*, *Richard II*, *Othello* – 'but the tragedy had to be kept out of the voice' – and all the sonnets he could remember, whistling hymns to it, playing it Gilbert and Sullivan and

Italian opera, and deciding, on reflection, that hawks liked Shakespeare best.

When I was a student I took a paper on Tragedy as part of my English degree. This was not without irony, for I was comprehensively tragic. I wore black, smoked filterless Camels, skulked about the place with kohl-caked eyes and failed to write a single essay about Greek Tragedy, Jacobean Tragedy, Shakespearian Tragedy, or indeed do much at all. *I'd like to write Miss Macdonald a glowing report*, one of my supervisors noted drily, *but as I've never seen her and have no idea what she looks like, this I cannot do*. But I read all the same. I read a lot. And I found there were myriad definitions of this thing called tragedy that had wormed its way through the history of literature; and the simplest of all was this: that it is the story of a figure who, through some moral flaw or personal failing, falls through force of circumstance to his doom.

It was the Tragedy paper that led me to read Freud, because he was still fashionable back then, and because psychoanalysts had their shot at explaining tragedy too. And after reading him I began to see all sorts of psychological transferences in my falconry books. I saw those nineteenth-century falconers were projecting onto their hawks all the male qualities they thought threatened by modern life: wildness, power, virility, independence and strength. By identifying with their hawks as they trained them, they could *introject*, or repossess, those qualities. At the same time they could exercise their power by 'civilising' a wild and primitive creature. Masculinity and conquest: two imperial myths for the price of one. The Victorian falconer assumed the power and strength of the hawk. The hawk assumed the manners of the man.

For White, too, falconry involved strange projections, but of very different qualities. His young German goshawk was a living expression of all the dark, discreditable desires within himself he'd tried to repress for years: it was a thing fey, fairy, feral, ferocious and cruel. He had tried for so long to be a gentleman. Tried to fit in, to adhere to all the rules of civilised society, to be normal, to be like everyone else. But his years at Stowe and his analysis and the fear of war had brought him to breaking point. He had refused humanity in favour of hawks, but he could not escape himself. Once again White was engaged in a battle to civilise the perversity and unruliness within himself. Only now he had put those things in the hawk, and he was trying to civilise them there. He found himself in a strange, locked battle with a bird that was all the things he longed for, but had always fought against. It was a terrible paradox. A proper tragedy. No wonder living with Gos brought him nearly to madness.

He is lost. The barn is a dungeon. He is swimmingly, drunkenly tired. A chill summer wind blows through the walls. White owls hunt outside: powdery, reed-thin shrieks under a low orange moon. He is an executioner, he thinks, and he should be wearing a mask. A black one that conceals his face. He has been measuring time in the bates of the hawk, in the hundreds of times he's lifted the screaming captive back onto the glove. The barn is the Bastille. The hawk is a prisoner. The falconer is a man in riding breeches and a checked coat. He stands in a Rembrandt interior. A pile of sticks and empty jars on the brick floor; cobwebs on the walls. A broken grate. A barrel of Flowers beer. A pool of light from the oil-lamp, and the hawk. The hawk, the hawk, the hawk. It is on his fist, all the sepia arrowheads on its pale breast dishevelled and frayed from his hands. The man is swaying backwards and forwards like a man on a ship, as if the ground beneath him pitched and rolled like the sea. He is trying to stay awake. He is trying to keep the hawk awake. The hawk is trying to close its eyes and sleep but the swaying pulls it back. I am free, the man is telling himself. *Free.* He stares at the cobwebs behind the exhausted hawk. I am in purdah, he thinks happily. I must not look the hawk in the eye. I must not punish the hawk, though it bates, and beats, and my hand is raw with pecks and my face stings from the blows of its bating wings. Hawks cannot be punished. They would rather die than submit. Patience is my only weapon. Patience. Derived from *patior*. Meaning *to suffer*. It is an ordeal. I shall triumph. He sways on his feet and suffers and the hawk suffers too. The owls are silent now. They quarter the Ridings over turf drenched with dew.

9

The rite of passage

The feathers down her front are the colour of sunned news-print, of tea-stained paper, and each is marked darkly towards its tip with a leaf-bladed spearhead, so from her throat to her feet she is patterned with a shower of falling raindrops. Her wings are the colour of stained oak, their covert feathers edged in palest teak, barred flight-feathers folded quietly beneath. And there's a strange grey tint to her that is felt, rather than seen, a kind of silvery light like a rainy sky reflected from the surface of a river. She looks new. Looks as if the world cannot touch her. As if everything that exists and is observed rolls off like drops of water from her oiled and close-packed feathers. And the more I sit with her, the more I marvel at how reptilian she is. The lucency of her pale, round eyes. The waxy yellow skin about her Bakelite-black beak. The way she snakes her small head from side to side to focus on distant objects. Half the time she seems as alien as a snake, a thing hammered of metal and scales and glass. But then I see ineffably birdlike things about her, familiar qualities that turn her into something loveable and close. She scratches her fluffy chin with one awkward, taloned foot; sneezes when bits of errant down get up her nose. And when I look again she seems neither bird nor reptile, but a creature shaped by a million years of evolution for a life she's not yet lived. Those long, barred tail-feathers and short, broad wings are perfectly shaped for sharp turns and brutal acceleration through a world of woodland obstacles; the patterns on her plumage will hide her in perfect, camouflaging drifts of light and shade. The tiny, hair-like feathers between her beak and eye – *crines* – are for catching blood so that it will dry, and flake, and fall away, and the frowning eyebrows that lend her face its hollow rapacious intensity are bony projections to protect her eyes when crashing into undergrowth after prey.

Everything about the hawk is tuned and turned to hunt and kill. Yesterday I discovered that when I suck air through my teeth and make a squeaking noise like an injured rabbit, all the tendons in her toes instantaneously contract, driving her talons into the glove with terrible, crushing force. This killing grip is an old, deep pattern in her brain, an innate response that hasn't yet found the stimulus meant to release it. Because other sounds provoke it: door hinges, squealing brakes, bicycles with unoiled wheels – and on the second afternoon, Joan Sutherland singing an aria on the radio. *Ow.* I laughed out loud at that. Stimulus: *opera*. Response: *kill*. But later these misapplied instincts stop being funny. At just past six o'clock a small, unhappy wail came from a pram outside the window. Straight away the hawk drove her talons into my glove, ratcheting up the pressure in savage, stabbing spasms. *Kill.* The baby cries. *Kill kill kill.*

Two days pass. I sit and walk, and sit and sleep, the hawk almost constantly on my fist. My arm aches and a damp tiredness grips my heart. A farming programme on the radio. Wheat, borage, rapeseed. Polytunnels and cherries. The hawk is alternately a hunchback toad, a nervous child or a dragon. The house is a tip. Scraps of raw meat decorate the bin. I've run out of coffee. I have forgotten how to speak. My mouth makes small, mumbled assurances to the hawk that all is well. She meets them with silence, with thready, nervous cheeps through her nose. As I walk she follows my feet with her eyes as if they were two small animals moving about the house with us. She is interested in flies, in specks of floating dust, in the way light falls on certain surfaces. What is she looking at? What is she thinking? I hear the click of the nictitating membrane that crosses her eyes as she blinks, and now I see them closely her eyes begin to disturb me. They look like discs of pale paper stuck to the side of her head, each with a hole-punched black pupil housed under a transparent dome like a bubble of water. The hawk is stranger than I'd thought. And calmer than I'd believed possible.

I'm starting to worry. Is there something wrong with her? She's oddly tame. Where is the lunatic I'd expected? For two days I've sat with her and not once, *contra* White, have I longed to dismember her and batter her to death. I'd expected a barrelling tornado of terror and wildness, some great and awful struggle of souls, but instead, as the light deepens and the late swifts outside ascend on flickering wings to bury themselves in the sky, I sit on a sofa watching a tired hawk go to sleep. The leading edges of her wings drop and rest against the glove. One downy grey eyelid slides up to cover an eye, then the other. Her shoulders fall; her head wobbles. The tip of her glossy black beak sinks into the feathers over her crop. Watching her doze in this vesper hour my eyes close too, but when sleep comes I am standing in the skeleton of a burned-out house, in white, blank air that glitters faintly with mica or frost. Around me are blackened joists and rafters. I put out a hand. Touch a piece of charred wood. Cold, furred, wrong. Rising panic. Refusal. A sense of absolute dismay. Then of toppling, the house collapsing into itself and on top of me. And we wake together, the hawk and I, her with a start of apprehension, a tightening of feet and feathers, and me with a slow, sickening disorientation that makes me fasten desperately onto the sight of the hawk to drag me back into a world with no ash in it. The same thoughts over and over. Why is she sleeping so much? Hawks sleep when they're sick. She must be sick. Why am I sleeping? Am I sick too? What is wrong with her? What is wrong with us?

Nothing was wrong with the hawk. She wasn't sick. She was a baby. She fell asleep because that's what babies do. I wasn't sick either. But I was orphaned and desperately suggestible, and I didn't know what was happening to me. For years I'd scoffed at White's notion of hawk-training as a rite of passage. *Overblown*, I'd thought. *Loopy*. Because it wasn't like that. I knew it wasn't. I'd flown scores of hawks, and every step of their training was familiar to me. But while the steps were familiar, the person taking them was not. I was in ruins. Some deep part of me was trying to rebuild itself, and its model was right there on my fist. The hawk was everything I wanted to be: solitary, self-possessed, free from grief, and numb to the hurts of human life.

I was turning into a hawk.

I didn't shrink and grow plumes like the Wart in *The Sword in the Stone*, who was transformed by Merlyn into a merlin as part of his magical education. I had loved that scene as a child. I had read it over and over again, thrilling at the Wart's toes turning to talons and scratching on the floor, his primary feathers bursting in soft blue quills from the end of his fingers. But I was turning into a hawk all the same.

The change came about through my grief, my watching, my not being myself. The first few days with a wild new hawk are a delicate, reflexive dance of manners. To judge when to scratch your nose without offence, when to walk and when to sit, when to retreat and when to come close, you must read your hawk's state of mind. You do this by watching her posture and her feathers, the workings of which turn the bird's shape into an exquisitely controlled barometer of mood. A hawk's simpler emotions are easily perceived. Feathers held tight to the body mean *I am afraid*. Held loosely they mean *I am at ease*. But the longer you watch a hawk the more subtleties you see; and soon, in my hypervigilant state, I was responding to the tiniest of cues. A frowning contraction of the crines around her beak and an almost imperceptible narrowing of her eyes meant something like *happy*; a particular, fugitive expression on her face, oddly distant and reserved, meant *sleepy*.

To train a hawk you must watch it like a hawk, and so you come to understand its moods. Then you gain the ability to predict what it will do next. This is the sixth sense of the practised animal trainer. Eventually you don't see the hawk's body language at all. You seem to feel what it feels. Notice what it notices. The hawk's apprehension becomes your own. You are exercising what the poet Keats called your chameleon quality, the ability to 'tolerate a loss of self and a loss of rationality by trusting in the capacity to recreate oneself in another character or another environment'. Such a feat of imaginative recreation has always come easily to me. Too easily. It's part of being a watcher, forgetting who you are and putting yourself in the thing you are watching. That is why the girl who was me when I was small loved watching birds. She made herself disappear, and then in the birds she watched, took flight. It was happening now. I had put myself in the hawk's wild mind to tame her, and as the days passed in the darkened room my humanity was burning away.

Three tentative raps on the front door. 'Hang on,' I call. A small voice inside me, resentful and savage, hisses, *Go away*. It is Christina with two takeaway coffees and the Sunday papers. 'So,' she says, settling herself in a chair by the fireplace. 'How's it going? Is the hawk OK?' I nod. I raise my eyebrows. I am vaguely aware this isn't enough to make a conversation. 'Mmm,' I say. The voice is not entirely mine. She hugs her knees and looks at me curiously. *I must try harder*, I think. So I talk about the hawk for a while, and then I can't speak any more. I stare at my paper cup.

I'm pleased to see her. *She shouldn't be here.* This coffee is good. *We should be alone.* These resentful thoughts surprise me. Manning the hawk is all about showing it new things. Christina is a new thing. 'I'm going to try something,' I tell her. 'Ignore the hawk. Just keep reading the papers.' I fetch a fresh piece of beef from the kitchen, sit with the hawk on the sofa, reach up and remove her hood. There's a moment of fast-beating incomprehension and the air in the room turns to ice. Tight-feathered, in savage irresolution, eyes like porcelain saucers, the hawk stares. My heart sinks. She is going to bate. But the moment stretches, and she does not. After a deal of cautious observation she decides that a human turning newspaper pages is something entirely fascinating.

An hour later all is calm and companionable. We're watching television. The hawk balances evenly on the balls of her feet, mesmerised by the flickering screen. Tiny white wisps of down still attached to the finials of her scapular feathers wave in the draught from the hall. Then, without warning, she bursts from my fist in a whirlwind of a bate. Papers fly. Christina flinches. *Shit*, I think. *I should hood her, let her rest. This is too much.* But I am wrong. Fear did not engender this bate. Frustration did. She picks at her jesses in displaced fury, then tears at the meat beneath her toes. She is hungry. The food is a wonderful discovery. She is a delicate, decisive gastronome. She picks, and bites, and swallows, and squeaks in happiness, and bites and swallows again. I am thrilled. But also indignant. This moment was to have been born of solitude and meditative darkness. Not this. Not daylight with another person in the room and *'Allo 'Allo!* on the television. Not in the presence of comedy Nazis and a soundtrack about giant sausages and the occupation of France. She narrows her eyes with pleasure, bristles around the nose, and her feathers soften into loose falls of ochre and cream. 'Has she done that before?' asks Christina. 'No,' I say. 'This is the first time.' Laughter from the television audience as an SS officer dressed as a woman hoves into view and the hawk finishes eating, lifts herself into a vast, frothy mop of feathers, holds them there for an instant and shakes them all back into place. A rouse. It is a sign of contentment. She has not roused before.

Now my hawk is tame enough to sit bareheaded. From her perch by the window she watches the curtains move over a carpet furred with dust. She won't yet be picked up without a bate. But I'm working on that. From the sofa I flick a thumbnail-sized scrap of steak towards her. It falls with a sticky *thwick* on the vinyl cloth beneath her perch. She looks down at it. Frowns. Turns her head to one side to inspect it more carefully. Then hops down with a scratch of talons and a rattle of feathers, picks the meat delicately from the floor and swallows it. Gone. For a while she stands there, as if trying to remember something she has forgotten, then bounces back onto the perch with brio, all shaggy trousers and waggy tail. I wait a while, then send another scrap of flesh her way. *Thwick. Hop. Swallow. Hop.* I lower myself to the floor and sit there for a while. Shuffling slowly sideways on my rump, I watch the hawk out of the corner of my eye. She tenses. I stop. She untenses. I move. She tenses. I stop again. I inch across the carpet until I reach that hair-fine juncture where any movement nearer will make her bate from the perch. Breathing as carefully as if I were about to take an extravagantly long rifle-shot, I slowly – so slowly – extend my garnished fist towards her. I can almost taste the hawk's indecision; the air is thick with it. But – joy! – she is looking at the food in front of her. She leans forward as if to pick it from the glove, but then something inside her snaps. With an awful clang of the metal ring of the perch against its steel base, she bates away from me. *Damn.* I take her up onto the glove for a few mouthfuls of food.

When she is settled back on her perch, we play the game again. *Flick. Hop. Flick.* She's solved the puzzle of where the food is coming from and some part of her is reconsidering my place in her world. She watches me intently as I inch towards her and again extend the garnished glove. She leans across and snaps up my gift of steak. My heart leaps. She takes another piece, and then another, smacking her glossy black chops.

As I sit there happily feeding titbits to the hawk, her name drops into my head. *Mabel*. From *amabilis*, meaning loveable, or dear. An old, slightly silly name, an unfashionable name. There is something of the grandmother about it: antimacassars and afternoon teas. There's a superstition among falconers that a hawk's ability is inversely proportional to the ferocity of its name. Call a hawk *Tiddles* and it will be a formidable hunter; call it *Spitfire* or *Slayer* and it will probably refuse to fly at all. White called his hawk Gos for short, but also awarded him a host of darkly grandiose other names that for years made me roll my eyes in exasperation. Hamlet. Macbeth. Strindberg. Van Gogh. Astur. Baal. Medici. Roderick Dhu. Lord George Gordon. Byron. Odin. Nero. Death. Tarquin. Edgar Allan Poe. *Imagine*, I used to think, amused and faintly contemptuous. Imagine calling your goshawk any of those things! But now that list just made me sad. My hawk needed a name as far from that awful litany, as far from Death as it could get. 'Mabel.' I say the word out loud to her and watch her watching me say it. My mouth shapes the word. 'Mabel.' And as I say it, it strikes me that all those people outside the window who shop and walk and cycle and go home and eat and love and sleep and dream – all of them have names. And so do I. 'Helen,' I say. How strange it sounds. How very strange. I put another piece of meat on my glove and the hawk leans down and eats.

10

Darkness

He pours another whisky into his emptied glass and broods over the day's events. He is free, but he has shackled himself to a madman. A lunatic. At the very least, a sufferer of intermittent delusional insanity. He turns down the beam of the paraffin lamp and sinks back into the chair, gloomily rereading the report he has written on the progress of his goshawk's education.

> 6.15–6.45 walked round + round Gos, holding out a leg, while he bated whenever I came too close. Came away without feeding him. This is not in the book. I have done the same thing, with the same results, for fifteen minutes in every hour since (until 6 o'clock at night).

He despised that rabbit leg. He despised the fur on it, the claws, the crown of pale flesh that grew dry and waxen as the hours passed. He despised it because the hawk did not want it. The hawk did not want him either. He had whistled to the hawk all day and his lips had grown dry as the whistle gave out and his solicitude had thinned to frustration and finally despair. Last night the frustration had reached such a pitch that he'd prevented Gos from regaining the fist after a bate – worse, gloried in the hawk hanging there, revolving slowly on his jesses. It was a terrible sin. He is full of shame. And worry. Gos's mutes are green. Does that mean his hawk is sick? Maybe that is why he did not want the rabbit. What should he do? *Starvation*, he thinks. That will cure the stomach upset, if it is one. Perhaps he shall give the hawk some egg tomorrow? But the most important thing of all is this: *he shall eat when he jumps for it, not before.*

White's plan would have worked, had he stuck to it. But he did not. By dawn Gos had been given the greater part of a rabbit to eat, and he had not jumped to the fist. Another resolution was broken. They all were. Even White's plan to keep the hawk awake for three days and nights had failed: he'd felt so sorry for Gos he kept returning him to his perch for short bouts of sleep. Freed from White's presence, Gos remembered how much better life was when not tied to a human who kept stroking it and talking to it and bothering it with slippery rabbit livers, and singing and whistling and moving glasses of liquid up and down. When he came to pick it up again the hawk was always as wild as ever.

Poor Gos. Poor, ragged, fearful, broken-feathered Gos. I thought of him often as I sat with my hawk. I saw him in black and white and a long way off, as if viewed through the wrong end of a telescope: a miniature, miserable hawk bating and twittering in distress on the grey lawns of a distant house. Gos was very real to me. But White was not. It was hard to imagine him with his hawk. Sitting with my own it was hard to imagine him at all. I looked at photographs, but they were all of different people: one was a pale-eyed man with a Shakespearian beard who'd written books under the pen-name James Aston, and another a thin young man with nervous eyes and a spare, haunted face who was Mr White the schoolmaster. There were photographs of White the countryman in an open-necked shirt and a tweed jacket, looking louche and amused. And photographs of White much later in his life: a corpulent, white-bearded English Hemingway, a woolly-sweatered Falstaff. I couldn't reconcile these faces. I read *The Goshawk* again as I sat with Mabel, read it many times, and every time it seemed

a different book; sometimes a caustically funny romance, sometimes the journal of a man laughing at failure, sometimes a
heartbreaking tract of another man's despair.

But one White was clear to me as I manned my hawk. It
was not White the falconer. It was the man who had, for the
first time in his life, discovered the joys of domesticity. A man
who painted woodwork the brightest of blues and reds, who
arranged feathers in jars on his mantelpiece and made curries
from prawns and eggs and spoons of thin-cut marmalade. I
saw him boiling his laundry in the copper on the kitchen
stove, and sitting in an armchair reading Masefield's *Midnight
Folk* with his setter Brownie sleeping at his feet.

And I saw him drinking. There was always a bottle at
White's side, and his battle with Gos made him drink all the
more. 'It was not that one drank enough to become incapable
or stupid,' he wrote, 'but alcohol now seemed the only way of
continuing to live.' As I sat with my hawk and puzzled over
White I wondered if it was alcohol that obscured him, blurred
him from view. I knew the notion was fanciful, but even so
there seemed some deep connection between White's drinking
and his evasiveness. And I was sure that it was the drink that
irrigated White's constant self-sabotage, for it is a common
trait of alcoholics to make plans and promises, to oneself, to
others, fervently, sincerely, and in hope of redemption. Promises that are broken, again and again, through fear, through
loss of nerve, through any number of things that hide that
deep desire, at heart, to obliterate one's broken self.

I opened the curtains the next morning. The brightness of the
room made me clearer, which concerned her for a while. But
when a broad stripe of sunlight fell across her back she raised
her feathers to greet it. Now, standing in a shallow bath next
to her perch, she nibbles her toes, takes precise and tiny bites
of water. She jumps back onto her perch and begins to
preen herself, contorting her body into the stylised shapes of

Japanese paintings of courtly goshawks. She runs her beak through one feather after another in quick succession: the sound is of paper being scored, or a pack of cards being shuffled. Then she stretches one broad wing behind her, drags it slowly back over her sunlit tail, and rouses, squeaking happily through her nose. I watch all this with a ravenous, gulping-down-champagne sense of joy. *Look how happy she is*, I think. This room is not a dungeon and I am not a torturer. I am a beneficent figure, one who crouches and stoops in anxious genuflection, bearing delicious treats of steak in my hand.

It is hubris. Less than an hour later I am certain that my hawk hates me and I am the worst falconer in the history of the world. No matter that Mabel is far tamer than any of the boys or books had told me she would be. *I've comprehensively failed her. The hawk is ruined.* I know this is true because she doesn't want to be hooded. Until now she has accepted the hood with equanimity. Earlier today I sensed a little thrum of disquiet in her heart and now it has exploded into outright rebellion. I bring the hood up to her head and she dodges it. Snakes her head. Contracts it into her neck. Ducks and runs.

I know why this is happening. To begin with the hood was a welcome refuge, but now she's decided I'm harmless it is merely something that stops her seeing, and she wants to see. Now, unhappy, unsettled, lifting one foot then the other, the hawk looks about the room for somewhere to go. Her mood is contagious; my heart flutters tightly, heavily in my chest. I have lost the ability to disappear. I try to remove myself by listening to the cricket on the radio but can't understand what the commentator is saying. I can only turn my attention from my unhappy hawk by thinking about the hood I'm holding. It is all she is thinking of too.

I remember hauling this hood out of my bag while looking for a pen before a university seminar a few months ago. 'What's that?' asked a colleague.

'A falcon hood,' I said, not looking up.

'Have you brought it in to show it to people?'

'No. It was just in my bag.'

'But can I look at it?'

'Absolutely, go ahead.'

She picked it up, fascinated. 'What an amazing thing,' she said, frowning under her straight-cut fringe. 'It goes over the hawk's head to keep it quiet, right?' And she looked inside, where the moulded leather was stitched with lines of hair-fine thread, and then turned it over in her hands, examining the bevelled opening for the hawk's beak and the plaited Turk's-head knot you hold it by, and the two long braces at the back that pull the hood open and closed. She set it back on the table reverently. 'It's so beautifully made,' she said. 'It's like a Prada shoe.'

Indeed. This hood is among the best of its kind. It was made by an American falconer called Doug Pineo and it weighs almost nothing. A few grams. That is all. Something about its perfect lightness set against the heaviness of my heart makes me giddy. I shut my eyes and my head is full of hoods. Modern American hoods like this one. Loose-braced Bahraini hoods of soft goatskin for passage sakers and peregrines. Syrian hoods. Turkmen hoods. Afghan hoods. Tiny Indian hoods in snakeskin for shikras and sparrowhawks. Huge eagle hoods from Central Asia. Sixteenth-century French hoods cut from white kidskin embroidered with golden thread and painted with coats of arms. They're not a European invention. Frankish knights learned how to use hoods from Arab falconers during the Crusades, and a shared love of falconry made hawks political pawns in those wars. When a white gyrfalcon owned by King Philip I of Spain broke its leash during the Siege of Acre and flew up to the city walls, the king sent an envoy into the city to request its return. Saladin refused, and Philip sent another envoy, accompanied by trumpets, ensigns and heralds, offering a thousand gold crowns for the falcon. Was it returned? I can't recall.

Did it matter? *No*, I think savagely. *They're all dead. Long dead*. I think of Saladin taking the king's falcon onto his own hand and covering its eyes with leather. *I own this. It is mine*. I think of fetish hoods. I think of distant wars. I think of Abu Ghraib. Sand in the mouth. Coercion. History and hawks and hoods and the implications of taking something's sight away to calm it. *It's in your own best interest*. Rising nausea. There's a sensation of ground being lost, of wet sand washing from under my feet. I don't want to think of the photographs of the tortured man with the hood on his head and the wires to his hands and the invisible enemy who holds the camera, but it is all I can see and the word *hood* like a hot stone in my mouth. *Burqa*, the word in Arabic. Hood.

I start speaking to the hawk – I think to the hawk – in a voice as low and reassuring as I can make it. 'When you travel in the car, Mabel,' I say, 'there'll be lots of frightening things out there and we can't have you crashing about while I drive. It is just to keep you feeling safe.' And then, 'It is necessary.' I hear myself say it. *It is necessary*. That is what I am telling myself. But I don't like it. Nor does she. Patiently I offer it again. 'Look,' I say carefully. 'Just a hood.' I move it slowly up to her feathered chin. She bates. I wait until she settles and move it up to her chin again. *Bate*. And again. *Bate. Bate. Bate*. I want to be gentle. I *am* being gentle, but my gentleness is a veneer on raging despair. I don't want to hood her. She knows it. On the radio the cricket commentator explains in gleeful detail why a batsman's defensive stroke has failed. 'Shut up, Aggers,' I snap, and try once again. 'Come on, Mabel,' I say beseechingly, and in another minute the hood is on, she is back on her perch, and I am slumped on the sofa. The world is burning and I don't want to touch it. *This is a disaster. A disaster. I can't do this. Not any of it. I am a terrible falconer*. I burst into tears. The hawk dissolves. I curl up, bury my face in a cushion and cry myself to sleep.

* * *

Forty minutes later Stuart is assessing the hawk with narrowed, practised eyes. 'Small, isn't she?' he says, dragging four fingers thoughtfully down one stubbled cheek. 'But she's a good-looking gos. Long body. Long tail. Bird hawk.'

By this he means my goshawk might be better suited to fly at pheasants and partridges than rabbits or hares.

'Yes.'

'How're you doing with her?' asks Mandy. She's sitting on my sofa rolling a cigarette, looking amazing, like a rural punk princess from an unlikely Thomas Hardy novel. I tell her that the hawk is surprisingly tame and everything's going well. But it is a dreadful lie. When they'd knocked on the door and roused me from sleep I knew I had to maintain some desperate fiction of competence. And so far I'd managed this, though there'd been a nasty moment when Mandy looked at me with concern in her eyes and I realised my own were red and raw. *It's OK*, I told myself. *She'll think I've been crying about Dad.* I pick up the hawk and stand there like someone with a present at a party and no clear idea to whom I should hand it. 'Lie down, Jess,' says Stuart. The black and white English pointer they've brought flops onto the rug and lets out a sigh. I unhood Mabel. She stands on tiptoe, the tip of her beak pressed to her spangled and silvery chest, looking down at this new phenomenon that is a dog. The dog looks at her. So do we. There is a curious silence. I mistake it for anger. For disappointment. For anything but what it is: astonishment. A look of wonder passes over Stuart's face. 'Well,' he says, eventually. 'You've got gold, there. I thought she'd freak out completely. She's very well manned.'

'Really?'

'She's so calm, Helen!' says Mandy.

It takes me a while to even half-believe them, but it helps that I manage to hood Mabel without too much fuss – and after two cups of tea and an hour in their company the world is bright again. 'Don't drag your feet,' Stuart says as they leave. 'Get her out of the house. Take her outside. Man her in the streets.' I know he is right. It's time for the next stage of training.

Carriage is what falconers call walking with a hawk to tame it, and all my books insisted it was the key to a well-trained gos. 'The key to her management is to carry, carry, carry,' wrote Gilbert Blaine. It was 'the grand secret of discipline' to Edward Michell. Back in the seventeenth century Edward Bert had explained that when you walk with a hawk 'her eye doth still behold change of objects', which is why carriage works – and why you can't tame a hawk by keeping her indoors. Such a hawk 'will endure nothing, because shee hath not beene made acquainted with any thing', he says. *Oh, Edmund Bert,* I think. *I wish it was still the seventeenth century. There'd have been fewer things out there to frighten my hawk.*

But I knew that wasn't true. There'd have been carts and horses and crowds and dogs and they'd have been just as frightening for a half-manned goshawk as buses and mopeds and students on bikes. The difference was that in 1615 no one would have paid me the slightest attention. Hawks on the streets of Cambridge would have been as unremarkable a sight as dogs on leads today. Walking with my hawk will be an open invitation for everyone to come up and stare, and enquire, and quiz me about the hawk, and what she is, and who I am, and why. And beneath my disinclination to engage in conversation there is a much simpler terror: people. Just people. I don't want to see people at all. After the door is closed I look at it for a long while, rubbing my cheek where the cushion had left a deep, indented scar.

Later that afternoon I take Mabel into the walled garden of my college house. Above us is a deep field of fast-moving cumulus. Branches lift in the breeze; leaves shift with a collapsing, papery flicker. The air is thick with sun and dust and dandelion seeds. There's too much light, too much contrast.

Too much noise and movement. I flinch at the hurry of it all. But the hawk? The hawk is unperturbed. She tips her head sideways to look up at the moving clouds – in daylight her irises are flat and shiny and slightly blurred, with pupils that dilate and contract like a camera lens as she focuses – zip-zip-zip – up to track a passing Cessna – and then she turns her head upside down to watch a fly, and then tracks another fly, and pulls abstractedly at the meat I hold in the glove, and watches other things way, way beyond my poor human vision.

The world she lives in is not mine. Life is faster for her; time runs slower. Her eyes can follow the wingbeats of a bee as easily as ours follow the wingbeats of a bird. *What is she seeing?* I wonder, and my brain does backflips trying to imagine it, because I can't. I have three different receptor-sensitivities in my eyes: red, green and blue. Hawks, like other birds, have four. This hawk can see colours I cannot, right into the ultraviolet spectrum. She can see polarised light, too, watch thermals of warm air rise, roil, and spill into clouds, and trace, too, the magnetic lines of force that stretch across the earth. The light falling into her deep black pupils is registered with such frightening precision that she can see with fierce clarity things I can't possibly resolve from the generalised blur. The claws on the toes of the house martins overhead. The veins on the wings of the white butterfly hunting its wavering course over the mustards at the end of the garden. I'm standing there, my sorry human eyes overwhelmed by light and detail, while the hawk watches everything with the greedy intensity of a child filling in a colouring book, scribbling joyously, blocking in colour, making the pages its own. And all I can think is, *I want to go back inside.*

11

Leaving home

Keys in pocket, hawk on fist, and off we go. Leaving the house that evening is frightening. Somewhere in my mind ropes uncoil and fall. It feels like an unmooring, as if I were an airship ascending on its maiden flight into darkness. Stepping over the low railings into the park I head for the thick black avenue of limes and the lamplit leaves beneath. Everything seems hot and clean and dangerous and my senses are screwed to their utmost, as if someone had told me the park was full of hungry lions. Night air moves in the spaces between the trees. Moths make dusty circles about the lamps. I look down and see each pale blade of grass casts two separate shadows from the two nearest lamps, and so do I, and in the distance comes the collapsing echo of a moving train and somewhere closer a dog barks twice and there's broken glass by the path and next to it a feather from the breast of a woodpigeon judging by its size and curl. It lies upon the grass as if held just above it, gleaming softly in the darkness.

'Bloody hell, Mabel,' I whisper. 'Who spiked my tea with acid?' Night has never looked like this before. I walk deeper into this lamplit world, wondering at my heightened perception and reassured by how unconcerned the hawk is. She does not look up. She couldn't care less about her surroundings. She is hunched busily over the rabbit leg in my glove. It is a *tiring* – a piece of sinewy, bony meat to keep her occupied as we walk, drawing her attention from the things around her. She pulls and picks scraps from it with the rapt concentration of a diner disassembling a lobster. Watching her I begin to relax. And straight away the emptied world is full of people.

But they are not people. They are things to shun, to fear, to turn from, shielding my hawk. They come towards us like tumbling rocks in a video game, threatening destruction with the merest glancing blow. My heart beats fast. Escape and evasion. I am here to show the hawk people, but from a safe distance merely, and those three men in pastel shirts are heading right towards us. I dodge behind a tree trunk and let them pass. As their backs enter Mabel's line of sight she sucks her feathers in so tightly she seems vacuum-packed in plastic. When they are gone she shakes her head nervously, cheeps once through her nose and starts eating again.

A minute later a woman swinging supermarket bags is upon us. There's nowhere to go. *Where did all these bloody people come from?* I look about in desperation. Mabel is now a pair of huge and haunted eyes, a ghost of bones and sinews, seconds from a bate. I hold her close to my chest and turn in a slow circle to block the woman from view. The woman doesn't see the hawk. What she sees is a weirdo in a tattered jacket and baggy corduroy trousers revolving on the spot for no good reason. She hurries past, fast. There's a sense of dreadful escalation. *It's fine*, I tell myself. *This is going well*, but blood sings loud in my ears. A bicycle hisses by. The hawk bates. I curse. Another bicycle. She bates again. My nerve breaks. I start back to the house. We are nearly at the door when a runner passes – he's come up silently behind us on his expensive trainers – and the hawk bates once again. I hate him for upsetting my hawk – actually hate him, am outraged by his existence. All the anger within me, the anger I didn't know was there, the anger the books call One of the Five Stages of Grief rears up in a towering instant of white-hot fury. I look at his retreating back and wish him death.

But then he breaks stride, turns back, and stops ten feet from us.

'Sorry,' I say, smiling and biting back ire. 'It's her first time out of the house, and she's still scared of people.'

'God, no. I'm sorry,' he says. 'I didn't see her.'

He's a person, I realise. A real person, skinny and bearded and wearing a blue T-shirt and with a water bottle in his hand and he is friendly and wary and a little in awe of the hawk. I think he might be a nice man.

'I hope I didn't startle you,' I begin apologetically. He grins and shakes his head.

'I was surprised! It's not something you see every day!'

I turn briefly to the hawk as she bends down to pull at the rabbit leg again. I open my mouth to speak. But when I look up he has gone.

It is bright, after heavy rain, and the crowds of closing time have gone. On this second expedition from the house Mabel grips the glove more tightly than ever. She is tense. She looks smaller and feels heavier in this mood, as if fear had a weight to it, as if pewter had been poured into her long and airy bones. The raindrop marks on her tight-feathered front run together into long lines like those around a downturned mouth. She picks fitfully at her food, but mostly she stares, taut with reserve, about her. She follows bicycles with her eyes. She hunches ready to spring when people come too close. Children alarm her. She is unsure about dogs. Big dogs, that is. Small dogs fascinate her for other reasons.

After ten minutes of haunted apprehension, the goshawk decides that she's not going to be eaten, or beaten to death, by any of these things. She rouses and begins to eat. Cars and buses rattle fumily past, and when the food is gone she stands staring at the strange world around her. So do I. I've been with the hawk so long, just her and me, that I'm seeing my city through her eyes. She watches a woman throwing a ball to her dog on the grass, and I watch too, as baffled by what she's doing as the hawk is. I stare at traffic lights before I remember what they are. Bicycles are spinning mysteries of glittering metal. The buses going past are walls with wheels. What's salient to the hawk in the city is not what is salient to man. The things she sees are uninteresting to her. Irrelevant. Until there's a clatter of wings. We both look up. There's a pigeon, a woodpigeon, sailing down to roost in a lime tree above us. Time slows. The air thickens and the hawk is transformed. It's as if all her weapons systems were suddenly engaged. Red cross-hairs. She stands on her toes and cranes her neck. *This. This flightpath. This thing*, she thinks. *This is fascinating.* Some part of the hawk's young brain has just worked something out, and it has everything to do with death.

'For the goshawk,' wrote White, 'the necessity was a long walk on the fist; as it always was.' But he walked as if the walking itself were the secret, not his attention to the feelings of his hawk. Even in the aftermath of my father's death my tattered heart knew that the secret to taming hawks was to take things slowly. To move from darkness to light, from enclosed rooms into the open air, to stand at a distance, first, and then grow closer, over many days, to this alien world of raucous voices and swinging arms, of bright plastic buggies and roaring mopeds. Day by day, foot by foot, mouthful by mouthful, my hawk would come to see that these things were not a threat, and would look upon them with equanimity.

But it was continuous murder for Gos. White walked because that was what the books said he should do, and so that was what he did, taking Gos outside even on the day he arrived. Forty-eight hours later he was walked to the Wheelers' farmhouse to meet 'all the family, barking dogs and all', and the next day they were out on the road meeting cars and cyclists. 'He bates repeatedly on these trips,' White noted in his day-book. On it went. He took Gos with him to the pub, took him fishing for carp, took him to Banbury in a motor car. 'He had to learn to stand that bustle,' wrote White, 'as we all have to do, however little we visit it.' And he did. Just as the despairing soul will finally comprehend its helplessness in the face of continuing horror and bear it because there is no alternative, so with Gos. He had no alternative. There was no softness in his taming. He had to learn to bear things through being frightened all the time, just as White had learned there was no escape in his own education.

Down the small roads and grassy rides and across fields damp with standing hay, White walked himself into the landscape. Whole days went past on foot, the novice austringer sinking gratefully into the rhythm and weather of the land. Walking home in the evening along the high-hedged Buckinghamshire lanes he watched 'the red moon perceptibly rising', which he 'had seen to sink as a yellow one at dawn'. At night the world became magical by virtue of its emptiness, and the Ridings a place of mists and stars and solitude. This was his patient excursion into the fields and back into the past.

Despite the eccentricity of a hawk on his fist, what White was doing was very much of his time. Long walks in the English countryside, often at night, were astonishingly popular in the 1930s. Rambling clubs published calendars of full moons, train companies laid on mystery trains to rural destinations, and when in 1932 the Southern Railway offered an excursion to a moonlit walk along the South Downs, expecting to sell forty or so tickets, one and a half thousand people turned up. The people setting out on these walks weren't seeking to conquer peaks or test themselves against maps and miles. They were looking for a mystical communion with the land; they walked backwards in time to an imagined past suffused with magical, native glamour: to Merrie England, or to prehistoric England, pre-industrial visions that offered solace and safety to sorely troubled minds. For though railways and roads and a burgeoning market in countryside books had contributed to this movement, at heart it had grown out of the trauma of the Great War, and was flourishing in fear of the next. The critic Jed Esty has described this pastoral craze as one element in a wider movement of national cultural salvage in these years; it was a response to economic disaster, a contracting Empire and totalitarian threats from abroad. It was a movement that celebrated ancient sites and folk traditions. It delighted in Shakespeare and Chaucer, in Druids, in Arthurian legend. It believed that something essential about the nation had been lost and could be returned, if only in the imagination. White, caught up in this conservative, antiquarian mood, walked with his hawk and wrote of ghosts, of starry Orion naked and resplendent in the English sky, of all the imaginary lines men and time had drawn upon the landscape. By the fire, his hawk by his side, he brooded on the fate of nations.

The cloud-base is low today. It does not matter. He is not flying today. He is walking. He is walking with his hawk, and he and Gos have traversed five fields to get here. Now he stands by the ruins of the chapel of St Thomas the Martyr. Once it was a chapel, then it was a house, and now it is a ruin, a great, collapsing carcass of stained ironstone. The roof is a broken ribcage heaped with rotting thatch. Lintels sag over windows and doors blocked with laths and limestone rubble. Great banks of nettles grow here, rich and green. Ash trees rise in lacy fists and the fields fall away each side. It is very quiet. He hears the ticking of a robin somewhere, like falling water. This place is soundly cursed against man, he thinks. The stink of the dead sheep he found dumped in a drain is still caught in his nose, a sorry, sodden wreck of fleece pullulating with maggots. He does not mind the smell. It is a bracing stench. It is the smell of mortality. He looks down at the rabbit-cropped turf. Beneath him, the people that lived and died and were buried here are here still, he thinks; their old bones would be grateful to see a goshawk again. He walks around the chapel, imagining the earth beneath him turning and muttering as it senses the familiar hawk above, as the bones of farm labourers mutter when agricultural machinery passes over their forgotten tombs.

> I thought of the small race now underground, strangers of a vanished species safe from comprehension, almost from imagination: monks, nuns, and the eternal villein. I was as close to them as anybody now, close even to Chaucer, 'with grey goshawk in hond'. They would understand my hawk with their eyes, as a farmer understood an elevator. We loved each other.

White's visit to Chapel Green was my favourite part of *The Goshawk* when I was young. It was a communion with something lost and forgotten, and somehow a hawk was at the heart of it. It always gave me a sense of kinship with White – although I couldn't imagine why farmers should have special knowledge of elevators. That made no sense at all. *Maybe he meant to write 'tractor'*, I thought, for I didn't know then what a bale elevator was, nor that White had been lately watching the Wheelers, who farmed the land around him, using one. But I could imagine the chapel quite clearly when I was small, and now it was clearer than ever. If I shut my eyes I saw White lifting Gos on his fist and shutting his own eyes very tight, as if it were possible for the whole mess of the twentieth century to slip aside, and the world of centuries before be resurrected, a lost community with him at its heart. He would have been loved. He would have been understood.

Looking back, and all for love. There was a telescope on my bookshelf at the far end of the room. A spotting scope in a green Cordura cover. I'd borrowed it from my father to go birdwatching and it had not been returned. I'd forgotten to bring it with me on that last visit. 'Next time,' he said, shaking his head with good-natured exasperation. There was no next time. I could not give it back. I could not apologise to him either. There was a time, perhaps the day after his death, or perhaps the day after that, when I sat on a train with my mother and brother. We were on our way to look for his car. It was a desperate journey. My hands clutched the coarse upholstery of the seat until my knuckles turned white. I remember buddleia, and trackside clinker, and a green gasometer, and Battersea Power Station as the train slowed. And it wasn't until we were standing on Queenstown Road station, on an unfamiliar platform under a white wooden canopy, wasn't until we were walking towards the exit, that I realised, for the first time, that I would never see my father again.

Ever. I stopped dead. And I shouted. I called out loud for him. *Dad*. And then the word *No* came out in one long, collapsing howl. My brother and mother put their arms around me, and I them. Brute fact. I would never speak to him again. I would never see him again. We clung to each other, crying for Dad, the man we loved, the quiet man in a suit with a camera on his shoulder, who had set out each day in search of things that were new, who had captured the courses of stars and storms and streets and politicians, who had stopped time by making pictures of the movings of the world. My father, who had gone out to photograph storm-damaged buildings in Battersea, on that night when the world had visited him with damage and his heart had given way.

The photographs he'd taken were still on the camera they handed to my mother at the hospital. The last photograph I saw only once. I never want to see it again. But I can never stop seeing it. Blurred, taken from a low angle, far too low; an empty London street. Sodium lights, dusk, a wall tipped sideways from the vertical and running into the distance; a vanishing point of sallow, stormy sky.

12

Outlaws

'Come on, Mabel!' I'm kneeling on the carpet and holding out a dead day-old cockerel chick. My freezer is packed with their sad, fluffy corpses, by-products of industrial egg production. Mabel loves them. She stares longingly at the one in my glove. I hold it just out of reach and whistle. 'You can do it!' I say. 'Jump!' But she is doing everything she can to avoid jumping. It is comical. She leans. She leans further. She stretches her neck as far as it will go and opens her beak hopefully. The food is just there. She can't reach it. She overbalances, scrambles upright. A change in tactics is required. She makes a cobra-strike grab for the meat with one great, grasping foot. Her reach is astonishing; her legs are almost as long as she is. One feathered shin flashes out, tawny as a lion's, and her talons very nearly catch on the glove. But not quite.

Now she is cross. She paces up and down. She stamps and grips her perch. Her black-feathered moustaches harden into frown-lines down her jaw, and I can feel her bristling. She snakes her head from side to side, reckoning distances. Something is changing in her. I sense it with a shiver. It is as if the room is darkening, contracting to a point. Then something happens. My hand is hit, hard, with a blow so unexpectedly powerful the shock is carried down my spine to the tips of my toes. Hitting someone's hand with a baseball bat would have a similar effect. She is on the glove, mantling her great, barred wings over it, gripping it fiercely and tearing at the meat. Disarticulated pieces of chicken disappear fast down her throat. I am delighted. She has crossed a great psychological gulf, one far wider than the ten inches of air between her perch and the glove she's landed upon. Not that she's landed on it: she's killed it. There is no mercy in that ratcheting, numbing grip. Mabel can keep up this pressure with no effort whatsoever. It is an effort for her to let go.

I choose my moment. When her head is up swallowing a mouthful of chick, I tug its remains through my palm and spirit it away. She looks down, then behind her, then at the floor. *Where did it go?* I persuade her to step back onto her perch. Then I hold the chick out once more, and further away. Instantly I feel that terrible blow. It is a killing blow, but there is something about the force of it that reminds me that I am alive.

I was alive, yes, but exhausted. I felt as if I were built of wool. Grey, loose-spun wool on an aching set of bones. My walks with the hawk were stressful, requiring endless vigilance, and they were wearing me away. As the hawk became tamer I was growing wilder. Fear was contagious: it rose unbidden in my heart as people approached us. I was no longer certain if the hawk bated because she was frightened of what she saw, or if the terror she felt was mine. And something else had happened on our walks. We had become invisible. The people passing by didn't stop, didn't look, sent not even a sideways glance in our direction. Some part of me began to believe that they didn't see us at all; that we were walking in another dimension, as if we were ghosts, or they were. I thought of those goshawks I'd seen as a child staring out at a winter afternoon from the world I now inhabited. And at night, at home, I stood at the window watching the lights outside, pressing my forehead against the pane to feel the faint ticking of summer rain through glass and bone.

Everyone saw us. Of course they did. A woman stalking the park with a bloody great hawk on her fist and a baleful stare on her face is hardly inconspicuous. Everyone saw us; they just pretended they hadn't. But some people were brave enough to look. The next morning, for example, standing in thin rain watching flotillas of umbrellas move across the park, I notice a man. He stands against a fence twenty feet away, hands resting equably on the wooden rail, watching us with a face as expressionless as if he were regarding horses in a field. I walk over and say hello. He is from Kazakhstan, he says, and we talk about my hawk, and about Kazakh falconers, *berkutchi*, who fly golden eagles from horseback as they have done for thousands of years. He has never seen the eagles, he says, because he lives in a city. In Almaty. He asks if my hawk has a hood. I give it to him. He turns it in his hands, nods at its workmanship, gives it back to me. Only then do we properly introduce ourselves. His name is Kanat. He asks where I will hunt with the hawk. 'On farmland a few miles from here,' I reply. He nods, looks searchingly at Mabel, and is silent for a long time. Then he spreads his fingers wide on the wooden rail and stares at the backs of his hands and at the cuffs of his brown leather jacket. 'I miss my country,' he says.

Soon after he leaves a cyclist skids to a halt and asks politely if he can look at the bird. He is absurdly handsome. He stands there with his Antonio Banderas hair, and his expensive technical jacket and titanium bike beaded with rain, and admires the hell out of her. 'She is *beautiful*,' he says. He is trying to find another word but it evades him. Beautiful will have to do. He says it again. Then he thanks me over and over again for the hawk. 'So close!' he says. 'I have never seen a hawk so close.' In Mexico he has only seen wild ones, and only far away. 'I like to watch them because they are . . .' And he makes a movement with one hand as if it were something lifting into the air. 'Free,' I say. He nods, and I do too, and in some wonder, because I am beginning to see that for some people a hawk on the hand of a stranger urges confession, urges confidences, lets you speak words about hope and home and heart. And I realise, too, that in all my days of walking with Mabel the only people who have come up and spoken to us have been outsiders: children, teenage goths, homeless people, overseas students, travellers, drunks, people on holiday. 'We are outsiders now, Mabel,' I say, and the thought is not unpleasant. But I feel ashamed of my nation's reticence. Its desire to keep walking, to move on, not to comment, not to interrogate, not to take any interest in something peculiar, unusual, in anything that isn't entirely normal.

I'm in an expansive, celebratory mood. Today Mabel flew four feet to my fist from the back of a chair in my front room. 'You're doing brilliantly,' I tell her. 'Time for a walk. Let's go and meet my friend's kids. They'll love you.' A few minutes later I knock on a door and my friend's husband opens it. My hawk flinches. So do I: this man was exceptionally rude to me once. But whatever. It doesn't matter. Maybe he was having a bad day. Forgive, forget. My friend isn't in. I stand before the door and tell him about the hawk. I tell him her age, her sex, her species, her name. I tell him that I'd thought her taming would be the kind of agonising battle I'd read about in *The Goshawk*. 'But it's been a total surprise,' I say. 'There's been no battle at all. Which isn't my doing, I'm sure. She's a freakishly calm hawk.' And the man inclines his head to one side, and smiles.

'Well,' he says, 'that'll be a gendered thing.'

'Gendered?'

'Yes. You're a woman, and she's female. Of *course* you get on,' he says.

He seems deadly serious. I stare at his curled hand on the

doorframe and heat rises in my face. *This is mockery.* For the first time in weeks, the hawk disappears from my mind as some part of me bunches up into one firm and unspoken sentence: *What an asshole.*

He's saying because I'm training a female hawk, there's some bond of sisterhood between us? *What the hell?* We're different *species*, for God's sake. 'I don't think that's a factor in my hawk's behaviour,' I say, and smile. It's a thin smile. The smile of the placator. It is a smile that is a veneer on murder. I rage my way home, heart bating wildly. Back in the house, hawk on her perch, I collect myself. My anger has gone: now I am fascinated. I pull all the falconry books off the shelves and pile them up on the floor. Then I sit cross-legged next to the hawk. 'Right, Mabel,' I say, 'Goshawks are boys' birds, are they? Let's see what the boys have said about you.' I pick up Humphrey ap Evans' *Falconry for You*, and read. 'She purrs and chirps to her master, rubbing her head against him. But she is proud and wild and beautiful: her anger is terrible to behold. She can be moody and sulky.'

Hmm.

Now I open Gilbert Blaine, and there I read of her 'peculiar and somewhat sulky disposition'. 'She will set her mind on making herself as disagreeable as she can,' he explained; 'will exasperate you to such a degree that you will long to wring her neck.' Then to Frank Illingworth's *Falcons and Falconry*: 'Never was there a more contrary bird than the gos! Her sole purpose in life seems to be to aggravate her owner.' 'Mabel, this is very dubious,' I say. Then I start on the Victorian falconers. Charles Hawkins Fisher did 'not like her or her kin', and Freeman and Salvin considered it 'a thousand pities that the temper of this bird is so very far from amiable; it is, in fact, sulky'.

'Sulky. Oh my God, Mabel. You know what you are? You're a woman. You're a hormonal woman!' It made such ghastly sense. It was why these falconers never wondered if

their own behaviour had anything to do with why their goshawks took stand in trees, or flew into fits of nerves, or rage,
or attacked their dogs, or decided to fly away. It wasn't their
fault. Like women, Goshawks were inexplicable. Sulky.
Flighty and hysterical. Their moods were pathological. They
were beyond all reason.

But reading further back I find that in the seventeenth century goshawks weren't vile at all. They were 'sociable and
familiar', though by nature 'altogether shye and fearfull'
wrote Simon Latham in 1615. They 'take exception' at 'rough
and harsh behaviour from the man', but if treated with kindness and consideration, are 'as loving and fond of her Keeper
as any other Hawke whatsoever'. These hawks, too, were
talked about as if they were women. They were things to win,
to court, to love. But they were not hysterical monsters. They
were real, contradictory, self-willed beings, 'stately and brave',
but also 'shye and fearfull'. If they behaved in ways that irri-
tated the falconer it was because he had not treated them well,
had not demonstrated 'continuall loving and curteous behaviour towards them'. The falconer's role, wrote Edmund Bert,
was to provide for all his hawk's needs so that she might have
'joye in her selfe'. 'I am her friend,' he wrote of his goshawk,
'and shee my playfellow.'

A more cynical eye might have seen these Elizabethan and
Jacobean men as boasting about their hawk-training skills;
old-school pick-up artists in a bar talking up their seduction
routines. But I wasn't cynical. They had won me over, these
long-dead men who loved their hawks. They were recon-
ciled to their otherness, sought to please them and be their
friends. I wasn't under any illusion that women were better
off in early-modern England, and assumed it was a fear of
female emancipation that had made goshawks so terribly
frightening to later falconers – but even so I knew which
kind of relationship I preferred.

I look at Mabel. She looks at me. So much of what she

means is made of people. For thousands of years hawks like her have been caught and trapped and brought into people's houses. But unlike other animals that have lived in such close proximity to man, they have never been domesticated. It's made them a powerful symbol of wildness in myriad cultures, and a symbol, too, of things that need to be mastered and tamed.

I close my copy of Bert's *Treatise of Hawks and Hawking* with a snap, and as the cover falls my hawk makes a curious, bewitching movement. She twitches her head to one side then turns it upside down and continues to regard me with the tip of her beak pointing at the ceiling. I am astonished. I've seen this head-turning before. Baby falcons do it when they play. But goshawks? *Really?* I pull a sheet of paper towards me, tear a long strip from one side, scrunch it into a ball, and offer it to the hawk in my fingers. She grabs it with her beak. It crunches. She likes the sound. She crunches it again and then lets it drop, turning her head upside down as it hits the floor. I pick it up and offer it to her again. She grabs it and bites it very gently over and over again: *gnam gnam gnam*. She looks like a glove puppet, a Punch and Judy crocodile. Her eyes are narrowed in bird-laughter. I am laughing too. I roll a magazine into a tube and peer at her through it as if it were a telescope. She ducks her head to look at me through the hole. She pushes her beak into it as far as it will go, biting the empty air inside. Putting my mouth to my side of my paper telescope I boom into it: 'Hello, Mabel.' She pulls her beak free. All the feathers on her forehead are raised. She shakes her tail rapidly from side to side and shivers with happiness.

An obscure shame grips me. I had a fixed idea of what a goshawk was, just as those Victorian falconers had, and it was not big enough to hold what goshawks are. No one had ever told me goshawks played. It was not in the books. I had not imagined it was possible. I wondered if it was because no one had ever played with them. The thought made me terribly sad.

In a letter to White, Gilbert Blaine explained that he didn't like goshawks because their 'crazy and suspicious temperament had alienated him from them, as it had most falconers'. 'Perhaps for this reason,' White wrote, years later, 'I had loved Gos. I always loved the unteachable, the untouchable, the underdog.' Gos was a queer thing, the opposite of civilised English hearts, and through him White could play many selves: the benevolent parent, the innocent child, the kindly teacher, the patient pupil. And other, stranger selves: through the hawk White could become a mother, a 'man who for two months had made that bird, almost like a mother nourishing her child inside her, for the subconsciousness of the bird and the man became really linked by a mind's cord: to the man who had created out of a part of his life'. And in White's notebooks, the ones written in green ink, he begins writing things late at night in a drunken, expansive hand that never make their way into his book because they are too revealing.

> The thing he most hates is to have his head stroked, the thing he most likes is to have his tail feathers pulled, stroked, pruned & sorted out. In fact, Gos shows much interest in his backward parts. He is a coprophilite, if not a pansy. He can slice his mutes 3 yards and always turns proudly round to look at them. I, however, who can pee continually for several minutes (and this he supposes to be some form of slicing) excite his interest and envy.

There are many ways to read *The Goshawk*, and one of them is as a work of suppressed homosexual desire – not for flesh, but for blood, for kinship. You can sense it is the book of a lonely man who felt he was different, who was searching for others like him. Falconry wasn't a particularly queer sport, though some of the falconers White corresponded with, like Jack Mavrogordato and Ronald Stevens, were gay. Perhaps Blaine, too: he never married. But falconers were a fellowship of men, a 'monkish elite', a 'small, tenacious sect', as Lord Tweedsmuir described them, who felt a love that other people did not understand. It was a love that was not considered normal, and it was not something they could help. Gilbert Blaine explained that 'deeply rooted in the nature of certain individuals [exists] some quality which inspires a natural liking for hawks'. The 'true falconer', he wrote, 'is born, not made'. And in years to come White would write of how falconry gave him a comforting sense of unspoken fellowship with like-minded men:

> It was not until I had kept some hawks by myself that I met another mature falconer, and saw his birds, and talked to him. Then, for the first time, I found the heart turning over with excitement at the spectacle of falcons in first plumage: found that neither of us needed to complete the grammar of a question or answer.

It was a revelation: he saw now that right back to prehistory there had been men like him. 'I thought it was right that I should now be happy to continue as one of a long line,' he wrote, musing on a photograph that showed a carving of an Assyrian falconer from three thousand years ago. He closed his eyes and imagined reaching back across the centuries to grasp 'that ancestor's bony hand, in which all the knuckles were as well-defined as the nutty calf of his bas-relief leg'.

To public-school men raised on tales of knights and chivalry, the sensation of time-travelling that falconry provoked could be overwhelming. When the countryside writer J. Wentworth Day went hawking with the British Falconers' Club in the late 1920s he wrote that with the marshes at your feet, 'the wind in your face, the hawk on your fist, you may know that you are, for a brief space, an heir of the ages. A minor page of history has turned back a thousand years.'

Trained hawks have a peculiar ability to conjure history because they are in a sense immortal. While individual hawks of different species die, the species themselves remain unchanged. There are no breeds or varieties, because hawks were never domesticated. The birds we fly today are identical to those of five thousand years ago. Civilisations rise and fall, but the hawks stay the same. This gives falconry birds the ability to feel like relics from the distant past. You take a hawk onto your fist. You imagine the falconer of the past doing the same. It is hard not to feel it is the same hawk.

I once asked my friends if they'd ever held things that gave them a spooky sense of history. *Ancient pots with three-thousand-year-old thumbprints in the clay*, said one. *Antique keys*, another. *Clay pipes. Dancing shoes from WWII. Roman coins I found in a field. Old bus tickets in second-hand books*. Everyone agreed that what these small things did was strangely intimate; they gave them the sense, as they picked them up and turned them in their fingers, of another person, an unknown person a long time ago, who had held that object in their hands. *You don't know anything about them, but you feel the other person's there*, one friend told me. *It's like all the years between you and them disappear. Like you become them, somehow.*

History collapses when you hold a hawk, just as it does for my friends with their small and precious objects. The vast differences between you and that long-dead person are forgotten. You cannot help but assume that they saw the world as you see it. And this has troubling ramifications. It is a small step from imagining you are the same as that long-dead falconer to presuming that the land you walk upon has been walked upon by people like you since time immemorial. And the ancestors falconers have chosen to imagine tend to have been a cut above the common crowd. 'Falconry is certainly of high descent,' wrote the falconer Gage Earl Freeman in 1859. 'Look at the pride – the honest noble pride – of ancestry!' When a friend countered this by saying his own love for falconry was 'perfectly independent of any feeling for antiquity or the middle ages, for which he cared nothing', Freeman's response was blunt. 'I believe he was mistaken.' But hawks did not always grant you communion with lords and earls and kings. At Chapel Green a hawk let White feel part of the community of a pre-Reformation English village. It made him feel at home.

When I was small I'd loved falconry's historical glamour. I treasured it in the same way children treasure the hope that they might be like the children in books: secretly magical, part of some deeper, mysterious world that makes them something out of the ordinary. But that was a long time ago. I did not feel like that any more. I was not training a hawk because I wished to feel special. I did not want the hawk to make me feel I was striding righteously across the lands of my long-lost ancestors. I had no use for history, no use for time at all. I was training the hawk to make it all disappear.

Tonight I take Mabel further afield. We get to Midsummer Common at about eight o'clock and we wander right across it, past the redpoll cattle grazing hock-deep in thistles, stop by the cycle path along the south side of the river and sit ourselves down on a wooden bench under an alder tree. My feet are wet, cold, stinging with thistle scratches. I clench my toes into my sandals and watch the river slide. This side of the bank is all narrowboats and cyclists but the far bank is fronted with concrete slipways and college boathouses. And on the slipway opposite a man in a tracksuit is cleaning the bottom of an upended racing boat. Walkers pass, cyclists pass fast, and he and I seem the only people here. The cyclists and shoppers don't see me, they don't see the hawk, and they don't see the man with the boat. I watch him work with his rags and bottles and his yellow bucket. Both he and I are concentrating our attentions on something important; both of us have a job to do. He has to clean and wax the shell of his boat, and I have to tame the hawk. Nothing else signifies. He wipes and waxes and polishes, and when this has been done to his satisfaction, the boat is shouldered and put back into the boathouse. He packs up the stuff on the slipway and leaves. Mabel doesn't care. She has something much more interesting to attend to: four mallards dabbling about in the grey water about twenty yards away. They float off in a little raft and we make our way home.

Now the light is thickening into real dusk and it starts to rain. And with the rain and the dusk comes the smell of autumn. It makes me shiver happily. But I have no idea what amazement is still to come. Because Mabel and I are about to witness an extraordinary phenomenon, an evening ritual I had no idea existed until today. Joggers! Like bats leaving their roost, their numbers build incrementally. First there are one or two, then a gap, then another one, and then three together. By the time Mabel and I are halfway home it feels as if we're in a nature documentary about the Serengeti. They are everywhere. Herds of them. They keep to the paths, though, which is good, because I can position myself and the hawk in a triangle of rough grass and chickweed just after the path splits into two. We stand there in the gloom and watch runners come up, split, and then stream past us. Of course they don't see us. We are motionless. 'Perhaps runners are like the dinosaurs in *Jurassic Park*,' I tell her. 'They can't see things that aren't moving.'

It is raining quite hard now, and the hawk's flat head is beaded with tiny gems of water that glow in the light from the sodium lamps. She balances on the balls of her feet, as she does when she's calm. Her pupils are wide and catlike in the dark. *What the hell*, I think. *She's jumped to the fist inside the house. I wonder if she'll do it out here.* Right next to us is a wooden barrier enclosing a young lime sapling. I plonk her down on the top of the post, and she jumps, *blam*, just like that, leash-length from the post to my fist for food. With the wind blowing the wrong way, with rain in her eyes, with joggers thundering past us, she jumps three times, and then rouses, sending raindrops in a spray of metallic orange around us both. Brilliant.

13

Alice, falling

The light is laid evenly on the grass, the cows are back in the fields after milking, and the far sky towards Buckingham builds towards dusk in dinted pewter clouds. Gos is perched twenty yards away on the railings of the well, and White is pleased with himself. He has solved the great and simple mystery of falconry: he knows now that the hawk will fly to him if it is hungry. It will misbehave if it is not. And now he has fashioned a creance from a long length of tarred twine – doubled in two to make it stronger, because it has a tendency to snap – and he has tied it to Gos's swivel. And now he is here, and the hawk is over there, and he is whistling the tune of the hymn that calls the hawk to him.

The Lord is My Shepherd.
I shall not want.
He . . .

He rubs his eyes. They have begun to ache. He has been whistling the tune for ten minutes now, the old Scottish melody to Psalm 23, and it is hard to keep to the right notes when your lips are dry and the mosquitoes are starting to bite.
The Lord is My Shepherd; I shall not want.
He does want. He wants very much.
He waves the glove again. The jointed rabbit leg waggles. *Come on, Gos! Come on!* He casts the hymn's sad notes once

more into the evening air. *Thou preparest a table before me in the presence of mine enemies.* Is the hawk looking at him? Surely he is. Why does he not come? He must be patient. The hawk will come.

He maketh me to lie down in green pastures. For an hour he stands there, sometimes giving up and lying down in the pasture among the cows, then getting up again and waiting for the hawk to fly to him. The hawk does not fly to him. He walks back to six yards from the well, holds out his fist and whistles again. Gos stares at him. He does not know what he is expected to do. The man does not know how to teach him. The minutes stretch. Now the waiting is too much to bear. He takes hold of the creance; tugs it. Then he pulls on it, dragging Gos forcibly from his perch. The hawk crashes to the ground, sits there for a few seconds and flies back up onto the railing. White pulls him down again. And again. And again. On the fourth time, the hawk, defeated, starts wandering about through the thistles towards him. White retreats. The hawk, confused, uncertain, follows. White retreats faster, waving the rabbit leg, and Gos starts to run. 'Skipping and leaping, fluffed full, a horrible toad, he bounded in my train,' White wrote; and 'the last two yards of the twenty-four were flown to the fist'. Later that evening he rewarded the hawk with a crop of rabbit. The day had been a success, he supposed, of a sort. He is beginning to understand how to bring his hawk into condition.

The condition of a hawk, White wrote, 'was evidently a matter of exquisite assessment which could only be judged by the austringer who knew his hawk, whose subconscious mind was in minutely contact with the subconscious mind of the bird.' It was a hard-won revelation, and it was a truth. Looking at Mabel I can see she's reached her flying weight: it is as obvious to me as a change in the weather. Agitation, nervousness, a tendency to bate from her perch when she was bored: all these are gone at two pounds and one and a half ounces, are replaced by a glassy calm, a flow of perfect attention as if everything inside her were exactly aligned.

You won't read the words 'flying weight' in antiquarian falconry books because the old falconers didn't use scales. They assessed the condition of their hawks by feeling their muscles and breastbones and observing their behaviour with sharp and experienced eyes. This is not an easy thing to do, and it is almost impossible for a novice falconer to grasp the subtleties involved in bringing a hawk into flying condition. White had no weighing machine and no mentor to teach him: he had to learn the old methods the hard way. I know that in one sense the weighing of hawks is a falling-off, a brute measure compared to the intuitive understanding that comes from really knowing your hawk. Still, I would not train a hawk without a set of scales. When I used to fly merlins, tiny falcons with needle talons and frames so voracious and delicate they resemble heated Meissen porcelain, I weighed them three times a day. I fussed interminably over the relative calorific value of quail and chicken and mouse; I could tell you how much weight my hawk would lose in an hour, in two hours, in three. Even an eighth of an ounce would make a difference to how my merlins flew. It is a grosser calculation with a goshawk, because Mabel is huge compared to a merlin. But still it is not easy to judge how much food, and of what kind, will bring her into perfect flying condition. Scraps of paper litter the kitchen table, jotted with weights and question marks. I am convinced I have these calculations pat, and I am out to prove it. At four o'clock we set off for my college cricket pitch and her first calling-off lessons. 'It'll be fine, Mabel. It's the long vacation. The place will be deserted. No dogs, no cows, no people. No one will bother us there.'

We stand uncertainly under the thatched roof of the pavilion. Behind us is a straggling copse of chestnut and limes and a ditch full of leaves and rainwater. The air about us is mild, still, pointed with tiny flies, the sky dull and flat as unpolished brass. There's an ill savour to the air. I am not sure I want to be here. On the other side of the pitch is a familiar building, a red-brick Victorian Camelot with crenellated battlements, mullioned windows, and a tiny Gothic tower. My office is up there on the top floor. Books, papers, a desk, a chair, a carpet of dove-coloured wool; air that always smells of sunbaked dust, even in winter when frost burns the glass and makes drop-shadows on the panes. I look at the blank façade and think of the letter I'd sent that morning to a German university telling them I couldn't accept the job they'd offered me that winter. I told them I was sorry, told them that my father had died and I needed to be here. But I was not sorry, and they were not the reasons for my refusal. *I can't go to Berlin in December*, I'd thought, appalled. *I have a hawk to fly.* Ambitions, life-plans: these were for other people. I could no more imagine the future than a hawk could. I didn't need a career. I didn't want one.

White doves fly up from the roof. I watch their wings flicker against the sky. Sudden vertigo. Something shifts in my head. Something huge. Then everything I see collapses into something else. I blink. It looks the same. But it isn't. This is not my college. Nothing about it feels familiar. It doesn't even feel like a college at all. Just a few acres of buildings, giant collector's boxes of brick and stone crammed with the detritus of centuries. In the chapel are painted angels whose faces are all the same, uncanny angels with swords and bright pre-Raphaelite plumage. There's a bronze Benin cockerel in the dining hall, and a skeleton in a cupboard in the Fellows' cloakroom, a real, yellowed skeleton held together with pins and twisted wire. Beyond my office building are a host of yew trees clipped into absurd wind-blown boulders. A bronze horse on one lawn, and a hare on another, and a metal book held to the ground by a sculpted ball and chain. Everything here is built from things pulled from dreams. A few weeks earlier scores of bay trees in pots were set out all over the college for an *Alice In Wonderland*-themed Ball; I'd watched students wiring flowers into their branches: soft fabric roses of white and pillarbox red.

In two months, I think, my college job will end. In two months I will have no office, no college, no salary, no home. Everything will be different. *But*, I think, *everything already is.* When Alice dropped down the rabbit-hole into Wonderland she fell so slowly she could take things from the cupboards and bookshelves on the walls, look curiously at the maps and pictures that passed her by. In my three years as a Cambridge Fellow there'd been lectures and libraries and college meetings, supervisions, admissions interviews, late nights of paper-writing and essay-marking, and other things soaked in Cantabrigian glamour: eating pheasant by candlelight at High Table while snow dashed itself in flurries against the leaded glass and carols were sung and the port was passed and the silver glittered upon dark-polished refectory tables. Now, standing on a cricket pitch with a hawk on my hand, I knew I had always been falling as I moved past these things. I could reach out and touch them, pick them off their shelves and replace them, but they were not mine. Not really ever mine. Alice, falling, looked down to see where she was headed, but everything below her was darkness.

Concentrate on why you're here, I tell myself. *You have a hawk to fly.* Ever since my father died I'd had these bouts of derealisation, strange episodes where the world became unrecognisable. *It will pass.* But I am spooked by what's just happened. My fingers shake as I thread the end of the creance through the swivel at the end of her jesses and tie it there with two miniature falconer's knots. I pull on them and they hold. Knots and lines. Material reassurances. I play out fifteen feet more creance and stow the rest of it deep in a zipped-up pocket of my hawking waistcoat to keep it secure. Then I pull her leash free from the swivel and tuck it into another pocket. Hawking waistcoats, like those of fishermen or photographers, are hardly clothes at all, just pockets hung in rows. The one at my right hip is lined in vinyl, and inside it are three dead day-old chicks, each skinned and torn roughly in half.

'Sit there – on you go.' The hawk hops onto the rail of the wooden veranda and turns to face me in a low boxer's crouch. I step back six feet, put half a chick in my glove, extend my arm and whistle. There is no hesitation. There is a scratch of talons on wood, a flowering of feathers, one deep downstroke, the brief, heavy swing of talons brought up and into play and the dull *thud* as she hits my glove. When she has finished eating we do it again, and this time I stand a little further away. Eight feet: three wingbeats, another reward. For a creature with the tactical intelligence of a goshawk this game is child's play. The third time I put her on the railing she is already airborne as I turn my back: a skip of my heart, a hastily extended glove and she is at my side, wolfing down the rest of her food, crest raised, wings dropped, eyes blazing, a thing of perfect triumph. I thread her leash back through the swivel and untie the creance. That will do for today. She flew perfectly. And I'm so pleased with how the lesson has gone I start singing on the way home. I serenade my hawk with 'My Favourite Things', with whiskers and kittens and brown paper packages tied up with string. It strikes me that this must be happiness. That I have remembered what it is, and how it can be done. But watching television from the sofa later that evening I notice tears running from my eyes and dropping into my mug of tea. *Odd*, I think. I put it down to tiredness. *Perhaps I am getting a cold. Perhaps I am allergic to something.* I wipe the tears away and go to make more tea in the kitchen, where a dead white rabbit is defrosting like a soft toy in an evidence bag, and the striplight flickers ominously, undecided whether to illuminate the room or cease working entirely.

* * *

These calling-off lessons teach the hawk to fly immediately to an upraised glove and a whistle. Rapid response is the key to success. If the hawk doesn't come straight away there's no point in waiting minutes on end, whistling and calling; it's better to end the training session and try again later. White did not know this, and it is one of the reasons why his first attempt to call Gos is so painful to read. But what upset me most about that sorry episode wasn't the wait that taught the hawk nothing, nor the sadistic tug on the creance that pitched poor Gos to the ground. It wasn't even that he'd taken so long to reward the hawk that it had no understanding that the food it was given was a reward at all. It was this: that once the hawk decided to walk towards him, White had run away.

But he returns and tries again. Two days later Gos is back on the railings and White is forty yards away, whistling and waving two ounces of butcher's steak in his hand. He pleads. He calls. He tries every voice he knows: his tone is command-ing, pandering, urgent, mad, soft, desperate, cross. 'Now, now,' he remonstrates. 'Don't be silly, come-along, be-a-good-Gos, Gossy-gossy-gos.' After ten minutes, Gos decides to fly. But the falconer's joy turns fast to horror, for what is approach-ing him is hardly a hawk at all. It is a 'hump-backed aviating Richard III', a ghastly aerial toad, and its glowing headlamp eyes are not focused on his outstretched fist, *my God*, but on his exposed and unprotected face. He begins to panic. Gos had hurt him a few minutes before, had jumped up to his shoulder and buried a foot in his neck. There was blood. There was a great deal of pain. He remembers the force of that blow, the agony of it, the reserves of patience it required for him not to dash the hawk to the ground and kill it, to wait, just to wait for the hawk to let go. *Closer*. Now it is five paces. It is almost upon him. Those great eyes are fixed on his. *Yea, though I walk through the valley of the shadow of death, I will fear no evil*. He cannot bear it. His nerve breaks. He shuts his eyes and ducks. Gos, vastly confused, veers off into the branches of a tree, misses his footing, drops awkwardly into a hedge.

White collects himself, retrieves the hawk, walks back to the railings and tries the whole lesson again. This time he will be brave. *This time.* As the hawk flies to him he holds his breath and tries to stand his ground:

> I braced the breast muscles not to flinch. It was too much. At two yards humanity became again the inherent coward, and cringed away to the right, averting face from the eyes of slaughter, humping shoulder, powerless to remain erect. But Gos bound to the shoulder with a decisive blow, stepped quickly down the arm, was feeding on two ounces of beef.

He had tried so hard not to be a coward. It was why he had hunted with the Grafton and learned to fly, and why he had swum around the St Leonards pier when he was small, and dived off the highest diving board at the Hastings Baths at school. He feels that old, sick horror. *Powerless to remain erect.* He *must* be brave. When he was small his mother had pleaded with him that he should 'grow up a big brave and honourable man' and it had conditioned him to fear the reverse. 'I felt myself incapable of being any of these noble things', he'd written. This was a test of manhood. Screwing his courage tight he calls Gos once more, from fifty yards this time, and this time he does not duck, even with terror flowing in all the courses of his veins. He is proud of the hawk for flying fifty yards, proud of himself for standing his ground. It is a victory worthy of celebration, and that night he drinks himself senseless. 'I cry *prosit* loudly and repeatedly,' he wrote, 'quaff fiery liquids of triumph, drink damnation to my enemies, and smash the glasses on the floor.'

It is fifteen days since the hawk arrived. I've washed my hair, applied some make-up, found some presentable clothes – that is, ones not dusted with dried hawk-mutes – and walked with

Mabel to my college for a summer lunch-party at the Master's
Lodge. At ten minutes past two I'm sitting at a long table on
a secluded English lawn giving an impromptu lecture on falconry while Mabel tears at a rabbit leg in my hand. The
Master of the college, a shrewd and genial man in an impec-
cably tailored suit, is listening intently to my speech. Next to
him is his mother, looking distinctly amused. Her grand-
children sit by her. And next to them, the Master's wife, an
elegant dark-haired lawyer, holding a glass of wine. She
catches my eye and grins. Two days ago on the way to the
supermarket I'd heard her shout my name and turned to see
her dismount from her bicycle with practised equestrian grace.
We'd talked for a while under tattered leaf shadows, and soon
I was in the kitchen of the Master's Lodge drinking tea. 'So,
Helen,' she said, 'we're having a lunch party on Saturday. Just
family. In the garden, if the weather's fine. What would be
marvellous,' she said, head tilted, 'would be if you came along
afterwards and brought your hawk. We've heard you're flying
her on the college grounds, and we'd *love* to meet her.' She
uncapped a black marker pen, wrote HELEN GOSHAWK on
a whiteboard, then hesitated, turned to me. 'Two p.m.?'

'Two p.m.'

She wrote the time in her elegant hand and smiled.

So now the hawk eats, the conversation continues, the sun
falls in pale planes on the ancient walls, the chirrups of
house martins drift down from above like distant fingertips
on glass, and I glory in it all. *How beautiful it is here*, I think,
and how supremely unlikely it is that I ever got to be here at
all, a state-school kid born to parents who'd never gone to
university, to whom Cambridge was the mysterious haunt of
toffs and spies.

'You must be a spy,' my father used to tell me. 'Must be.'
He'd watched me as a child sneaking about with binoculars,
hiding for hours in bushes and trees. I was the invisible girl;
someone tailor-made for a secret life.

'No, really I'm not,' I'd say for the hundredth time. 'I'm not!'

'But of course you'd say that.' And he'd laugh delightedly, because there was no way I could persuade him otherwise.

'It's a job, Dad,' I'd say, rolling my eyes. 'I teach people English and the History of Science. I sit in a library, read books, do my research. That's all it is. I'm not something out of a John le Carré novel.'

'But you could be,' he'd say, stressing the *could*, and part of him not joking at all.

My father had revelled in the thought that I might be a spy, for it was a life he understood, being only a hair's breadth from his own. One day he'd handed me a miniature silver camera. 'It takes special film,' he said gleefully, flipping open the back and showing me where the miniature spool fitted in its matchbox-sized casing. Over the years he'd rigged up infra-red light-beams to photograph nocturnal wildlife, staked out the love-nests of cabinet ministers, tracked and photographed the movements of nuclear waste on secret midnight trains, climbed over fences, sneaked cameras into places he, and they, should not have been. Patience, detection, subterfuge and record. What historians did for a living was far more mysterious to him than the work of spies.

My vision blurs. We carry the lives we've imagined as we carry the lives we have, and sometimes a reckoning comes of all of the lives we have lost. The summer lunch recedes. I cannot pull it back. Fog seeps in from the rugby pitch where Prideaux strode. Slow, white breaths. There's a hush in my head; it grows louder. 'I am not a spy,' I'd told my father. 'I'm a historian.' But watching everyone around the table, their faces entranced by my hawk, it seems I'm not even that any more. *I am the Fool*, I think, dully. *I used to be a Research Fellow, a proper academic. Now I am in motley. I am not Helen any more. I am the hawk woman.* The hawk pulls on the rabbit leg. Wasps circle her like electrons. They land on her feet, on her nose, seeking shreds of rabbit flesh to take back to their paper nest in some nearby Cambridge loft. She flicks them away with her beak and I watch their yellow-and-black striped abdomens spinning through the air before they right themselves and fly back to the hawk. This summer lunch feels deeply unreal. Shadows of damask and silver, a photogravure in an album, something from Agatha Christie, from Evelyn Waugh, from another time. But the wasps are real. They are here, and they are present. So is the hawk, the sun at their centre. And me? I do not know. I feel hollow and unhoused, an airy, empty wasps' nest, a thing made of chewed paper after the frosts have murdered the life within.

Sometimes a reckoning comes of all the lives we have lost, and sometimes we take it upon ourselves to burn them to ashes. In the evenings, by the light of the Aladdin lamp, in the soft white glow of its fluorescing mantle, White is doing his old life to death. He is committing the murder in a novel he'd started writing at Stowe, and now it is nearly finished. The book is called *You Can't Keep a Good Man Down*, and it is the story of the decline and fall of a public-school head-master called Dr Prisonface. Prisonface is terrified of life; he is a chameleon, a mirror, existing only through his reflection in the eyes of others. He loses his job at the school. He woos and is rejected by a boyish dark-haired barmaid, flees in ter-ror from the advances of her mother. He flies with drunken aviators descended from Romantic poets. He tries to teach Hollywood moguls how to be Gentlemen and is humiliated when they mow down grouse with tommy guns. The book is a vicious satire on the educational system and the cult of the English Gentleman, but it is also a psychological exorcism, a caustic narrative written to burn away his former life. White called Prisonface to life in order that he should suffer, be punished, mocked, reduced to rags and die. From head-master to private tutor, from farmworker to beggar, he fails at everything he attempts. Everyone he meets on the way lectures him on why he is useless and unreal, and the book's narrator, too, puts the boot in at every opportunity.

Towards the end of the book, limping and homeless, Prisonface meets a mysterious man on a country road. The man has saturnine, strangely carved features, and walks in darkness, a black dog by his side. He is a supernaturally suave figure: Prisonface is drawn to him, drawn to his power, recognising in it 'the wisdom of certainty, the happiness of reality, the mastership of right'. The stranger had once been a schoolmaster too, at a place called Golden Gates, but left because he could not bear the people teaching there. Now he is married, lives in a cottage in the woods and is content. The man is White's vision of his future self: a White freed, a White triumphant, a man who lectures Prisonface, over several pages, on the failings of the school system: 'To anybody who has spent two months training a goshawk, knowing that it will be fatal even to give the creature even a cross look,' the man says, 'it seems very extraordinary that the complex psychology of a human being can be taught with a stick.'

Sitting by the lamp, White finishes writing the speech that is perhaps the least cruel, the most humane in the whole book. He is speaking to his past self with pity and compassion.

'You went back to school voluntarily from the University because you still needed to go to school, because there was something still to find. You went back under the hen's wing for safety, because you were still too small a chicken, but also in search of something: you want the talisman that would make you fit to leave.'

'What am I searching for?'

'That you will only know when you find it.'

'Is it wisdom or manhood?'

'Perhaps it is love.'

Perhaps it is love. Perhaps it is. I imagine him writing those lines in his small kitchen, the light wet on the oilskin tablecloth, the night close against the window. He will stoke the fire in a little while. First he will write a little more. His hawk is sleeping. All the leaves on the trees of the Ridings are still tonight, all unmoving out across Three Parks Woods, across Stowe Woods and Sawpit Woods, over the Black Pits ponds, the carp slumbering deep in the waters. There is peace here. He is a wicked man. A free man. A man who is cast out, the man who fell. *Feral. Ferox. Fairy.* A man who is content with his lot. He puts the pen down to pour another drink, then picks up his pen and writes some more. He writes of Dr Prisonface asking the mysterious man his name, and of the man telling him it is Lucifer. Lucifer the light-bringer, the fallen angel, the devil incarnate.

14

The line

The expression on Christina's face is unusual. It's not a
happy face, but it's not unhappy either. Tense, certainly. It is
fierce, ambivalent and brave. Today she'd come out to watch
the hawk fly and in a burst of inspiration I decided to recruit
her as my under-falconer. She'd borne my grief-spurred
strangenesses with great good grace over the last few months
but nothing could have prepared her for this. 'The problem
is, I can't get away fast enough,' I tell her. 'She flies after me
as soon as I start walking away. But she has to come longer
distances before I can fly her loose. Can you hold her for me,
out on the pitch, so I can call her from your fist?'

'You'll have to show me how,' she says, paling.

'It's easy, really.'

I give her my spare glove, put the hawk on it and bend her
fingers into the right shape to hold the jesses.

'Turn your back to me – yes, like that. Perfect. Now she
can't see me. So I'm going to walk over there. When I shout
OK, turn right, stick out your arm and open your hand, so
she can fly.'

She bites her lip, nods.

'Make sure you turn the right way; you don't want to get
the creance caught round your legs.'

She holds the hawk with cautious concentration, as if it were
a pitcher full of some caustic agent. She stands straight-backed,

still and composed, a small figure fifteen yards away in skinny black jeans, T-shirt and bright red sneakers.

'OK!'

She turns, and Mabel bursts towards me, dragging the creance behind her, flying so low her wing-tips almost brush the turf. With each deep wingbeat her body flexes and swings but her eyes and head are perfectly, gyroscopically, still, fixed and focused on my glove. The silvered undersides of her wings flash as she spreads them wide, her tail flares, she brings her feet up to strike and she hits the glove feet-first like a kickboxer.

'Was that OK?' shouts Christina.

I give her a thumbs-up, and she responds the same way: for a moment we are two traffic controllers on the flight deck of an aircraft carrier.

We do it again. And again. The next day brings heavy rain so we fly her loose between us in the front room of my house, back and forth from fist to fist, over the rug, past the mirror, under the light, wings sending up draughts that leave the lampshade swinging wildly. By the fourth day the hawk is flying twenty-five yards to me, will come without hesitation from the ground, from Christina's fist, from tree branches, from the roof of the pavilion. 'Thank you so much for your help,' I tell her as we walk from the field. 'You know, I think we're nearly there. Once she flies a full fifty yards I'll let her loose.' The thought brings a squirmy, high-pitched joy. *I mustn't rush. I cannot wait.*

I had called so many hawks before, but calling Mabel was different. I stood there, raised my arm, and whistled the whistle that meant, *Please come. This is where you want to be. Fly to me. Ignore the towering clouds, the wind that pushes the trees behind you. Fix yourself on me and fly between where you are and where I am.* And I'd hear my heart beating. And I'd see the hawk crouch and fly. I'd see her drop from the perch, speed towards me, and my heart would be in my mouth. Though she was still on the creance, I feared the faltering. I feared the veering off, the sudden fright, the hawk flying away. But the beating wings brought her straight to me, and the thump of her gripping talons on the glove was a miracle. It was always a miracle. *I choose to be here*, it meant. *I eschew the air, the woods, the fields.* There was nothing that was such a salve to my grieving heart as the hawk returning. But it was hard, now, to distinguish between my heart and the hawk at all. When she sat twenty yards across the pitch part of me sat there too, as if someone had taken my heart and moved it that little distance. It reminded me of Philip Pullman's children's fantasy series *His Dark Materials*, in which each person has a *daemon*, an animal that is a visible manifestation of their soul and accompanies them everywhere. When people are separated from their daemons they feel pain. This was a universe very close to mine. I felt incomplete unless the hawk was sitting on my hand: we were parts of each other. Grief and the hawk had conspired to this strangeness. I trusted she would fly to me as simply and completely as I trusted gravity would make things fall. And so entrenched was this sense that the hawk flying to me was part of the workings of the world that when things went wrong, the world went wrong with it.

She'd left Christina's fist with all the joy and certainty in the world. I watched her approach and waited with happy anticipation for the solid *thwack* of her landing on my glove. But it did not come. Instead, she snatched at the food in my fist with one down-dropped taloned foot, and kept flying, fast, out and away from me. I could feel the failure in her, the sense that she hadn't got what she wanted, and I could feel, too, that what had just happened had spooked her, and that now she was flying away from it, and me, as fast as possible. I grabbed hold of the creance and ran with her, putting resistance on the line until she was brought to earth, crest raised, wings spread wide, feet planted in the turf, beak open, panting in fury. I held out my fist and she flew straight up onto it as if nothing had happened at all.

'She must have been scared by something,' I said. 'Let's try it again.'

And again the hawk came, low and fast, and again she snatched at the glove and kept flying. Again I brought her to earth.

'Why is she doing it?'

'I don't know. I don't know.'

This had never happened before. Over the years I'd had hawks that ignored me. Hawks that turned their back on me. Hawks that flew reluctantly, flew badly, or didn't fly at all. It never worried me. These hawks weren't at their flying weight, that was all, and this was easily fixed. But this was different. This was a hawk desperately eager to fly to me, but with a last-second terror of landing on my glove. It was incomprehensible. I telephoned Stuart. 'I don't know what's wrong. Does she need more manning? Is she too high in weight?'

I was as bewildered as a child.

'What should I do?'

There was a long pause, and then a longer sigh.

'Are you feeding her chicks?' he said.

'Yes.'

'Stop feeding her chicks! They're too rich for her at this stage. She'll be fine, she's nearly there. Just feed her rabbit. It won't hurt her, but it'll stop this problem.'

All the trust I had left in the world rested in the fact that the hawk wanted to fly to me. Now she was scared to land on my fist – *she didn't trust me* – and I could not explain to Stuart how awful this felt. I thanked him. I had asked for advice, and he had given it, simply and precisely. *This is the problem. This is how you fix it.* But I didn't believe him. *It can't just be the food. I have done something bad*, I thought miserably. *Something terrible.*

The next day a plague of moorhens had come out of the messy copse behind the pavilion and were running all over the pitch like a flock of feathered black mice. Moorhens! Birds that can neither fly well nor run fast, they are such easy prey for goshawks that falconers avoid flying them out of a sense of sporting fair play. Mabel had never seen them before, but she looked upon them now as if they had been designed by a kindly deity for her personal delectation. I wasn't surprised; I'd already discovered that all sorts of predatory taxonomies are buried in a baby goshawk's brain. A few days earlier I'd seen her looking at a small drawing of partridges in a book I'd left open on the floor. Intrigued, I picked up the book and held it in front of her. She kept her eyes fixed on the picture, even when I moved the book about in the air. *No way!* I thought. The drawing was in ink; it was stylised and sparse: it caught the feel and form of partridges, but there was no colour or detail to it. I flipped through the book, showed her other drawings: finches, sea-birds, thrushes. She ignored them all. Then I showed her a drawing of a pheasant. Her black pupils dilated; she leaned forward and stared down her beak at it, as fascinated as she had been with the partridges. I was amazed. Amazed that she could understand two-dimensional images, and even more amazed that something deep in her brain saw these sparse inked curves as fitting the category *gamebirds* and had pronounced them worthy of interest.

Right on cue I hear a soft clucking noise, and a thin peeping, and Mabel's head swings round, and mine too, and we see – just there, just ten feet away – a hen pheasant and a line of cheeping, half-feathered poults squeezing themselves under a railing on their way towards the grass. The pheasant sees Mabel and stops dead. She has never seen a goshawk before, but instantly perceives the danger she is in. She crouches to fly, realises this would leave her chicks behind, then considers sitting down and pretending to be a rock, and when she realises the futility of this manouevre – her lacy beige back does not match the sunlit grass, and the hawk has already seen her – all hell breaks loose. She stretches her neck high, puffs out her cheek feathers, beak open in panic, and runs pell-mell out across the pitch. Her chicks follow her desperately, six ungainly clockwork dinosaurs. I am bewildered – there is no safety out there, nowhere to hide, unless the pheasant thinks that putting her chicks amongst the distant moorhens would give them a faint, statistical chance of escape.

Mabel. Oh God, Mabel. Mabel is bating at them, bating so hard, wings beating so furiously, that she hangs horizontally in the air. The breeze is cold in my face, my fist pulled towards the fleeing pheasants. She bounces back onto my hand, beak open with exertion, fixes me with a white-hot, angry eye, then bates towards them again. *Not here, not now! Mabel! I can't. I can't let you catch one. It is against the laws of God and Man and . . . College.*

I try to keep her on my fist – which is like trying to balance a very tall and unstable pile of precious china plates – execute a smart volte-face to block the pheasants from view, and in the excessively polite voice that only ever falls on me at times of enormous stress I ask Christina if she 'might possibly chase the pheasants back into the bushes? And perhaps the moorhens too?' She grins, and shepherds the pheasants back into the garden behind the railings. Then she sprints off across the pitch towards the moorhens. Meanwhile Mabel is standing on tiptoe, jumping up and down, craning her neck over my shoulder to see where they have gone, and I'm trying to stop her from seeing, and largely failing, and I turn my head and see Christina running across the field, arms windmilling, and before her, scores of moorhens rushing back into the woods, wings open as they run, like small boys playing aeroplanes, and I start giggling uncontrollably. This is *ludicrous*. I'm holding tight onto Britain's deadliest hawk while someone chases all the gamebirds away. *My God*, I'm thinking. *If any of my falconer friends find out about this, they'll never speak to me again.*

Once the pitch is clear of temptation I call Mabel as usual. She flies to my fist perfectly, a whole thirty yards. But on the second and third flights she clouts the glove hard with both feet, skies up, tries to turn in mid-air, wobbles, stalls, then ends up on the ground a few feet away, panting, wings dropped, looking as if she is going to explode. All my laughter is gone. Now I know why austringers have, for centuries, been famed for cursing. I curse. It is my fault this is happening. I know it is. I hate myself. I try to keep calm. I fail. *Damn, damn, damn.* I'm hot, incredibly bothered, pushing hair from my eyes with rabbit-flesh-specked fingers, cursing to high heaven, and to top it all I see a man in white shirt-sleeves and a black waistcoat striding towards Christina, his shadow dark before him. It is one of the college porters, and he is not happy. The set of his shoulders is unmistakable. They start talking. From this distance I can't hear what's being said, but she is waving one hand towards me, and I suppose she is explaining to him that I'm not a random trespasser, but a bona fide College Fellow, and what I am doing is not against the rules.

From his demeanour I don't think he believes her.

They stop talking as I approach. He recognises me. I recognise him. 'Hello!' I say brightly, and explain what I am doing with a hawk on this hallowed ground.

'Hmm,' he says, eyeing Mabel with suspicion. 'Are you going to catch students with it?'

'Only if they're causing trouble.' Then I whisper conspiratorially, '*Let me have the names.*'

It is the right answer. A shout of laughter. He is fascinated by the hawk, and wants to know more about it, but he is working and duty calls. 'Excuse me,' he says, and he sets his shoulders once again, narrows his eyes into the sun, and stalks off towards some poor tourists who've decided to have a picnic on the corner of the college rugby pitch.

I flew her later in the day. I flew her earlier. I fed her rabbit with fur and rabbit without. I fed her chicks that I'd gutted and skinned and rinsed in water. I reduced her weight. I raised it. I reduced it again. I wore different clothes. I tried everything to fix the problem, certain that the problem couldn't be fixed because the problem was me. Sometimes she flew straight to my fist, sometimes straight over it, and there was no way of knowing which it would be. Every flight was a monstrous game of chance, a coin-toss, and what was at stake felt something very like my soul. I began to think that what made the hawk flinch from me was the same thing that had driven away the man I'd fallen for after my father's death. Think that there was something deeply wrong about me, something vile that only he and the hawk could see. And every evening I wrote in the journal I'd kept since the hawk arrived. I made notes in terse, impersonal shorthand, detailing the weather, Mabel's behaviour, measurements of weight and wind and food. They read like aviation reports, things to be broadcast in clipped tones from the Air Ministry roof:

> 2lb 1½oz light winds, sunny, 4 p.m. 35 yards four flights quick response, overshot last two. Washed chicks.

But they were changing.

> 2lb 1½oz clear, slight breeze, 4.30 p.m. three flights 35 yards overshot every time. Awful. Rabbit. ???!!

They were no longer entirely about the hawk.

> Dull. Headache. Hard to get out today. Am I ill? 2lb 1¼oz

rabbit three flights 25 yards overshot on last why? Have to fix this what am I doing wrong?

Sun, stiff breeze. 4 p.m. Rabbit, but same as yesterday 20 yards OK – at 25 overshot twice: 2lb 1¼oz rest of day horrible because I had to see people, have to pretend everything fine. On and on. Wish they would FUCK OFF AND LEAVE ME ALONE.

The anger was vast and it came out of nowhere. It was the rage of something not fitting; the frustration of trying to put something in a box that is slightly too small. You try moving the shape around in the hope that some angle will make it fit in the box. Slowly comes an apprehension that this might not, after all, be possible. And finally you know it won't fit, know there is no way it can fit, but this doesn't stop you using brute force to try to crush it in, punishing the bloody thing for not fitting properly. That was what it was like: but I was the box, I was the thing that didn't fit, and I was the person smashing it, over and over again, with bruised and bleeding hands.

Rage crouched inside me, and anything could provoke it. One weekday morning I laboured into town under a sky the colour of wet cement to meet an Uzbek student I'd worked with on a research trip to Central Asia the previous winter. A quiet, neat man, a nice man. I'd camped with him in frozen deserts, eaten lamb-stuffed quinces at roadside shacks on the Silk Road, stood with him on the banks of the Syr Darya river. He had lately arrived in Cambridge and he wanted to see me. I sat down with him at a café table. I liked him. I knew I should talk to him, but couldn't remember how. I tried a few words. They sounded wrong. I stuck a watery smile on my face and turned my head towards the window, desperately trying to remember how to have a conversation. And there, behind the plate glass of the bank across the street, a woman in a grey uniform was standing on a chair in her stockinged feet, reaching up to peel a huge vinyl sticker of a singing skylark from the glass. It had been advertising some kind of financial offer. Now the offer was finished, and so was the lark. She picked at its open beak with her fingernails, then started pulling its head from the window. Inch by inch the bird disappeared; first it hung there, decapitated, printed wings spread wide, then each wing was stripped from the glass, hacked at with fingers and a plastic scraper, until the last feather of its tail was gone. She screwed the skylark into a ball, and threw it to the floor.

Blind, cold, shaking fury. I felt it rise. I hated that woman. I wanted to burst into the bank, scream at her, pick up the tangled ball that was a skylark and take it home. Smooth it out, save it from harm. Across the table my student friend was looking at me with the same expression of baffled concern that the waiter had worn on the night my father died. That also made me angry. I was angry with the woman for tearing down the skylark and angry with this nice, innocent man who gave me no cause to be angry at all. I mumbled an unsatisfactory apology, told him that 'things have been hard since my father died', and 'it isn't your fault' and 'I'm sorry, and this is awful, but I really have to go'. I walked past the window as I crossed the street. The woman was back on her chair, smoothing a new sticker out against the glass: a giant arrow that pointed at nothing. I could not meet her eye.

Then I started crashing my father's car. I didn't mean to: it just happened. I backed up against bollards, scraped wings against walls, heard the sound of metal squealing in agony over and over again, and I'd get out of the car and rub the new gouges dumbly with my fingers, as if somehow that might fix them, though they ran through the paint to the metal below. 'Are you punishing your father's car because he left you?' asked a psychoanalytically-minded and fairly tactless friend. I thought about that. 'No,' I said, embarrassed because my answer was so much less interesting. 'It's that I don't know what shape my car is any more.' It was true. I couldn't keep the dimensions of the car in my head. Or my own, for I kept having accidents. I cracked cups. I dropped plates. Fell over. Broke a toe on a door-jamb. I was as clumsy as I had been as a child. But when I was busy with Mabel I was never clumsy. The world with the hawk in it was insulated from harm, and in that world I was exactly aware of all the edges of my skin. Every night I slept and dreamed of creances, of lines and knots, of skeins of wool, skeins of geese flying south. And every afternoon I walked out onto the pitch with relief, because when the hawk was on my fist I knew who I was, and I was never angry with her, even if I wanted to sink to my knees and weep every time she tried to fly away.

15

For whom the bell

'Bloody hell, she's calm, Helen,' Stuart says. 'I can feel her heartbeat. She's not bothered at all.' His head is bowed low over the table, fingers spread wide over the closed wings of my hooded hawk. He holds her upon a kitchen cushion as firmly and as gently as if she were made of glass. 'Good,' I say, shifting her covert feathers carefully aside to reveal the base of her tail. Here, just before the long feathers join her body, the quills are hollow and translucent, and I'm about to glue and tie a bell the size and shape of an acorn onto the topmost pair. It doesn't take long. I tug on it gently to check it is secured, then take the hawk back onto my fist. She rouses and the bell sounds loud in the bright room. It does not seem to concern her at all.

Bells are among the most ancient of falconry technologies. For years I'd bought bells from Pakistan, hand-hammered from brass to a design of immense antiquity, but the one Mabel wears is American; modern, small and light, hand-made from nickel silver. When she flies free it will tell me where she is. Bells were traditionally attached to hawks' legs on tiny leather straps called bewits, but a tail-mounted bell is much better for a goshawk, for they have an invariable habit of shaking their tails when they land. You can stand with your back to a tree with a gos in it and trace its movements from branch to branch behind you through sound alone.

But bells aren't foolproof: their sound is dulled by wind and distance, and a motionless hawk is silent, so when Mabel flies free she'll also wear a tiny radiotransmitter, and I'll carry the receiver that picks up its signal over my back in a black cloth case. Even with these double precautions the thought of taking her off the creance fills me with dread. I had never lost a hawk. I'd never expected to. But once she is free, I'm convinced that Mabel will rocket away from me and disappear for ever. I'm even more certain of this when I fly her a few hours later. This time she doesn't even snatch at the food in my glove, just flies straight past me until she's brought down to earth.

Disconsolate, I carry her back to the edge of the village playing fields. Stuart watches me approach, looks critically at the hawk. He rubs the back of his neck with one hand. His face, tanned and lined by years of sun and wind, is thoughtful and grave.

'It might be the bell, do you think?' I say. 'Freaked her out a bit?'

He frowns. 'It's a new place, too. But she's not ready yet, Helen. Not yet.' He feels her breastbone speculatively. 'She needs to come down more. She's still too fat. You're feeding her rabbit? Just rabbit?'

I nod miserably.

He looks at me, considering. 'Tell you what, Helen, come out on the hill with me tomorrow,' he says. 'I'll be going up there to fly the tiercel. We'll get her out into the fields, away from streets and houses. She needs space.'

'That would be brilliant, Stuart.'

'I'll pick you up at five.'

'Thank you. Thank you so much.'

'She needs to come down a bit more, Helen.'

He was offering to help, and I was unprepared for how this made me feel. I'd flown scores of hawks. I'd taught falconry to beginners. I'd written papers on it, had lectured on its venerable history. But now I bowed my head before Stuart. He knew what to do. He knew about goshawks and I did not. I felt weak with relief at not having to be an expert any more. There he was, rolling a cigarette, reassuringly calm and kind, a proper, generous friend; and it was there, standing on the edge of a village playing field, that I gratefully stepped into novicehood again, as if I had never seen a hawk in my life.

'Need to excel in order to be loved,' White had written in his dream diary. But there is an unspoken coda to that sentence. What happens if you excel at something and discover you are still unloved? White was triumphant: Gos had come a whole hundred yards on the creance, was ready to fly free: he could say truthfully now that he had trained a hawk. But something terrible was caught up in his triumph. For the first time since the hawk arrived White felt exposed. Being a novice is safe. When you are learning how to do something, you do not have to worry about whether or not you are good at it. But when you have done something, have learned how to do it, you are not safe any more. Being an expert opens you up to judgement. In his hawking day-book White began writing about critics and how he might 'avoid the kicks which frighten me'. He felt it necessary to explain that his self-satisfaction was not egotism, but 'actually a horrible surprise at being good at anything after having been so bad at living for 30 years'. And all the authoritarian figures in his life under whom he had lived in fear coalesced in his imagination into an elderly falconer with a waxed moustache who would read his book and consider him a fool. He knew he must explain to that man that what he had written was only the book of a learner. The words in his day-book read very like a prayer.

May I hope that this book will receive the oblivion of those austringers on the one hand, and of those critics on the other, who realise that indifference and a supposition of non-existence sometimes are the most killing weapons. May I hope that some will realise that I am only a man.

He is only a man. Success is a pressure. He cannot quite bear it. It boils and bubbles. And without knowing it, quietly and cruelly, he begins to sabotage his success, because success cannot be borne. It is so very easily done.

Stuart pulls off the road onto a farm track to the west of the city. The evening is warm, but there's a torn-paper whiteness behind the sun that speaks of frost to come. I unhood the hawk. Her pale eyes stare out across a hillside of stubble and chalky till, at slopes cut with hedgerows crisped at their edges into shot-silk taffeta. She sees skeletal teasels and fencewires. Larks calling overhead. A discarded twelve-gauge shotgun cartridge by my feet. *Red.* She glances down at it, then up, fixing her gaze on something three fields away, delighted at this enlargement of her world. When Stuart takes her upon his fist she leans back and stares up at him with almost comical dread, head sunk deep into her shoulders. But soon she relaxes; for all his strangeness there is a kindness to him, an ease and proficiency in his dealings with her that quickly reassures. We unwind the creance and call her across the bare field. She flies badly, of course. I see that flinch as she approaches, that moment where all conviction and trust slides away and I am revealed to her as a monster. Once again I grab the creance and bring her to earth. Her feet sink into the friable loam; she looks down in wonderment at her half-obscured toes.

Stuart is firm with me. Tells me she needs to be keener. I cannot bear it. I get him to swear that my hawk won't die in the night.

'Of course she won't,' he says, blue eyes crinkling into something between a smile and a frown.

'Are you *sure*?' I say pathetically. I am horribly worried that I am starving her to death.

He extends a hand and feels Mabel's breastbone, her ribcage, the muscles under her wings.

'She's *fine*, Helen.'

'Honestly?'

'*Yes.*'

I trudge back to the car, staring down at my feet.

Then Stuart stops dead.

'Stuart?'

'Look!' he says. 'Look at that!'

'What?' I say, turning and shading my eyes. 'I can't see anything.'

'Look towards the sun.'

'I am!'

'Look *down*!'

Then I see it. The bare field we'd flown the hawk upon is covered in gossamer, millions of shining threads combed downwind across every inch of soil. Lit by the sinking sun the quivering silk runs like light on water all the way to my feet. It is a thing of unearthly beauty, the work of a million tiny spiders searching for new homes. Each had spun a charged silken thread out into the air to pull it from its hatch-place, ascending like an intrepid hot-air balloonist to drift and disperse and fall. I stare at the field for a long time. It reminds me of an evening last autumn on that trip to Uzbekistan. I'd been sitting on the ground outside my tent wondering if the terrible smell was a decomposing cow, or something much worse. Before me were miles of marsh and desert and in the far distance the Fergana Mountains, fading into haze. Then I saw the strangest things hanging in the air, and I could not work out what they were. They looked like white question marks, and they disobeyed the laws of physics alarmingly. There was no wind at all, yet they hovered, and sank, and rose with supernatural slowness. What the hell? I ran after one. I walked up to it so that it was within six inches of my nose, and I still couldn't understand what it was. It was as long as my hand from wrist to finger-tip; it was white, and squiggly like the doodle you make with a running-out pen, and made of some material I couldn't identify. I thought of manna, and soda, of ash and silly string. And then I looked very, very closely, as it rose very, very slowly upwards, and there, from the base of this white frothy squiggle, was an almost-invisible line. And right at the bottom of the line was a spider exactly this size, the size of the word *Ah*.

The next day I left Mabel at home and took a train to London. I didn't want to leave her, and I didn't want to go. I remembered the city after my father's death as a ghastly place, pale and caustic under toppling clouds. But now, rounding the corner of Fleet Street, I found the city wasn't empty any more. It was a dark and fathomless warren of litter and glass, bankers and traders streaming through its sunken lanes. Sills, barricades, alleys. Tipping gutters, anti-pigeon spikes, pavements patterned with spots of trodden gum. And then, suddenly, St Bride's Church, caged behind railings on a raised platform of green-stained stone. The picture editor of my father's newspaper was there, waiting with my mother and brother at the door. I had not met him before. Blue eyes in a fierce, sad pugilist's face, a strong handshake, a pinstripe suit. He'd set up this meeting: the newspaper was organising a memorial service for my father, and we'd come here to discuss it with the canon of the church. And so in the vestry office we talked of hymns, of invitations, of readings and speakers and songs. I said I would make a speech. We talked some more. My mother sat very upright in a grey sweater and pink gilet, her hair carefully brushed, her face taut and pale. *Oh Mum*. James was even paler. He shot me a tight smile. My eyes prickled and burned. He turned to the canon. 'I work as a designer,' he said. 'I could design the Order of Service?' The canon nodded and pushed a handful of printed booklets across the desk towards us. 'These are from past services,' he said, dipping his head in a gesture of unconscious, anxious tenderness. 'They might help you with your father's?' I picked up the nearest. On its cover was a smiling middle-aged stranger in a piano-keyboard tie. I looked at his face for a long time, pressing the pad of one finger hard into the corner of the stiff cover to make a tiny flare of pain to cover the ache in my heart.

When we got up to leave the canon pressed business cards into our hands. Business cards. *Absurd*. The tie. The incongruity. *This. All this.* I looked back at the office. Strip-lights and pinboards, coat-hooks and fax machines. Diaries and schedules. The offices of death. I felt laughter rising inside me. I tried to stifle it. It came out as a broken cough. This had happened before; once, on the morning Mum and I had to choose my father's coffin, sitting in wing-back arm-chairs in the undertaker's office before a small vase of salmon-coloured roses. Dim light. A cramped room. A sti-fling hush. The undertaker handed us a laminated folder, and it fell open onto a page of coffins painted with football colours, with photorealistic spitfires, golf-courses, saxo-phones and trains. We'd laughed then as I laughed now. The coffins, like the tie, made the small loves of life ridiculous in death, the business card made the memorial mundane. The laughter was because there was no way of incorporating these signs of life into the fact of death. I laughed because there was nothing else I could do.

On the way home I felt a great and simple sadness. I missed my dad. I missed him very much. The train curved and sun-light fell against the window, obscuring the passing fields with a mesh of silver light. I closed my eyes against the glare and remembered the spider silk. I had walked all over it and had not seen it. I had not known it was there. It struck me then that perhaps the bareness and wrongness of the world was an illusion; that things might still be real, and right, and beautiful, even if I could not see them – that if I stood in the right place, and was lucky, this might somehow be revealed to me. And the sun on the glass and the memory of the shining field, and the awful laughter, and the kindness of that morning's meeting must have thinned the armour of silence I'd worn for months, because the anger was quite gone now, and that evening as we drove to the hill, I said in a quiet voice, 'Stuart, I'm not dealing very well with things at the moment.'

I said, 'I think I'm a bit depressed.'

'You've lost your father, Helen,' he said.

'I'm training a gos. I suppose it's quite stressful.'

'You've *lost your father*. And you're doing OK with the gos,' he added. 'You might not see it, but you are. She'll be flying free, soon. She's nearly there, Helen. Don't be so hard on yourself.'

I hadn't told him everything. I hadn't confessed the unpaid bills, the letters from the bank, the impossible nights, the mornings in tears. But I had told him something. I looked at Mabel. Her head drooped forward. She looked indescribably mournful in her hood. I stroked her craggy, snake-scale toes. She was asleep. I touched the hood, very gently, and felt the whole weight of her sinking, sleeping head against my fingers. *Perhaps I should ask Stuart to take us home*, I thought. I was so impossibly tired; there seemed no point in flying her at all. But when I unhooded her out on the hill, Stuart, noticing her oddly upright stance, the pale feathers fluffed over her toes, the rising feathers on her crown, the shackly, possessive grasp of her feet on the glove, raised his eyebrows and asked, 'What does she weigh?'

'One pound and fifteen ounces.'

'Look at her,' he said. 'She's a different hawk today.'

She was. I called her. I had lost hope in her coming but I called her all the same. And she flew to me. She flew like a promise finally kept. She raced towards me, wings flickering across fifty yards of flint-strewn earth, hit the glove and stayed. I gave her back to Stuart and called her again. Three times she flew to my fist the whole length of the creance with total conviction. There was no hesitation, no faltering. The hawk flew to me as if I were home.

'You've hit her flying weight,' Stuart said approvingly. 'A couple more days of this and we'll get her flying free.' Of course he was right. I had miscalculated her flying weight for weeks. But the narcissism of the bereaved is very great. I thought that the reason the hawk had flown to me was because I had confessed how bad things were. It had made me feel better – and it was this that had made me less offputting to my hawk. *I must try to be happier*, I told myself. *For the hawk's sake I must.*

16

Rain

White is making a trap. It is not easy. There is a testing practicality to this that pleases him. He has stripped an ash-wand of bark and bent it into a U. He's given it leather hinges, covered it with two yards of knotted strawberry netting, and made it into a bow-net like the ones the old falcon-trappers used. He's going to bait it with a tethered blackbird and catch one of the hawks in Three Parks Wood. Or try to. He'd first seen them a month ago, and they'd never quite left his mind. They were nothing like Gos; they were small, fast, sharp-winged. Aerobatic. They'd raced round a tree wing-tip to wing-tip in a perfect vertical bank, exactly like aircraft round the pylons at the Hatfield air race. An aviator's dream; a dream of the future. He reaches to pick up the reel of line that will pull the net over the hawk he will draw to earth. And he remembers an old nightmare. Fleeing in terror from a gang of thugs, he'd leapt into an aeroplane and piloted it up towards safety. There was danger in the dream, a net of telegraph wires strung above that blocked his ascent to freedom. He is not sure what the hawks are. He knows they are not kestrels. It would be too much to hope for peregrines. Perhaps they are sparrowhawks.

White's hawks in the wood weren't sparrowhawks. They were hobbies: tiny dark-hooded migratory falcons with rust-red trousers and thin white brows. Fantastically rare in the 1930s, they are much commoner today. They catch small birds and insects in mid-air: it would have been impossible to trap one with a blackbird tethered to the ground. But White thought they were sparrowhawks, and out in the wood he built a hide of poles and branches and pegged the trap fifteen feet away, strewing it with dust and leaves to hide it. He was neglecting Gos, and he knew it. The sparrowhawks were a new craze, his 'insensate El Dorado'. He told himself he was catching one for Peter Low, a boy he'd taught who'd lost a pet sparrowhawk. He told himself he was catching them because training Gos was too easy, and he had to test himself against something harder.

I think now that White's quest for the hawks was his final test of Gos: he was behaving like a fearful man who has finally won someone's love and, unsure whether that love can be trusted, decides it is safer to obsess about someone else. But when I was small his actions were incomprehensible. 'WHY?' I'd howled. 'Why did he abandon his goshawk? I would *never* have done that!' My mother was wiping the bathroom mirror. I could see her face in it, and behind it my own, pale and outraged. It was my first reading of the book. I'd reached the bit about the sparrowhawks and I was too upset to read any more. I'd jumped from my bed and gone looking for reassurance.

'Is this the Goshawk book you've been telling me about?'

'Yes! He's got his hawk ready to fly free but then he starts making traps to try and catch some sparrowhawks and goes off and leaves the hawk behind and it's *stupid*.'

A long pause.

'Maybe he was tired of his hawk,' she said, the hand with the cloth in it now pressed to the sink.

This made no sense at all.

'But how could he be tired of a hawk?'

And now she saw I was upset, and she put down the cloth and drew me into a hug.

'I don't know, Helen. Perhaps he was a silly man.'

Gos's small feral head, tipped and streaked and patterned like a cat's, looks about in puzzlement. *This is not what normally happens.* His sharp black beak opens and closes. He is hungry. He hops along the railing around the well, gripping it tight with toes and claws. Flakes of rust fall. *Hungry.* He hops further, looking down the long line of the creance and still not finding the man at the end of it where he always is. Where was he? Gos needed vantage to see. So he flew across to the nearest tree. There was a branch just above him. He flew up to it. Hawks hate to sit on a lower perch when a higher one is offered, and so he hopped and scrambled onto the one above him, and then onto another, and another, laddering up the tree, pulling the creance behind him. Soon he sat at the very top of the unclimbable oak, the world offering itself to him; the skies fletched with pigeons, the fields sinking towards Stowe, the roof of the palace and its glittering lakes and all its obelisks and temples and classical avenues, all the lines of sight cut into the landscape by men two hundred years ago, with his small hawkish face looking down upon it as if this view, this perfect view, was the reason it was made.

White had only left Gos on the railings for a minute. He'd heard the farmer's car and ran across the field to tell Mrs Wheeler about his new wireless set. When he got back Gos was not on the well but on top of a tree, a shadow against the sky, and the twigs and branches below him woven and tangled with twine. He whistled, waved food, but the hawk didn't move. He panicked and pulled on the creance and it made Gos bate and the twine more tangled than ever. He started to worry the creance would snap. 'It had hardly any breaking strain,' he wrote. 'It had already been broken twice.' The hawk was held tight; powerless, White called for someone to help him. But the arrival of the farmer's son in a white shirt carrying a ladder made the hawk bate even more. Soon Gos was hanging upside down in a cocoon of fraying string, feathers breaking in his struggle to free himself, before finally he hung unmoving, exhausted, immobilised, a feathered fly in a tarred and knotted web. It was an hour and a half before White entangled his jesses with a screwhook fastened to the end of a salmon rod, dragged him down to the ground and got him back on his fist. *You bloody little sod*, White hissed at Gos. The hawk, he wrote, looked at him angrily, 'as if it had all been my fault'.

A couple more days and I'll fly her free. A couple more days. But then a series of summer storms send cold water running in sheets along the ruffled tarmac and shell the roof with twigs and leaves. It is terrible flying weather. So instead of going out to the hill I exercise Mabel in the park. I tie the swivel to the creance and lower her to the ground – she jumps to the grass crab-wise and looks up at me, hunched and baleful – then I put a scrap of food on my glove, raise it high in the air, and she flies vertically up to eat it. Then we do it again. And again. High-jumping like this is an old falconer's way of manning and muscling-up a hawk in relatively enclosed spaces; it's good exercise for the hawk and fun to do. It is also hard to do: Mabel is frighteningly fast. It is far from my walks with the hawk along twilit streets. There is something of the street performance about it, and it brings in the crowds. They stand, tonight, in a loose semi-circle twenty feet away. A mother crouches by her child, pointing at the hawk. 'Isn't it regal?' she breathes. Mabel is far from regal; she's gulping down bits of day-old chick with strange choking squeals. Next to the mother and child is a bus driver on his way to the depot, two hooded teenagers, and a girl taking pictures on her mobile phone. But they don't bother me, because I'm concentrating on this. *Grass, glove. Grass, glove. Grass, glove, grass.* The rhythm becomes a heartbeat. The crowds recede.

Then I come down with a fever. The sickness defeats all purpose, all purchase on the hawk. I feed her on the sofa, put her back on her perch and watch her drift into the place where goshawks go when they've eaten. It is very far away. I wave my hand in front of her face. She appears not to see it at all. Her eyes seem as remote from thought or emotion as a metal dish or a patch of sky. *What is she thinking? What is she seeing?* I wonder. I shut my eyes and guess. Blood, I am sure. Smoke, branches, wet feathers. Snow. Pine needles. More blood. I shiver. And the days pass and the fever continues. The rain continues. It dampens the house. Wide parchment stains bleed across the wall in the hall and front room. The house smells of stagnant water in the coal-cellar, hawk mutes, and dust. Nothing is moving, nothing improving, nothing heading anywhere. I am packing up boxes to leave, still not knowing where I'd live when the house was gone. In a fit of bitter misery I make a fort out of an old cardboard wardrobe box in the spare room upstairs and crawl inside. It is dark. No one can see me. *No one knows where I am. It is safe here.* I curl up in the box to hide. Even in my state of sickness I know this is more than a little strange. *I am not going mad,* I tell myself. *I'm ill. That is all.*

17

Heat

The days of rain are followed by heat and insomnia and white nights that go on for ever. Outside at three in the morning a woman is calling 'William! William!', over and over again in a hoarse, stagey whisper. I have no idea why she is whispering; her hammering on William's front door is waking the street. I give up after that, go downstairs, tiptoe past the sleeping hawk, sit outside on an upturned flowerpot and smoke a cigarette. A thick black sky, clear stars, an end-of-summer sky. Mabel had flown perfectly for the last two days; she'd come fifty yards instantly to my upraised fist. Everything was accelerating now towards that crucial point. Point in the sense of time. Point in the sense of aim. Point in the sense of something so sharp it hurts. Flying the hawk free, unencumbered by the creance, nothing stopping her headlong flight out and away but the lines that run between us; palpable lines, not physical ones: lines of habit, of hunger, of partnership, of familiarity. Of something the old falconers would call love. Flying a hawk free is always scary. It is where you test these lines. And it's not a thing that's easy to do when you've lost trust in the world, and your heart is turned to dust.

At a more sensible hour I stumble into town in search of coffee. The park has been ravaged in the night. Great handfuls of bedding plants have been pulled out of the ground by drunken lads on a rampage; all the sapling limes along the path are wrenched and snapped in half. I look down at a heap of crushed and wilting marigolds, and wonder if I might replant them. But the roots look dry, the leaves already curled, so I walk on to the café, sit down at a table by the window with a newspaper and a coffee. There's an article about climate change. An unprecedented summer melt in the Arctic. The Northwest Passage is open. Permafrost is melting. Ecosystems failing. Horrible news, and wildly important, but I can't concentrate on the paper: I keep looking up because outside the window is a line of people. It's not a line like a ticket queue or an airport line, or any line I've seen before. A woman with perfectly straight bobbed grey hair and close-pursed lips grips a binder of loose papers. The man next to her holds one too. They're staring into the middle distance and no one is saying a word. I don't see the panic beneath the silence for a while, but then the panic is all I can see. When she passes my table I ask Dagmara the barista if she knows what is going on. She shrugs her shoulders. 'I just asked one of them. It's a bank. The Northern Rock. They are taking their money out because it is going bankrupt.' I frown at the unmoving line. Something about it reminds me of Mabel mantling her wings over food. *Mine. Mine mine mine.* I've never seen a bank run before. It's something from the Wild West or a grey, blowsy print of Weimar Berlin. When I was an undergraduate we were told that history had ended, and we all believed it. When the Berlin Wall fell, what history was made of was over. No more Cold War. No more wars. And yet here it was, and is, and all of it falling apart. Endings. Worlds dissolving. Weather systems, banking systems, the careful plans of municipal gardeners. Families, hearts, lives. Distant wars and small trees wrenched in two. I look at the line of people and all their fierce possessiveness and all their hidden terror at the thought that their bulwarks against death might be lost. Money. Security. Knots and lines. The ends of things. And it is sitting there with a cooling coffee that I think seriously for the first time about what I am doing. What I am going to do with the hawk. Kill things. Make death.

I had hunted with hawks for years before death meant anything to me at all. Perhaps I was then to all intents a child. I'd never considered what I was doing was cruel. I was a spectator, not a killer. Wild hawks hunted; so did mine. There seemed no useful moral difference. And falconry for me was about revelling in the flight of the hawk, never in the death it brought. But when my hawk caught things I was pleased – partly for the hawk, and partly because I had, as a child, bought into that imagined world of tweed-clad Victorian falconers, where death was visceral and ever-present and hedged with ceremonial formalities. When I watched those men with goshawks put the dead pheasant in the bag all those years ago I saw a kind of ease that bespoke centuries of social privilege and sporting confidence.

And the vocabulary I'd learned from the books distanced me from death. Trained hawks didn't catch animals. They caught *quarry*. They caught *game*. What an extraordinary term. *Game*. I sat quietly watching the line and wondered. I would hunt with this hawk. Of course I would. Training a goshawk and not letting it hunt seemed to me like raising a child and not letting it play. But that was not why I needed her. To me she was bright, vital, secure in her place in the world. Every tiny part of her was boiling with life, as if from a distance you could see a plume of steam around her, coiling and ascending and making everything around her slightly blurred, so she stood out in fierce, corporeal detail. The hawk was a fire that burned my hurts away. There could be no regret or mourning in her. No past or future. She lived in the present only, and that was my refuge. My flight from death was on her barred and beating wings. But I had forgotten that the puzzle that was death was caught up in the hawk, and I was caught up in it too.

* * *

'To him I am still the rarely tolerated enemy, and to me he is always the presence of death,' White wrote of Gos in his notebook. 'Death will be my last failure.' His neglect had made Gos wild again, and the hawk had become death to him because it could not be beaten. For six weeks he had struggled with it and the struggle had been as Jacob's with the angel. 'I have lived for this hawk,' he wrote in despair. 'I have gone half bird myself, transforming my love and interest and livelihood into its future, giving hostages to fortune as madly as in marriage and family cares. If the hawk dies almost all my present me dies with it. It has treated me today as if I were a dangerous and brutal enemy never seen before.'

Perhaps the final blow, when it came, was born of simple exhaustion. His hawk had beaten him, and he could not bear to fight it any more. But I think that it was more than this, much more. When I think of the tragedy of White and Gos I think of a small boy back in India standing in front of a wooden play-castle his father has made for his birthday. It is a big castle, big enough to get into, and his father has fixed a real pistol barrel to the battlements. It is to fire a salute for his birthday, but the little boy stares at it in dread. His father has forced him to stand in front of the castle, and he knows he is to be executed. There is nothing he can do. He is powerless. He cries silently, inconsolably, knowing that his father will shoot him, knowing he is about to die.

What must it be like to live in a world where you cry because you believe your father will kill you on your birthday, a world in which you are beaten, daily, for no reason? A world in which you write a letter to your mother in India enclosing your school photograph, and she writes back to tell you that your lips are 'growing sensual', and that you should hold them in, with your teeth if necessary? I cannot imagine White's childhood of terror and shame, but I can understand how it made him see the world as controlled by cruelty, by dictators and madmen. I can see how that power-less child in front of the play-castle never quite stopped believing that he was going to be shot.

For it was not just his fear of success that made White sabotage the training of his hawk. Underlying the whole long affair was a deep repetition compulsion, the term Freud used to describe the need to re-enact painful experiences in order to master them. But with the hawk the re-enactment was the tragedy. 'He has been frightened into insanity, being, like all predatory people, by nature terrified at heart,' he wrote of Gos. What had he done? He had taken something wild and free, something innocent and full of life, and fought with it. The cost of his mastery would be to reduce it to a biddable, broken-feathered, dull-eyed shadow of the bird it was meant to be. Gos had been meant to fly slantwise across dark valleys of German pines, to slay and ravine and be his own wildest self. White had thought he could tame the hawk without breaking its natural spirit. But all he has done is try to break it, over and over again. He thinks of Gos tangled in the tree, hanging there in the branches, trapped, powerless, entirely unable to move.

It wasn't conscious. None of it was conscious. But the disaster was inevitable. White saw that the hawk was himself, a bird that was a 'youth who had been maddened by every kind of clumsiness, privation, and persecution'. And he understood, finally, terribly, that what he had done was become the persecutor, no matter how many times he told himself otherwise. The hawk was the child in front of the play-castle. He was his father. *He was his father.* He was the dictator, not the hawk. And so the great tragedy rolled to its conclusion, and the final blow, of course, fell from simple sentiment.

Low clouds move fast over the Ridings. It is raining hard. The cattle lie under the trees in the gale, their flanks dark and soaked, their breaths steaming in the air. White goes out to the barn where Gos is tied to his perch in shadow. Guilt uncoils in his heart. The hawk has no choice but to sit where he is told. He has no freedom at all. So White puts a bow-perch in the ground just outside the door, ties six yards of twine – the tarred twine with no breaking strain, the twine that has already snapped twice, the dangerous, poor quality twine – to Gos's swivel, then ties the other end to the perch in the barn. This way, he tells himself, his hawk can fly out-side and then fly back inside when he wants. Pleased that he's given Gos more freedom, he returns to the house.

The rain is relentless. It is not a day to try to trap the hawks. It is a day for comfort. He will make it up to Gos. He will pace up and down the kitchen with him, feed him tid-bits, make him love him again. Gos likes music: he will play him songs on the wireless. But he finds the wireless has died. He bicycles to Tom's, borrows his telephone to order a new battery. Then he pedals back. Rain and rooks. A man on a bicycle in a high wind who decides he must concentrate on small things today. Big things are too difficult. What he will do is repaint the woodwork in the passageway, and then perhaps the kitchen door. When the passageway is done he examines his handiwork with a critical eye. It looks well. Now for the kitchen door. *Blue paint*, he thinks. His father used to like painting things in bright and clashing colours. He knows he has inherited the vice. So he goes into the barn to fetch it. Gos bates from him, first upwards to the rafters, then straight out of the open door. When White leaves the barn, the paintpot in his hand, he looks for Gos sitting on his perch. But the perch is empty. Gos is not there. His hawk is gone. Gos has gone and the frayed end of the twine lies snapped upon the ground.

PART II

18

Flying free

Tonight. The weather is perfect, the hawk's weight too. I race about the house, fizzing with anticipation, filling my morning with small and mundane tasks. I scrub mutes from the vinyl cloth on the floor, whistle happily, wash and dry my hair. But some invisible needle is picking away inside me: as the afternoon wears on, things begin to unravel. First I fight with my mother on the phone for no good reason, then when Christina arrives to see the hawk fly I snap at her for no reason whatsoever. Picking up my hawking waistcoat in the kitchen I hear her say *gridlock* but the word doesn't register at all. I should have listened. There'd been a horrendous crash on the A14 outside Cambridge. Stuart had been stranded in its aftermath, stuck in his Land Rover under a flyover stanchion, air ambulances roaring overhead through roiling clouds of smoke. He'd called me. Told me he was running late because of a crash, but that was all. 'I'm going up the hill now,' he said. 'Coming?'

'Yes,' I said. 'See you in twenty minutes.'

But the accident had been so appalling it had closed not only the main road but the roads around it too. All the rush-hour traffic crossing Cambridgeshire had to come through the centre of the city. Forty minutes later we're no more than a quarter of a mile from the house and I am shaking with monstrous frustration. Poor Christina sits silently in the back. Mabel bates. I cannot bear it. She bates again. I shout at her.

She does not know the noise is directed at her, but I hate myself for shouting, and that guilt sits on top of the other guilts and all those sit on top of the knowledge that the accident that caused this must have been terrible indeed. The air in the car turns solid as glass. I take deep breaths and stare out of the window. It is a beautiful evening. This makes things worse. I watch starlings coast over the shopping centre, watch the sun, sinking, sinking, and the smooth air furring at its edges into the shade of a woodpigeon's breast, all delicate greys and torpid pinks. I turn on the traffic news. Turn it off. Mabel bates again, disturbed by the unaccustomed stops and starts and engine silence. Every bate ratchets up my stress another notch. I call Stuart on my phone. He's waiting for us. I fume. The car inches. I look down and notice I'm nearly out of petrol, which adds a whole, delightful other dimension to the ticking minutes.

By the time we get to the hill I'm practically catatonic. There, at the top of the hill, is Stuart's Land Rover. We walk up the track. It's getting dark. Mabel looks ragingly keen to fly for the three minutes it takes to walk up there, and I start to relax. But she takes one look at the nylon kite that Stuart has been using to help train his falcon to climb high into the sky – takes one look at this triangular splash of fluttering primary colours, looks me in the face, and then bates. *Bate. Bate. Bate.*

Stuart persuades me not to go home. 'We'll find something for her to fly at,' he says. 'She'll settle down.' She does, a bit. So do I. I try to unkink my knotted shoulders and take deep gulps of cooling air. I am stressed. I don't normally fly hawks free like this. Normally I'd call her to the fist on the creance as usual, then untie the creance and fly her once or twice without it. Only later would I try flying her at quarry. But I defer to Stuart's knowledge: he knows about goshawks and he's done this many times before.

Time passes. It's now getting on for a thick, gloomy evening. Smoke is everywhere on the horizon. A yellow crescent moon tilts, out of focus, up there in something that looks like a plate of agar. Swimmy dusk. Bats flit. Trees gather darkness to themselves. Mabel's swivel and leash are in my pocket, I have swapped her jesses for thin flying jesses that will not catch on twigs or branches, and I grip them tightly between my gloved fingers. I have walked, under Stuart's instructions, to a triangle of rough ground just one side of a copse of trees. It is a thick patch of thistles and dry seedheads, and we trudge through it. I am mute with stress, enraged by what is happening and powerless to stop it. It is dark. What the hell am I doing? The hawk's pupils are huge. Her eyes are almost completely black. I cannot believe how stupid this is. I want to go home. *I want to go home.* And Stuart starts beating up towards me, mushing the thistles and grasses with a stick to push any hidden rabbits or pheasants towards us so Mabel can see them. *This is ridiculous. I don't want to be here, and I don't know why I'm letting this happen. I shouldn't be loosing this hawk. I should just* – there is a movement behind me and to my right, and the hawk peers, seeing something running, and then bates at the spot. *Oh!* And I let her go. And immediately I wish I had not. Suddenly my hawk is free. She flies powerfully for a few seconds, dips at whatever it was, which has gone, and then starts to fly in circles, sailing like a moth, a giant hawkmoth. She gains height. There is a terrible crepuscular hush. I can see her long head turning to look at me, and her tail fanning and flexing as she turns. I'm in some kind of fugue state. The gap between me and the hawk is something I feel like a wound. She is circling, and looking at me, and seems uncertain about coming back. Stuart is standing here. Christina is standing there. I am standing right here, shouting and whistling at the hawk. The dark, that she can fly in circles, that everything's unclear: these things are discoveries for her. She's trying to work out what to do. The new ground. The angle of incidence between up here and down there, where Helen's hand and heart are.

She finally pitches with her back to me on the apex of a young beech tree; the crown bends almost double under her weight. All I can see is her shape, all angles and shoulders, and I feel the confusion that animates her entirely. I call her. She leaps from her awkward perch and comes through dusk towards my upraised fist. All is too strange. She bounces off the glove, cutting it merely, and starts circling again. She ends up deeper in the wood, perched again – but, happily, facing my way. Through the gloom and the flocked leaves I can see her yellow nose, and something of her accipitrine crouch. I know her eyes are on me. So out goes the fist. I pile one chick, two chicks, three chicks on it. Whistle. Call. 'Come on, Mabel!', slapping my gloved hand in animate will.

At this point, space-time is folded and scrunched into direct relations. Trigonometry. Goshawk glide-path to my fist, and Goshawk intentionality, which I am sure is also derivable in mathematical terms. My beating, horrified heart, and my soul feeling like water at four degrees; heavier than ice, falling to the bottom of the ocean.

And suddenly, she is back on the glove, I feel soaked in iced water, and I cannot believe she's not lost. I feel like White: a tyro, a fool, a beginner. An idiot. 'Never mind,' says Stuart. He knows I am in pieces. I catch the flash of his grin in the darkness. 'She's too high, and it's getting dark. But you got her back, right? That's always a good end to the day.' I can barely speak. I croak a reply. The adrenalin fits and fizzes in my veins as I walk back to the car, and I'm still not sure how I managed to drive home.

The air is dark and full of water. He is soaked to the skin. Gos is nowhere to be seen. He is tying pieces of rabbit to all the places where the hawk had been. They are like prayers, like the tattered ribbons pagans tie to winter twigs. His hands are very white against the coruscating green of the wind-blown bark of empty oaks. He has run out of rabbit.

He has no lure. He has no meat but liver. He'll ask Mrs Wheeler to buy some steak for him in Buckingham. Standing by the farmhouse door he listens. 'Rooks observed to be mobbing, or a solitary crow sitting on the dead branch of some tree, cawing or jerking about uneasily, are an almost certain sign that the lost hawk is not far away,' he'd read in Blaine. Nothing. Then a single caw, loudly repeated. *There.* A couple of hundred yards away is a crow, circling the top of a tree, cursing at the bird beneath it. On the topmost branch sits Gos, tiny at that distance, his familiar blunt-shouldered form hunched against the gale. White runs to the tree and stands under it waving a piece of liver and a handkerchief as a lure while flashes of water spread on the further fields. The rain falls on the glades, avenues, and all the temples and obelisks of Stowe, and Gos sits there, imperious, indecisive, and horribly soaked, for White's constant stroking had taken the waterproofing oil from his feathers. The gale buffets his perch. It is not comfortable here. It is not comfortable at all. He opens his wings, intending to fly down to the man with the food in his hand. He leaves the tree, turns in mid-air, starts to descend. White's heart, beating. The hawk approaching. Then the wind fills his wings and pushes, and the hawk, who has no skill and does not know how to fly in a gale like this, is sucked away downwind and is gone.

There is a time in life when you expect the world to be always full of new things. And then comes a day when you realise that is not how it will be at all. You see that life will become a thing made of holes. Absences. Losses. Things that were there and are no longer. And you realise, too, that you have to grow around and between the gaps, though you can put your hand out to where things were and feel that tense, shining dullness of the space where the memories are.

I was a lucky child. Until I saw that pheasant die in a

winter hedge, all I knew of death came from books – and one kind in particular. I was looking at a whole shelf of them now. That morning I'd filled the car with boxes, put Mabel on her passenger-seat perch and driven back to my parents' house for the weekend. *My parents' house.* I supposed it was my mother's house now. I had come back because I was preparing to move. A dear friend had offered me his house while he and his family went to China for a few months, and I was impossibly grateful to them, but the prospect of losing my beautiful college house was hateful. I stacked the boxes in the garage then sat with my mother in the kitchen while Mabel loafed and bathed and preened on the sunny lawn. We drank tea, reminisced, talked about Dad and times gone by. There was a lot of laughter. It was good to see her. But it was not easy to be there. We sat in chairs that Dad should be sitting in, drank from cups he had drunk from, and when I saw his careful handwriting on a note pinned by the back door it got too much. Much too much. I ran into my old room, sat on the little bed and hugged my knees, pain worming around inside my chest like a thing with a million tiny teeth and claws.

I looked up at the top of my old bookshelves. There, dusty and unread for years, were all the animal books of my childhood. I'd loved these books. They were rich with wildness, escape and adventure. But I hated them too. Because they never had happy endings. Tarka the otter was killed by hounds. The falcons died of pesticide poisoning. A man with a spade beat to death the otter in *Ring of Bright Water*; vultures tore out the Red Pony's eyes. The deer in *The Yearling* was shot, the dog in *Old Yeller* died. So did the spider in *Charlotte's Web* and my favourite rabbit in *Watership Down*. I remember that awful dread as the number of pages shrank in each new animal book I read. I knew what would happen. And it happened every time. So I suppose it wasn't a surprise to eight-year-old me that Gos snapped his leash and was lost in the wind and rain. I greeted it with sad resignation. But it was dreadful all the same.

But I hadn't trained a hawk then, and I had no understanding of loss. I did not know how White felt. Now I did. I sat on my bed and it pressed on my chest like a weight the size of a hill. I felt it. For the first time I understood that vast blankness that shuttered his heart in horror. 'I cannot remember that my heart stopped beating at any particular time,' he wrote in his diary. 'The blow was so stunning, so final after six weeks of unremitting faith, that it was tempered to me as being beyond my appreciation. Death will be like this, something too vast to hurt much or perhaps even to upset me.'

His heart is torn in half. The pigeon in his hand is rigid with terror; it has turned from a bird to a thing of iron and feathers. Its red eye is blank, its little beak panting. He steels himself and throws it high in the air towards the hawk in the tree. The pigeon he'd bought to trap the hawks in the wood – such irony – rises up, trailing the creance behind it. Gos stoops upon it like a vast predatory butterfly, but then pulls away and swings into the next tree. White pulls the pigeon to earth, picks it up, follows, and throws it out again. He fishes for Gos with the pigeon as a fisherman casts lures for a pike. He has been doing this for a while now, and each time the hawk's stoop brings it closer to the pigeon and White's waiting hands. He bends to pick the pigeon from the ground, exhausted, wings spread, its flight feathers so wet they look like fraying pencils. He knows this terrified bird can barely fly. He knows that the next time he throws it into the air the hawk will catch it. Just one more time. But he cannot do it. He *knows* this pigeon. He had tamed it. It had sat companionably on his finger. It was his friend. His world is broken; he is breaking his Word. It is brute cruelty. He cannot do this any more. He remembers a passage in Blaine's book on capturing hawks while they sleep, hugs the soaking pigeon to his breast and leaves Gos to nightfall. He returns with a ladder, a rope, a torch and the salmon rod he'd used once before to hook Gos down from a tree. He stands under the tree, trembling with hope of success, when Graham Wheeler, the farmer's lad who had come to help, runs up. Gos takes fright and slips from the tree into darkness.

For days he walks the Ridings and sees him, sometimes, soaring over the trees in distant, expanding circles. His soul is still tied up in the hawk. He can see that Gos is happy. *He deserves to be free*, thinks White, and wishes him well in his life in the wild. But death waits for Gos, White knows: his jesses and swivel, the accursed accoutrements of his former subjection, will get snagged on a branch, and he will struggle, and hang, and starve, and die. Should fate see fit to deliver the bird back into his hands, he vows, he should treat him differently: as a partner not his slave. His remorse is bitterly deep. He is lonely without Gos. He misremembers Blake. *Love asketh but himself to please, To bind another to his delight, Joys in another's loss of ease, And builds a hell in heaven's despite.*

Later that afternoon I walked with Mabel up a narrow lane to a nearby farm. I'd had permission to fly my hawks there years ago. Did I still? Probably not. I didn't care. There was something splendid in the thought that what I was doing was surreptitious, underhand, slightly criminal. I raised my binoculars and scanned the fields. No tractors, no farm-workers. No dog-walkers. No one out for an evening stroll. And so off we crept, Mabel and I, off to the top wood, where the rabbits used to be. We sneaked around the corner of a blackthorn thicket. There. About thirty yards away, a little way out from the margin of the wood: three of them in silhouette, ears glowing backlit by the sun, crouching to feed. And next to them, a cock pheasant, ankling his way slowly past.

Grief had spurred me to fly the hawk, but now my grief was gone. Everything was gone except this quiet sylvan scene. Into which I intended to let slip havoc and murder. I stalked around the edge of the wood, crouching low, holding my breath. My attention was microscopically fierce. I'd become a thing of eyes and will alone. Mabel held her wings out from her sides, her head snaking, reptilian, eyes glowing. It felt like I was holding the bastard offspring of a flaming torch and an assault rifle. Soft grass underfoot. One hand out to steady myself, we picked our way around to the final corner. And then I slowly extended my gloved fist out from the screen of brush.

The hawk left the fist with the recoil of a .303 rifle. I stepped out to watch. Saw a chain of events so fast they snapped into a comic strip: *frame, frame, frame*. Frame one: goshawk spluttering from the fist in bars and pinions and talons. Frame two: goshawk low to the ground, grass streaking along under her. Chocolate wings, beating strongly, hump-backed. Frame three: rabbits running. Frame four: the pheasant, too, crouching and running into the wood's safe margin.

But it wasn't safe. Split-second, ink-starred decisions in the hawk's tactical computer. She slewed round sling-shot style, heel-bow, soaking up g-force like a sponge. Closed her wings and was gone. Sucked into the black hole of the wood, beneath a low-hanging larch branch. Everything disappeared. No rabbits, no pheasant, no hawk. Just a black hole in the wood's edge. It had gone very quiet. There was the distant *coc-coc-coc* of a scared pheasant.

I ran into the wood and shivered. We'd been hawking in the soft, woolly haze of a sunny autumn evening. Soft grass, meadow brown butterflies; a comfortable, easy light. Walking into the wood, the temperature dropped by five degrees, and the light by several stops. It was dark. And cold. Outside, a late summer evening in England. In here, Norway. I half-expected to feel grains of snow pattering through the needles. I stood, slightly unnerved. Looked about. Nothing. No hawk. What should I do now?

I stood very still and listened. Strained to hear through the dark. Listened so hard the air became particulate: sound no longer sound, but compression waves through trillions of molecules of air. But there was no sound at all. Dead, muffled silence between larch trunks. And then, some way off to my left – a long way off – I heard a scuffle and breaking sticks and the unmistakable sound of hawk bells. I broke through brush, blindly. I thought I'd heard a squeal in the sound; maybe she had caught a rabbit. Silence again, except for my breathing hard and smashing through the branches of a fallen tree, blind and brute, to get to the spot.

I saw her before I heard her. She came running out from a tangle of thornbushes capping a huge warren. Came at a run, barrel-chested, and flung herself up to my fist. Everything apart from her yellow-tinted cere and feet was black and white. Blackthorn, black needles, the hawk's white chest, black teardrop feathers, black talons. Black nose. White tailings of chalk from where the rabbits had dug. When she came back to my fist she had chalk mud on all her toes. It covered my glove as she ate, made small white marks like the letters of half-forgotten words that as she ate were smeared and erased and written all over again.

It had been a long while since I'd hunted with a hawk, but I didn't remember it being like this. I was sure it had never been like this. I was astounded by the radical change in subjectivity it had instilled: how the world dissolved to nothing, yet was so real and tangible it almost hurt. How every passing second slowed and stretched, catching us out of time: when I stepped back onto the road to walk home I was astounded how low the sun had fallen. We'd been out for less than an hour. It had felt like years.

The falconer and scientist Professor Tom Cade once described falconry as a kind of 'high-intensity birdwatching'. I thought it was a nice phrase, and an accurate one. But now I knew this was wrong. What I had just done was nothing like birdwatching. It was more like gambling, though the stakes were infinitely bloodier. At its heart was a willed loss of control. You pour your heart, your skill, your very soul, into a thing – into training a hawk, learning the form in racing or the numbers in cards – then relinquish control over it. That is the hook. Once the dice rolls, the horse runs, the hawk leaves the fist, you open yourself to luck, and you cannot control the outcome. Yet everything you have done until that moment persuades you that you might be lucky. The hawk might catch her quarry, the cards might fall perfectly, the horse make it first past the post. That little space of irresolution is a strange place to be. You feel safe because you are entirely at the world's mercy. It is a rush. You lose yourself in it. And so you run towards those little shots of fate, where the world turns. That is the lure: that is why we lose ourselves, when powerless from hurt and grief, in drugs or gambling or drink; in addictions that collar the broken soul and shake it like a dog. I had found my addiction on that day out with Mabel. It was as ruinous, in a way, as if I'd taken a needle and shot myself with heroin. I had taken flight to a place from which I didn't want to ever return.

19

Extinction

Falconers have a word for hawks in the mood to slay: they call the bird *in yarak*. The books say it comes from the Persian *yaraki*, meaning power, strength and boldness. Much later I was amused to find that in Turkish it means an archaic weapon and is also slang for penis: never doubt that falconry is a boys' game. I'm back in Cambridge now, and as I carry Mabel up the stony track to the hill each day I watch her come into yarak. It is disturbingly like watching her slow possession by a demon. Her crest feathers rise, she leans back, tummy feathers fluffed, shoulders dropped, toes very tight on the glove. Her demeanour switches from *everything scares me* to *I see it all; I own all this and more*.

In this state she's a high-tension wire-strung hawk of murderous anticipation, wound so tight she bates at anything that moves – things she's not a hope of catching: flocks of larks, distant racing pigeons, even a farmyard tomcat – and I hold her jesses tight and don't let her go. But when a hen pheasant rockets up from my feet I do. She chases it fiercely but it has too much of a head start; after fifty yards she slows, turns in mid-air and comes back to me, planing over the top of a hedgerow ash to land gently upon my fist. On another day she bursts downhill in pursuit of a rabbit and is about to grab it when the rabbit stops dead in its tracks. She overshoots and crashes into the ground; the rabbit jinks, doubles back on itself and runs uphill to the safety of a hole. She leaps back into the air to resume her pursuit but the rabbit is gone. She alights, confused and crestfallen, on the grass.

I'm crestfallen too. It's not that I'm baying for blood. But I don't want Mabel to get discouraged. In the wild, young goshawks will sit for hours hidden in trees waiting for an easy opportunity to present itself: a fledgling crow, a baby rabbit. But it is September now: nature's easy pickings are grown. And while most goshawkers have a dog to help them find game, or a ferret to bolt rabbits for their hawk to chase, I do not. All I can do is walk with the hawk and hope we find something to catch. But I am a liability; her senses are far better than mine. We walk past a gully under a hedge where there are rabbits and rats and God knows what, all covered with brambles and briars and robins' pincushions set on briar stems like exotic fruit, their vegetable hairs brushed green and rose and carmine. She dives from my fist towards the undergrowth. I don't know she's seen something – so I don't let her go. Then I curse my pathetic human senses. Something was there. A mouse? A pheasant? A rabbit? With a stick I poke about in the gully but nothing comes out. It is too late; whatever it was has gone. We walk on. Mabel stops looking murderous and assumes an expression of severe truculence. *How the hell*, I imagine her thinking, *am I supposed to catch things with this idiot in tow?*

I return exhausted from our latest attempt: a hellish, traumatic afternoon, fractious, gusty and sour. I'd met Stuart and Mandy out on the hill. 'I'll run the dogs for you,' he said. 'See if we can get a point for her.' But Mabel wasn't having any of it. She bated and twittered and glared. She hated the dogs, she hated it all. I hated it too. I fed her up and drove us home. Then I started pulling clothes from a wardrobe, attempting to transform myself into a cheerful, civilised person who does things like go to art galleries. I brush the burrs from my hair, wash my face, shrug on a skirt, push the sleeves of a cashmere jumper back to my elbows, paint a black line over each eyelid. Foundation. Mascara. A smear of lipsalve to seal my wind-dried mouth, a pair of shiny boots with heels that make me worry that I can't run in them – for running seems essential these days – and I check the result in a mirror. It is a good disguise. I'm pleased with how convincing it seems. But it's getting late, and I'm running against the clock. I have twenty minutes to get to a gallery for the opening of an art exhibition. I'm supposed to give a talk about it in a few weeks' time and I have to see the bloody thing first. I battle with sleep as I drive, and by the time I reach the gallery doors my knees are ready to give way.

I expect a room of paintings and sculpture. But when I open the doors there's something so unexpected inside my brain turns cartwheels. It is a full-sized bird hide built of rough-hewn pine, and it is – I read the sign – an exact copy of a real structure in California. Seeing it in the gallery is as disconcerting as opening a fridge door and finding a house within. The hide is dark inside and packed with people peering through a window in one wall. I look out of it too. *Oh!* I see the trick. It is a neat one. The artist has filmed the view from the real hide, and is projecting it onto a screen beyond the window. It shows a soaring California condor, a huge, dusty-black carrion-eating vulture rendered nearly extinct by persecution, habitat destruction and poisoning from lead-contaminated carcasses. By the late 1980s only twenty-seven birds remained, and in a last-ditch effort to save the species they were trapped and taken into captivity so that their domestic-bred young could be used to repopulate the wild. Some people tried to stop this happening. They believed honestly and sincerely that once all the birds were captive, condors would cease to exist. These birds are made of wildness, they argued. A captive condor is a condor no more.

I watch the condor for a while. It makes me impatient. My head is packed with real skies and real hawks. I'm remembering live condors I'd met at a captive-breeding centre years before: vast, loose-feathered, turkey-necked birds with purpose and curiosity; avian hogs in black feather-boas. Precious, yes, but complicated, real, idiosyncratic, astonishing. The condor on the gallery screen was nothing like them. *Helen, you are an idiot,* I think. *That is the whole point of this exhibition. The whole point of it, right there in front of you.*

I think of what wild animals are in our imaginations. And how they are disappearing – not just from the wild, but from people's everyday lives, replaced by images of themselves in print and on screen. The rarer they get, the fewer meanings animals can have. Eventually rarity is all they are made of. The condor is an icon of extinction. There's little else to it now but being the last of its kind. And in this lies the diminution of the world. How can you love something, how can you fight to protect it, if all it means is loss? There is a vast difference between my visceral, bloody life with Mabel and the reserved, distanced view of modern nature-appreciation. I know that some of my friends see my keeping a hawk as morally suspect, but I couldn't love or understand hawks as much as I do if I'd only ever seen them on screens. I've made a hawk part of a human life, and a human life part of a hawk's, and it has made the hawk a million times more complicated and full of wonder to me. I think of my chastened surprise when Mabel played with a paper telescope. She is real. She can resist the meanings humans give her. But the condor? The condor has no resistance to us at all. I stare at the attenuated, drifting image on the gallery screen. It is a shadow, a figure of loss and hope; it is hardly a bird at all.

The other exhibit is perfectly simple. It is a bird lying on its back in a glass box in an empty room. Seeing it makes all my soapbox musings fade and fall away. It's a parrot, a Spix's macaw. There are none left in the wild now and the last captive birds are the focus of desperate attempts to keep the species alive. This one is long dead. Stuffed with cotton wool, a small paper label tied to one of its clenched dry feet, its feathers are the deep blue of an evening sea. It might be the loneliest thing I have ever seen. But leaning over this spotlit skin in a glass coffin, I don't think of animal extinction at all. I think of Snow White. I think of Lenin in his ill-lit mausoleum. And I think of the day after my father died, when I was shown into a hospital room where he lay.

But this isn't him, I thought, wildly, after the woman closed the door. *He isn't here.* Someone had dressed a waxwork of my father in hospital pyjamas and a patterned duvet. Why would they do that? It made no sense. It was nonsense. I took a step back. Then I saw on his arm the cut that would not heal and stopped. I knew I had to speak. For ages I could not. Physically could not. Something the size of a fist was in my throat and it was catching the words and not letting them out. I started to panic. Why couldn't I speak? *I have to speak to him.* Then the tears came. They were not like normal tears. Water coursed in sheets down my cheeks and dripped to the hospital floor. And with the water came words. So I leaned over the bed and spoke to my father who was not there. I addressed him seriously and carefully. I told him that I loved him and missed him and would miss him always. And I talked on, explaining things to him, things I cannot now remember but which at the time were of clear and burning importance. Then there was silence. And I waited. I did not know why. Until I realised it was in hope that an answer might come. And then I knew it was over. I took my father's hand in my own for the last time, squeezed it in a brief goodbye and quietly left the room.

The next day out on the hill Mabel learns, I suppose, what she is for. She chases a pheasant. It crashes into the brambles beneath a tall hedge. She lands on top of the hedge, peering down, her plumage bright against the dark earth of the further slope. I start running. I think I remember where the pheasant has gone. I convince myself it was never there at all. I know it is there. Clay sticks to my heels and slows me down. I'm in a world of slowly freezing mud, and even the air seems to be getting harder to run through. Mabel is waiting for me to flush the pheasant, if only I knew where it was. Now I am at the hedge, trying to find it, constructing *what will happen next* scenarios in my head, and at this point they're narrowing fast, towards point zero, when the pheasant will fly. I cannot see Stuart and Mandy any more, though I know they must be there. I'm crashing through brambles and sticks, dimly aware of the catch and rip of thorns in my flesh. Now I cannot see the hawk because I am searching for the pheasant, so I have to work out what she is doing by putting myself in her mind – and so I become both the hawk in the branches above and the human below. The strangeness of this splitting makes me feel I am walking under myself, and sometimes away from myself. Then for a moment everything becomes dotted lines, and the hawk, the pheasant and I merely elements in a trigonometry exercise, each of us labelled with soft italic letters. And now I am so invested in the hawk and the pheasant's relative positions that my consciousness cuts loose entirely, splits into one or the other, first the hawk looking down, second the pheasant in the brambles looking up, and I move over the ground as if I couldn't possibly affect anything in the world. There is no way I can flush this pheasant. I'm not here. Time stretches and slows. There's a sense of panic at this point, a little buffet of fear that's about annihilation and my place in the world. But then the pheasant is flushed, a pale and burring chunk of muscle and feathers, and the hawk crashes from the hedge towards it. And all the lines that connect heart and head and future possibilities, those lines that also connect me with the hawk and the pheasant and with life and death, suddenly become safe, become tied together in a small muddle of feathers and gripping talons that stand in mud in the middle of a small field in the middle of a small county in a small country on the edge of winter.

I stare at the hawk as she grips the dead pheasant, and her mad eyes stare right back at me. I'm amazed. I don't know what I expected to feel. Bloodlust? Brutality? No. Nothing like that. There are thorn-scratches all over me from where I dived through the hedge, and an ache in my heart I can't place. There's a sheeny fog in the air. Dry. Like talc. I look at the hawk, the pheasant, the hawk. And everything changes. The hawk stops being a thing of violent death. She becomes a child. It shakes me to the core. She is a child. A baby hawk that's just worked out who she is. What she's for. I reach down and start, unconsciously as a mother helping a child with her dinner, plucking the pheasant with the hawk. For the hawk. And when she starts eating, I sit on my heels and watch, watch her eat. Feathers lift, blow down the hedge, and catch in spiders' webs and thorn branches. The bright blood on her toes coagulates and dries. Time passes. Benison of sunlight. A wind shifts the thistle stalks and is gone. And I start crying, soundlessly. Tears roll down my face. For the pheasant, for the hawk, for Dad and for all his patience, for that little girl who stood by a fence and waited for the hawks to come.

20

Hiding

White rushes from the house. The postman brought him news of agitated rooks in nearby woods. Breathless, he runs to the trees. Gos is not there. Of course he is not. He cannot find the sparrowhawks either. He thinks he hears them sometimes, but perhaps the calls are owls. He exists, now, in a landscape of hearsay; there are rumours of hawks like rumours of war. He stares at the sky. He litters the country with traps. He sits for days on end in the woods, from dawn until dark, cramped and shivering in his hide. Nothing. He buys a gamekeeper's pole trap with jagged metal jaws. He files away the teeth designed to break hawks' legs and pads its spring-shut jaws with felt. Then he makes another trap, a falconer's trap from a description in a book: a noose of running twine around a ring of upturned feathers, and in the centre of the ring a teth-ered blackbird. He'll hide with one end of the twine in his hand, and when the hawk takes the bird, he'll pull, so the twine slips over the feathers and catches the hawk by its legs. It might work, if he can trap a blackbird to use as bait. He cannot trap a blackbird. He despairs. He starts a letter. *Dear Herr Waller*, it begins. He writes in English because his Ger-man is poor. He asks the man who'd sent him Gos for another hawk. He knows it might be too late in the year to get a young one, and passage hawks – those trapped when already on the wing – are few and far between. But he ends the letter with hope, takes it to Buckingham and posts it to Berlin. He waits for a reply, he waits for the hawks, he waits in penance and suffers for his sins. Nothing comes and there is no answer.

My job was over. It was time to move. I was already an emotional mess, but the stress of the move pushed my dysfunction to spectacular proportions. The new house in the suburbs was nothing like the old house in the city: it was huge and modern, with a vast front room for the hawk to sleep in and lawns to sun herself upon. I filled the freezer with hawk food and a stack of frozen pizzas. Dragged my clothes upstairs in their plastic sacks, dumped them in a pile by the bedroom door. The rain came again, thin and sour, and I spent my first day there sprawled on the sofa with a notepad on my knees, failing to write my father's memorial address. *I have five minutes*, I kept thinking, dully. *Five minutes to speak of my father's life.*

The house was full of toys: alphabet blocks and jigsaws, plush animals in boxes, pictures in felt-tip pen and glitter pinned to the kitchen walls. It was a family house and there was no family in it. The emptiness I felt was my own, but in my madness I began to feel the house didn't want me, that it missed its family and was mourning their loss. I stayed out longer with Mabel, found it harder and harder to return, because out with the hawk I didn't need a home. Out there I forgot I was human at all. Everything the hawk saw was raw and real and drawn hair-fine, and everything else was dampened to nothing. The landscape built meanings in my head that felt like pressures, like light, like gifts: sensations impossible to put into words, like the apprehension of danger, or someone reading over your shoulder. Everything became more complicated but strangely simple too. The hedgerows that were once hawthorn, blackthorn, maple and ash were now all of a piece and nameless, wrought of the same stuff as me; they felt like inanimate people, no more or less important than the hawk, than me, or anything else on the hill. Sometimes my phone rang and I'd answer it. The effort to drag myself out of the bright nimbus of land cut with lines of strategy and hawkish desire was terrible. It was usually my mother. She had to say everything twice, to begin with, as if she were coaching me in how to return from this strange hedgerow ontology to more ordinary humanity.

'Hello!' she'd say.

Silence.

'Hello?'

And Mabel would be on my fist, tail fanned, shoulders dropped, staring through me and the phone, and her attention catching on everything serially. *Field-fence-fieldfare-wing-flick-pheasant-feather-on-path-sun-on-wire-twelve-woodpig-eons-half-a-mile-distant-tick-tick-tick* and Mum's saying:

'How are you?'

'Fine, Mum. How are you?'

'I'm OK. Have you heard from James?'

Her voice was slow and deep compared to the constant indexical chatter of things and I couldn't hear what she was really saying because there were twelve woodpigeons half a mile away and the hawk was looking at them and so was I. I could not hear my mother's pain. I could not feel my own.

We'd come to a different place today, a field on the other side of town overrun with rabbits. It took less than a minute for Mabel to grab one deep in a drift of nettles. Hawks don't retrieve their prey: you must run to them, let them eat a while, then take them back onto your fist for a reward of food. I ran, bent down, parted the stinging stems, picked the rabbit up with the hawk, and put them both down on the grass. Now the rabbit is dead, its pelt bunched between the hawk's gripping talons, but blood upwells as she breaks into its chest, and I cannot stop watching it, this horrible, mesmerising, seeping claret filling up the space, growing jelly-like as it meets the air, like a thing alive. It *was* a thing alive. I want to sit and think. This is a great mystery. I feel something pressing against my own chest, leaning in, a question wanting an answer. But there's no time for contemplation: I have to get her back on the glove, or she'll stuff her face and won't fly tomorrow. It's time for the ancient falconer's trick to stop a hawk from feeling she's been robbed of her prize. First I cut off one of the rabbit's hind legs and hide it behind my back, then lay handfuls of grass in a stack by my side. Then I hold out the leg in my glove, throwing the grass over the rabbit to hide it. The hawk looks down, sees grass at her feet, looks up, sees food, leaps straight to my fist and eats.

And as I tuck the rabbit into the back pocket of my waistcoat the noise begins. First it is a low, dopplering growl. It dies away, returns. Engines. Big engines, growing louder. The note climbs to a vast marine roar – and a Second World War bomber, a Flying Fortress, emerges from behind the trees. Woodpigeons spray from the tops of the oaks in terror. Pheasants crow, shadows flicker, the remaining rabbits bolt to their holes. I feel an urgent need to hide. But Mabel gives the monstrous thing a single, indifferent glance and continues to eat. I'm astonished. How can the hawk not see it as a threat, this vast, impossibly heavy whale of a plane? She comes right overhead, absurdly low; she is painted a deep USAAF wartime green, and as she banks through the sun-furred air I see the bomb bay and the gun turret on her belly. The size of her, the deep thrumming drone of her four Pratt & Whitney engines, the sense that she is alive, an animal – all these things hold me transfixed. I sit back on my heels and stare, my fear forgotten. And two lines fall into my head.

> Consider this, and in our time
> As the hawk sees it, or the helmeted airman:

The poet W. H. Auden had written those lines in 1930, and I hadn't thought of them for years. To have the commanding view of the hawk and airman: to be lifted free from the messy realities of human life to a prospect of height and power from which one can observe the world below. To have safe vantage, from which death may descend. *Safety*. I think of the American airmen stationed here seventy years ago flying aircraft just like this one, scrambling to the ice-boxes that were cockpits, wearing heated suits that didn't work, breathing oxygen through rubber hoses that furred with crystalline ice, so that at altitude they had to bend and crush them between their fingers to get sufficient oxygen to breathe. They slept on cots in an alien land of rain and fog, dressed in silence for dawn briefings before running to their ships, holding the throttles forward, tight-chested as the engines spooled up, climbing through cloud, eyes locked on the manifold pressure gauges and the rpm displays, navigators calling headings in degrees. And then the hours of flight to and from Germany where they dropped their appalling cargo through skies thick with exploding shells. One in four did not complete their tour of duty. The sky was not a place of safety, no matter how commanding their view. What happened to them was terrible. What they did was terrible beyond imagining. No war can ever be just air.

The hawk is on my fist. Thirty ounces of death in a feathered jacket; a being whose world is drawn in plots and vectors that pull her towards lives' ends. She finishes the last scraps of rabbit, strops her beak, rubs strands of pale fur onto the glove. Then she shakes her feathers into place and gazes up at the empty sky where the bomber had been. And I feel it then, the tug. How did Auden's poem go, after those lines?

The clouds rift suddenly – look there

I look. There it is. I feel it. The insistent pull to the heart that the hawk brings, that very old longing of mine to possess the hawk's eye. To live the safe and solitary life; to look down on the world from a height and keep it there. To be the watcher; invulnerable, detached, complete. My eyes fill with water. *Here I am*, I think. *And I do not think I am safe.*

My father had grown up in that war. For the first four years of his life he and his family had lived under the bombers streaming over in stacked formations, cut with searchlights at night or in scrawls of ragged contrails that glowed in the upper air by day. What must it have been like to see those tiny crosses passing overhead? You know that some are trying to kill you. Others defend you. Knowing which was which must have had, in the language of the time, great danger valency. Your life was caught up in these small and migrant machines. Like all your friends you make Airfix models, spend your pocket money on *Aeroplane Spotter*. You memorise the position of engines, learn the lineaments of tail position, shape, engine note, fuselage. And so plane-spotting became Dad's childhood obsession. Numbering, identifying, classifying, recording, learning the details with a fierce child's need to know and command. When he was older he cycled to distant airfields with a bottle of Tizer, a Box Brownie camera, a notebook and pencil. Farnborough, Northolt, Blackbushe. Hours of waiting at the perimeter fence, a small boy looking through the wire.

I must have inherited being a watcher from Dad, I thought idly. Perhaps it was inevitable that with Dad's propensity to stare up at the slightest engine note, raise a pair of binoculars to distant contrails, my tiny self would emulate him, learn that looking at flying things was the way to see the world. Only for me, it wasn't aeroplanes. It was birds.

Now I've come to realise that we were watching the same things: or at least, things that history conspired to make the same. Since the dawn of military aviation, birds of prey had been thought of as warplanes made flesh: beings of aerodynamic, predatory perfection. Hawks fly and hunt and kill: aircraft do the same. These similarities were seized upon by military propagandists, for they made air warfare, like hawks, part of the natural order of things. Falconry's medieval glamour played its part, too, and soon hawks and aeroplanes were deeply entangled in visions of war and national defence. There's an extraordinary example of this in Powell and Pressburger's 1944 film *A Canterbury Tale*. In the opening scenes a party of Chaucerian pilgrims crosses the downs on the way to Canterbury. A knight unhoods a falcon and casts it into the air. The camera lingers on its flickering wings – a quick cut – and the falcon's silhouette becomes a diving Spitfire. We see the knight's face again. It is the same face, but now it wears the helmet of a modern soldier as it watches the Spitfire above. The sequence is powered by the myth of an essential Britishness unchanged through the ages, and it shows how powerfully hawks could marry romantic medievalism with the hard-edged technology of modern war.

Sitting there in the grass, listening to distant engines under a misty October sky, I thought of my father standing on the bombsite in my dream. He had stood and waited, as a boy. Had been patient and the planes had come. And I remembered, then, a story he'd told us one Saturday morning over breakfast. It was a good story. In a small way, it made my dad a hero. I felt a flood of gratitude. There'd been weeks of panic, of not knowing what to say in my father's memorial address, and now I knew this story would be at the heart of it. 'Thank you, Dad,' I breathed.

In White's little grey notebook with the snake on its cover there are nightmares of aeroplanes too. They loom 'silver-gold through the blue haze' towards him; he dives underwater, looks for cellars to hide in, but they can always find him, always know where he is. They drop high explosives and poison gas, step-dive down to render him dead. They were the dream-terrors of a boy who grew up at the mercy of violent authority: his father, his schoolmasters, the prefects, and now the dictators dragging the world to war. In *England Have My Bones* White explained that he had learned to fly because he was scared of aeroplanes.

Perhaps his fear was not only of falling; perhaps his lessons were an attempt to conquer his fear of persecution by assuming for his own the airman's eye. And just as he'd fought with his fear of the aeroplane, so he had tussled with Gos. For Gos was the dark and immoral child of ancient German forests. He was a murderer. He had all the glamour of the dictator. His laws were those of Hitler and Mussolini; he was the violence and irrationality of fascism made flesh. 'He was a Hittite,' White wrote later; 'a worshipper of Moloch. He immolated victims, sacked cities, put virgins and children to the sword.' I began to see, now, how you could read *The Goshawk* with a different eye: as something like a war. Siegfried Sassoon had seen it, recognised the battle that raged in its pages. When it was published White sent him a copy but he confessed that he could not read it. He had started to, but flunked it. 'I now flinch from anything frightful,' he explained, 'and what I read was agonising.'

White's politics were deeply unfortunate. He loathed capitalism, and while he'd flirted with Communism at Stowe, loving its revolutionary fervour, he began to fear it, for if the revolution came, it would take away his individuality and he was sure that was all he had. Now he wondered if he might be a fascist. He was not sure. He hated nationalism, but certainly did not believe people were equal. He did not like Hitler. But he did not like the British government either. He had a child's vision of apocalyptic redemption: he believed that war, when it came, would bring waste and murder and the ruin of civilisation, but that war would be worthwhile if we could emerge from the ruins with wisdom.

One had to choose one's side. Democracy against fascism. The rational against the irrational. Blood or peace. People or rabbits. White chose to shoot rabbits, rather than people, and he chose to fight the war in person with a hawk. Through Gos, he battled the dictator in himself. And for him the hawk was a salutary thing, for he believed that war came from society's repression of innate human urges. Because the hawk could not dissemble he was a 'tonic for the less forthright savagery of the human heart'.

And so the war was fought, here, in a kitchen and a barn, a garden and a wood. To and fro across the disputed territory the battle onward raged. When White understood that he was the dictator he tasted defeat, engineered the hawk's loss and pushed it away. Then came a new stage in the war: his retreat to forest bunkers. From these miniature shelters, he hoped to bring down the hawks of the air that flew like the aeroplanes in his dreams.

Years before, back in those happy times of safety in St Leonards, his greatest thrill had been when his grandparents took him to Hastings Caves and the guide led them underground into the curious halls of smuggler-carved sandstone. 'At a particular point in the journey under the earth,' he wrote, 'as we children and the nannies and the ordinary holiday trippers stood mute in the silent, sound-absorbing sand, the guide used to put out his candle – and there we were in the utter darkness as well.' He treasured that memory. For a boy who always felt imperilled, that pitch-black cave was a refuge, and he returned to it in his imagination again and again. He dreamed of tunnels and caves as sanctuaries. He called his cottage in the woods his badger's sett. In *Gone to Ground* he made an underground bunker save a field of hunting folk from the end of the world; and in *The Queen of Air and Darkness*, the second book of *The Once and Future King*, he wrote of Merlyn's imprisonment for centuries in the cave beneath the hill. The imprisonment is in Malory, but Merlyn's foreknowledge of his fate is not. 'It will be charming to have a rest for a few hundred years,' he announces to the astounded king.

A return to the womb would be one way of seeing this obsession with dark and private spaces. But White saw them not as the womb of the mother he despised, but as refuges under the ground; they were safe because they were hidden from the persecutor's hunting eyes.

He has made himself a grave. It is a skeletal coracle of slim ash poles covered with a wet blanket sprouting with mustard and grass. He'd scattered the seeds on the wool and waited for them to grow. This morning he toiled like a tortoise with the shell on his forehead and shoulders, took it out to the wood, arranged the blanket over it and lay on the ground inside. He has no tobacco. He cannot smoke. He can barely move. He has been here for hours, shivering with cold, lying in wait for hawks that would not come. It is a vigil, an ordeal, just as those long nights with the hawk. Another thunderstorm crosses the Ridings. The sky is rusty water and the trees have blurred to ink. Fat raindrops hammer on the blanket and soak through his steaming clothes; there is wet wool and sweat and the electric scent of the storm carried in with the rising wind. He is closer to them now, those long dead men who understood him. He lies in a grave like them. He holds his breath as poachers walk past, men who know the forest in all its perfect parts, men who have the instinctive ability to read the landscape. They do not see him. He has become invisible. It is something like a miracle. The suffering of his body is as naught to the joy of being free from the pain of being seen.

21

Fear

It was always there, kneeling by Mabel on her prey, that the thoughts came, when I wondered how I could be doing this, how I could be hunting at all. I hate killing things. I'm loath to tread on spiders and get laughed at for rescuing flies. But now I understood for the first time what bloodthirstiness was all about. It was only when I was aligned with the hawk's eye that it made sense, but then it made more sense than anything else in the world. When I saw birds fly overhead I'd turn my head and follow them with a kind of longing.

Hunting with the hawk took me to the very edge of being a human. Then it took me past that place to somewhere I wasn't human at all. The hawk in flight, me running after her, the land and the air a pattern of deep and curving detail, sufficient to block out anything like the past or the future, so that the only thing that mattered were the next thirty seconds. I felt the curt lift of autumn breeze over the hill's round brow, and the need to tack left, to fall over the leeward slope to where the rabbits were. I crept and walked and ran. I crouched. I looked. I saw more than I'd ever seen. The world gathered about me. It made absolute sense. But the only things I knew were hawkish things, and the lines that drew me across the landscape were the lines that drew the hawk: hunger, desire, fascination, the need to find and fly and kill.

Yet every time the hawk caught an animal, it pulled me back from being an animal into being a human again. That was the great puzzle, and it was played out again and again. How hearts do stop. A rabbit prostrate in a pile of leaves, clutched in eight gripping talons, the hawk mantling her wings over it, tail spread, eyes burning, nape-feathers raised in a tense and feral crouch. And then I'd reach down and put my hand on the bunched muscles of the rabbit, and with the heel of one hand at the back of its head where the fur was soft and tawny, I'd pull once, twice, hard on its back legs with the other, breaking its neck. A fit of kicking, and the eyes filming over. I had to check the rabbit was dead by very gently touching its eye. Everything stopping. Stopping. Stopping. I had to do this. If I didn't kill the rabbit, the hawk would sit on top of it and start eating; and at some point in the eating the rabbit would die. That is how goshawks kill. The borders between life and death are somewhere in the taking of their meal. I couldn't let that suffering happen. Hunting makes you animal, but the death of an animal makes you human. Kneeling next to the hawk and her prey, I felt a responsibility so huge that it battered inside my own chest, ballooning out into a space the size of a cathedral.

For years I'd explained that I'd rather eat hawk-caught food than things that have had a blind and crowded life in a barn or battery cage. One minute the rabbit is there, twitching its nose in a field that smells of nettles and grassy roots, then it is running, and then it is caught, and then it is dead. I'd told people that there are no injuries in hawking: either things are caught or they escape, and I'd told them, too, that nothing is wasted: everything the hawk catches is eaten by the hawk or me. If you choose to eat meat, I'd said, this is the best way I know to get it.

But these arguments seemed petty now, and pointless. They had nothing to do with what it was like. To be there, with a hawk and a caught rabbit that twitched and kicked and died. And the world biting into me. The serious, every-thing puzzle that was death and going away. 'But how could you?' people asked. Someone said it was a way of destroying the world a piece at a time after my father's death. 'Were the rabbits you?' another asked. No. 'Were you killing yourself?' No. 'Were you sorry?' Yes. But the regret wasn't that I had killed an animal. It was regret *for* the animal. I felt sorry for it. Not because I felt I was better than the animal. It wasn't a patronising sorrow. It was the sorrow of all deaths. I was happy for Mabel's success and I mourned the individual rab-bit. Kneeling by its corpse I'd feel a sharp awareness of my edges. The rain prickling on my collar. A pain in one knee. The scratches on my legs and arms from pushing myself through a hedge that had not hurt until now. And a sharp, wordless comprehension of my own mortality. *Yes, I will die.*

I learned that momentary shouldering of responsibility that allowed me to reach down and administer the *coup de grâce* to a rabbit held tight in Mabel's feet. A part of me had to click into place and there was another part of me I had to put far away. There's no better phrase than the old one to describe it: *You have to harden your heart.* I learned that hardening the heart was not the same as not caring. The rab-bit was always important. Its life was never taken lightly. I was accountable for these deaths. For the first time in my life I wasn't a watcher any more. I was being accountable to myself, to the world and all the things in it. But only when I killed. The days were very dark.

They darkened further. Driving back to the house one after-noon I passed a huddle of walkers staring at a rabbit crouched in the grassy verge on the other side of the road. They were upset. Their shoulders were hunched in concern. I pulled in a little further up the road and waited. I did not want to talk to them, but their concern pulled at me. They knew the rabbit was sick and wanted to do something, but no one knew what that could be, and no one was brave enough to get near it. For minutes on end they stared at it, unable to intervene, unwilling to leave. Then they walked on. When they were gone I got out of the car and went up to the little lump of fur. It was a small rabbit. Its muscles were wasted, its head covered in tumours, its eyes swollen and blistered. It was matted with mud. It could not see. 'Oh rabbit,' I said. 'I'm so sorry.' Leaning down I hardened my heart and put it out of its misery.

The rabbit had myxomatosis. It arrived in Britain in 1952 and in two years the virus – originally from South America, but already introduced by humans to Australia and Europe – killed ninety-five per cent of the British rabbit population. Tens of millions of rain-soaked corpses littered the roads and fields, and their disappearance had huge effects on the countryside: rabbit-grazed grasslands grew thick with scrub and predator populations crashed. Rabbits have recovered since, though never to the numbers that we once thought normal. And while the virus is less virulent now, outbreaks still occur.

That small rabbit sat huddled in my mind. It would not go away. It felt like a revenant, something pulled from the past, from back when I was small and the countryside was in crisis. It wasn't just the rabbits dying. Hawk populations were in freefall from agricultural pesticides. Skeletal elm trees were chopped down and burned. The otters were gone, rivers were poisoned, there were guillemots drowning in oiled seas. Everything was sick. And we'd be next. I knew it. All of us. I knew that one morning there'd be a siren, then a double flash of light on the horizon and I'd look up and see a distant mushroom cloud, and then, on the wind, the fallout would come. Invisible dust. And then everything would be dead. Or we'd go back to the Stone Age, and live in rags huddled around ruins and smoking fires. But even that slim dream of survival was dashed. 'Are we going to build a nuclear fallout shelter under the garden?' I asked my parents one afternoon after school. They looked at each other. Maybe they didn't understand, I thought, so I went on. 'In the leaflet it says we should build a shelter under the stairs and there's not very much room under ours for you and me and James.' There was a long pause, then they gently told me that our house was very close to several very important military targets. 'There's no point in worrying,' they said. 'There'll be no fallout. If there's a war, we won't even know about it. We'll be instantly vaporised.' This, needless to say, did not help at all. I scratched my name on bits of slate and buried them as deep as I could in the garden, under the earth. Maybe they'd survive the apocalypse.

The archaeology of grief is not ordered. It is more like earth under a spade, turning up things you had forgotten. Surprising things come to light: not simply memories, but states of mind, emotions, older ways of seeing the world. The rabbit was a ghost from the apocalypse of my childhood, and later that week another appeared. This one was not a rabbit, but a book. I had pulled it from my friend's shelves: a new edition of J. A. Baker's *The Peregrine*, the story of a man obsessively watching wintering wild peregrines in the Essex countryside of the late 1960s. I'd not read it for years. I remembered it as a poetic celebration of nature. But as I started reading it I found it was not like that at all. *This, I thought with a chill, comes from the same place as that rabbit.* I saw in it the writer's awful desire for death and annihilation, a desire disguised as an elegy for birds that flew through poisonous skies, falcons as searing-bright and pewter-flashed as reflected sun, already things of memory before they were ever gone.

I was frightened of Baker and what he meant. I was not as frightened of White. Despite his disaster with Gos, despite his desire for cruelties and his dreadful politics, White fought hard against death. He loved the small things of the world, and knowing war was coming, he lived in hope of miracles. In Baker's book I saw no hope at all. For him the world was dying, and his hawks were icons of extinction: ours, theirs and his own. There was no struggle in him. He shared the falcons' fate; had no choice but to follow them. He was lured towards them just as the gulls and plovers in his book rose helplessly towards the peregrine's killing strike, just as the compass-beaks of all the small birds hiding in hedges pointed in fear towards the magnet that was the falcon in the air. There were no place names, no people in his book. They'd fallen away. I understood this better now, for I knew the pull of the hawk, and I knew how the world could disappear in the light it cast. But his hawks were made of death. Troubled, I hoped my hawk was life. I hoped it very much.

I'd never believed in Baker's falcons, because I'd met real ones before I'd ever read his book: cheerful, friendly falconer's birds that preened on suburban lawns. But most of my bird-loving friends read Baker's book before they ever saw a live one, and now they can't see real peregrines without them conjuring distance, extinction and death. Wild things are made from human histories. When I was a child I hated what White had thought of his goshawk. But Gos's hawkish ghost moved behind the patterned, living feathers of my own. And there were still darker ghosts behind him.

A few years ago I visited a friend who was at that time the president of the British Falconers' Club. We chatted over tea and biscuits. We talked about the history of falconry for a while, and the history of the Club, and then he said, 'Come and look at this.' And he pulled open a cupboard, and there, right at the back, half-obscured by the usual household bits and bobs, I saw it.

'*Oh God*,' I said. 'Gordon, is that it?'

He looked at me and nodded. 'I hate it,' he said. 'I can't bear to have it in the house.'

I crouched down and pulled it out. It was a bronze falcon standing on a vertical plinth, heavy, stylised, and slightly worn around its wings.

'Shit, Gordon. This freaks me out,' I said.

'Me too,' he replied.

The statuette was very valuable, and very beautifully made, but it was a thing that both of us wished had never been made at all.

In 1937 Gilbert Blaine and Jack Mavrogordato were invited to the International Hunting Exhibition in Germany. They travelled to Berlin with a display of British falconry: stuffed falcons on perches, falconry equipment, photographs, books and paintings. I suspect their last-minute attendance was partly diplomatic cover: travelling with them was Britain's pro-appeasement Foreign Secretary, Lord Halifax, who'd been invited to the event for secret talks with Hitler.

There were no more than fifty falconers in the whole of Germany, but the symbolism of falconry was flourishing in the Reich. On the cover of the exhibition catalogue a stylised, naked Übermensch held a golden hawk upon his fist. The national falconer's association, the *Deutscher Falkenorden*, had been given state patronage, and a vast half-timbered State Falconry Centre, the *Reichsfalkenhof*, had recently been built in the forest at Riddagshausen. In Berlin Blaine and Mavrogordato walked through halls whose walls were hung thickly with thousands of antlers and draped in red banners sewn with swastikas. They admired the German hawks, falcons and eagles sitting on perches in the halls, but they were less impressed by the open-air falconry demonstrations. They watched a saker falcon catch a tethered pigeon, and an eagle thrown at a rabbit so tame it sat nibbling grass until the eagle landed.

Only two countries had falconry exhibits in the Berlin exhibition. Germany won first prize for theirs, and the British

Falconers' Club came second. That bronze falcon I'd pulled from Gordon's cupboard was their award. It had been sent to the club after the exhibition by Hermann Göring. Göring: Hitler's right-hand man, commander-in chief of the *Luftwaffe*, the Jägermeister of the Reich, the man who'd set the Reichstag on fire. Falconry delighted him. It wasn't only that he considered it the Romantic sport of ancient Teutonic kings. Hawks themselves were a natural elite, the perfect naturalisation of Nazi ideology: living paragons of power and blood and violence that preyed guiltlessly on things weaker than themselves. Göring's portrait of his favourite hawk, a white gyrfalcon standing on a cliff, is utterly true to the conventions of Nazi portraiture: bathed in morning sunlight, its wings half open, the falcon stares coldly into the distance. And Göring had a trained goshawk, too: I had seen it stuffed and mounted on a branch in an American archive years before. It was a big goshawk in adult plumage, still wearing jesses and bells, its dry toes locked around a dusty branch. It was beautifully mounted. Someone had taken very good care to make it look alive. I stared into its glass eyes, chilled to the bone, and wondered if it was related to Gos. There was every chance that it was a cousin of White's hawk, for the man who'd painted Göring's gyrfalcon, the man who headed the *Deutscher Falkenorden*, who had arranged falconry's state patronage and designed the *Reichsfalkenhof*, was Renz Waller. And he was the man who'd sent White Gos; the man to whom White had written pleading for another hawk. And who wrote back to him a few weeks later saying he would certainly try to 'get for you a other passager Gos'.

A new hawk! Full of excitement, White uncapped his pen and wrote *Plan for a Passage Gos* on the inside cover of his new copy of Bert's *Treatise*. He mapped out detailed training plans, and they rang with new authority. 'Watch her that night, keeping her constantly in motion,' he wrote. 'Have an assistant to take turns at this.' But the new hawk was not to be. The day before it was due to arrive White was rushed to hospital with appendicitis – as if his body was rebelling against the prospect of another weary battle. The thought of the surgeon's knife was a terror to him. 'It made me feel cleaner in some obscure way,' he wrote to John Moore after the operation. 'I think I am brave and master of my soul after all.' He had survived the crisis, and returned to his cottage. For a while he courted the night nurse, Stella, who had tended him at the hospital – but he thought her a wholly alien creature, and when he saw she might truly want him, he spurned her cruelly.

The winter was long and dark. There was something mythical about its slow progression from snow to thaw, to snow again, to mud and misery and sickness, as if in living through it, he was passing through many ages. Hope returned with spring. He filled the house with orphans: squab pigeons and doves, a tawny owl called Archimedes and a pair of baby badgers. Then in April White drove to Croydon to pick up a new hawk. He called her Cully. She was in a dreadful state. On being trapped half her tail feathers had broken off, along with most of the primaries on her left wing. White frowned over diagrams in falconry books, cut buzzard feathers to size, and glued and sewed these replacements into the trimmed quills of her wings and tail. *Imping*, they called it: he knew it was one of the falconers' Great Arts. But it was a bad job, the fixing, and all the bating in her eight weeks of training left her tail-less, part-winged, barely able to fly.

But fly she did. The hawk flew free. Heart in mouth, he flew her free. Finally he would hunt with a hawk he had trained himself. His dazzling dreams of self-sufficiency, his dreams of innocent cruelty: both were within his reach. But it was getting late in the season, and he knew that Cully should be put down to moult. Hawks shed and replace all their feathers once every year, and during this time they are not flown, but loosed in a spacious enclosure and fed *ad libitum*. But he needed this one success. And one evening out on the Ridings, after days of fruitless stalking, he loosed his tattered hawk at a rabbit on Tofield's Riding and after a hapless, ragged flight – at one point running after the rabbit, rather than flying – Cully grabbed it by the head. White rushed to the scene, took his hunting knife and pinned the rabbit's skull to the ground. Desires that had never flowered in his courting of the nurse were unleashed in a wave of darkness. 'Think of Lust,' he wrote, of killing the rabbit. 'Real blood-lust is like that.'

22

Apple Day

Oh God. What am I doing here? I'm sitting on a white plastic picnic chair under the shade of a marquee roof. Ten feet behind me Mabel resembles a shadow cast on water; her wings are crossed as tight as swords and her eyes bloom huge with horror. I know how she feels. *Too many people*, I think, fidgeting on my seat. *Too many people.*

'So, Helen,' Stuart had said. 'The landowner's asked us to bring some hawks along for Apple Day at the farm.'

'Apple Day?'

Stuart told me that it was a tiny country fair, a celebration of rural history, farming and local food. 'We're not flying, just weathering the hawks in a marquee so members of the public can see them. I'll take my tiercel. Greg's bringing his barbary. Alan's coming up with some eagles. Can you bring Mabel?'

'Yes, of course,' I said. 'No problem.' I could do this. I'd worked in a falconry centre, for God's sake. All I did for months was show people hawks. But as the day drew closer I started to fret. *How will Mabel cope?* Two months ago she was a bomb-proof, crowd-proof goshawk. But goshawks aren't like other hawks: they need constant carriage to stay tame. Now we're living in the empty suburbs we've not seen people for weeks. She's forgotten how not to be scared of people. *And so have I.* My teeth are clenched so tight in the face of the crowds I feel pain blossoming up my jaw.

After twenty minutes Mabel raises one foot. It looks ridiculous. She is not relaxed enough to fluff out her feathers; she still resembles a wet and particoloured seal. But she makes this small concession to calmness, and she stands there like a man driving with one hand resting on the gear-stick. She looks pathetically small next to the birds beside her. To her left is a golden eagle, a hulking great thing with chest-feathers like armoured scales and taloned feet the size of human hands. To her right is a male martial eagle, an antelope-killing black and white monster with piercing white eyes. It is enormous, bigger than most of the dogs walking past the mesh fence in front of the marquee, and it watches them them go by with its black chrysanthemum-petalled crest raised in idle speculation of murder.

Stuart has brought his tiercel peregrine. Greg has brought his barbary falcon, a tiny jewelled dusty-blue and copper falcon with thin golden toes. While it preens he sits cross-legged, chatting with members of the public, his red cashmere jumper holed wildly at the elbow. Alan the eagle-man is drinking tea from a plastic cup, resting an arm on the tall perch of a saker falcon, which looks up at him with a mild and playful eye.

I can't sit still. I go for a walk round the fair. It is not very big, but it is full of surprising things. Smoke from an oil-drum barbecue curling through drying chestnut leaves. Beneath the tree an ancient wooden cider press pouring apple juice into cups. The crushed apples fall into mounds of oxidising pulp beside it and the man working the mechanism is shouting something to the craggy plantsman on the next stand with stripling trees for sale. I find a cake stand, a face-painting stand, a stand of vivaria full of snakes, spiders and stick insects the size of your hand. A stall of orange pumpkins by an ice-cream van. A boy kneeling by a hutch staring at a rabbit under a paper sign that says MY NAME IS FLOPSEY. 'Hello, Flopsey,' he says, bringing his hand up to the wire. I walk into a white marquee, and inside, in dim green shade, find trestle-tables displaying hundreds of apple varieties. Some are the size of a hen's egg; some are giant, sprawling cookers you'd need two hands to hold. Each variety sits in a labelled wooden compartment. I walk slowly along the apples, glorying in their little differences. Soft orange, streaked with tiger-spots of pink. *Charles Ross. Berkshire pre 1890. Dual use.* A little one with bark-like blush markings over a pale green ground. *Coronation. Sussex 1902. Dessert.* Miniature green boulders, the side in shadow deep rose. *Chivers Delight. Cambridgeshire 1920. Dessert.* Huge apple, deep yellow with hyperspace-spotting of rich red. *Peasgood's Nonsuch. Lincolnshire 1853. Dual use.*

The apples cheer me. The stalls have too. I decide the fair is a wonderful thing. I wander back to my chair, and as Mabel relaxes, so do I. I wolf down a burger, gossip with my falconer friends. Stories are told, jokes are made, old grievances aired, the qualities and abilities and flights of various hawks discussed in minute detail. It strikes me suddenly how much British falconry has changed since the days of Blaine and White. Back then it was the secretive, aristocratic sport of officers and gentlemen. In Germany, falconry had fed into the terrible dreams of an invented Aryan past. Yet here we are now in all our variousness. A carpenter ex-biker, a zookeeper ex-soldier, two other zookeepers, an electrician and an erstwhile historian. Four men, two women, two eagles, three falcons and a goshawk. I swig from a bottle of cider and this company is suddenly all I'd ever wished for.

'Excuse me? Is that a goshawk?'

He's in his forties, with glasses. A thickset, cheerful man holding a wriggling toddler. 'Hang on, Tom,' he says. 'We're going to get an ice-cream. I just want to talk to this lady for a second.'

I grin. I know how it feels to hold onto a creature who wants to be somewhere else. And then my heart falters, just a little.

No father, no partner, no child, no job, no home.

Get over yourself, Helen, I hiss inwardly.

'It's yours?' he says. 'Wow.'

I tell him about the goshawk. He listens. Then his face turns serious and sad.

'You are so lucky,' he says. 'I've always wanted to do falconry. All my life. I've got books and everything. But I've never had the time.' There's a pause. 'Maybe one day.' He hugs Tom a little closer. 'Come on then, you,' he says, and they walk away to the ice-cream van.

White air and aching bones. Another migraine. I swallow a dose of codeine and paracetamol. My head still hurts. There's a brumous, pewter light outside, as if someone had stuck tracing paper against the glass. I go back to bed. *Must fly goshawk*, I think when I wake. *Must fly goshawk.* But I'm finding it so hard to move that secretly I'm hoping the hawk's weight is wrong, or the weather is. I have no excuse to stay in bed this time: both hawk and weather are fine.

We drive into a strange, windless, sunny afternoon that makes everything resemble hollow metal models painted with enamel. Clouds, swags of leaves, houses. All in the same plane, like a stage-set, and riveted together. The air smells of woodsmoke. I am inexpressibly tired. I park the car on the grassy verge near the field, change Mabel's jesses, unhood her, and she snaps into yarak in an instant. She knows where she is. And here we are. And there are the rabbits. She leaves the fist. As soon as she does the pain in my head recedes and my exhaustion fades. Her flight is getting much more stylish. I am still astonished by how fast she is. When I watch her scaly, foreshortened, hunched flight away from me towards a distant target, I swear that the world around her slows. She seems to be moving at precisely the right speed, and everything around her – rabbits running, leaves falling, a pigeon flying overhead, all these things slow down as if they're moving through liquid.

I am becoming fascinated by her quality of attention. I'm

starting to believe in what Barry Lopez has called 'the conversation of death', something he saw in the exchange of
glances between caribou and hunting wolves, a wordless
negotiation that ends up with them working out whether
they will become hunter and hunted, or passers-by. I am
wondering whether my goshawk does this. Mabel back on
the fist, I walk towards three rabbits. They are sitting on the
grass, right there, no more than ten yards away. Closer. Five
yards! Mabel is in raging yarak, but is ignoring them. She's
staring with interest at the other end of the field. Something
out there, a good six or seven seconds' flight away. 'Mabel!'
I murmur. 'Look!' And I try to angle my hand so her head
turns towards the rabbits underneath her nose. One of them
hops about. *It is just there.* She still ignores it. I don't understand. She cranes her neck to the other end of the field, again.
And then my fist is empty. She's gone, flying to the far side of
the field, very low, very fast, dancing about the tops of the
short nettles, missing one rabbit, making split-second calculations and attention-switches, then crashing down on
another. These are the rabbits she has been conversing with.

I run towards the spot. I can't see her anywhere. *Where is
she?* There are nettles everywhere, but it's only regrowth, a
mere three inches high. *Where is my hawk?* I hold my breath.
Silence. And then I hear muffled, muffled bells. And finally I
spot her head, snaking up out of the nettles. *What the–* She
looks like she's broken, crushed, as if gravity had suddenly
increased tenfold; her wings fanned, feathers bent upwards
along their vanes from the pressure. Ah: I see now. Her wings
are spread to brace herself against the ground, because she
has hold of the rabbit, and the rabbit is down the hole, and
she's holding on and bracing with all her might to stop herself being pulled underground. Her beak is open with the
effort. I reach down the hole, feel my way along her impossibly long shins and encounter a rabbit foot. She has it,
but only just. I grab the leg, and try to work out how to

extract the rabbit from the hole. I pull a little, and the rabbit kicks. Goshawk squeaks. I change the angle, and slowly, like an evil, rural conjuror, pull the rabbit out of the hole, and toss it onto the grass. Mabel stamps and dances, changes her hold from hind leg to head, and the rabbit is still. She is in such a rage that she stamps up and down on the rabbit for ages, once it's dead, and then starts plucking it. She plucks for minutes and soon we are surrounded by a deep circle of soft grey fur.

The conversation of death. The sentence kept coming to mind. I'd think of it at odd moments – while taking a bath, scratching my nose, leaning to grab a mug of hot tea. My subconscious was trying to tell me something and though it was shouting very loudly indeed, I didn't hear what it was saying. Things were going wrong. Very wrong. One afternoon Mabel leapt up from her perch to my fist, lashed out with one foot and buried four talons in my bare right arm. I froze. Blood was dripping on the kitchen floor. I could do nothing. Her grip was too powerful. I had to wait until she decided to let go. The pressure was immense, but the pain, though agonising, was happening to someone else. *Why has she footed me?* I thought wildly, after she released her grip and continued as if nothing had happened at all. *She has never been aggressive before.* I was sure I'd done nothing to provoke her. Is she overkeen? Is the weighing machine broken? I spent a good quarter of an hour fussing about with piles of tuppences, trying to calibrate it. There was nothing wrong with it at all. But something was wrong with me. It wasn't just a hawk-inflicted injury. I was becoming vastly anxious. I jumped in panic when the postman knocked on the door; recoiled from the ringing phone. I stopped seeing people. Cancelled my gallery talk. Deadlocked the front door. Out on the hill I fled from walkers, dodged behind hedges when farm vehicles drove up the track. Some days I lay in bed in so much mysterious pain I began to believe the only explanation was a terminal disease.

You could explain what it was like by running to books and papers. You could read Freud, you could read Klein. You could read any number of theories about attachment and loss and grief. But those kinds of explanations come from a world the hawk wasn't in. They aren't any help. They are like explaining how it feels to be in love by waving an MRI scan of a lovestruck brain. You have to look in different places.

The anthropologist Rane Willerslev once lived for a year in a Yukaghir community in north-eastern Siberia and became fascinated by how their hunters saw the relationship between humans and animals. The hunters, he wrote, think 'humans and animals can turn into each other by temporarily taking on one another's bodies'. If you want to hunt elk, you dress in elkskins, walk like an elk, take on an elk's alien consciousness. If you do this, elk will recognise you as one of their own and walk towards you. But, Willerslev explained, Yukaghir hunters consider these transformations very dangerous, because they can make you lose sight of your 'original species identity and undergo an invisible metamorphosis'. Turning into an animal can imperil the human soul. Willerslev included the story of a hunter who'd been tracking reindeer for many hours and ended up in an unfamiliar camp, where women he did not know gave him lichen to eat and he started forgetting things. He remembered his wife but could not remember her name. Confused, he fell asleep, and it was only when he dreamed he was surrounded by reindeer urging him to leave that he saw what he had done.

That story made me shiver when I read it, because that was what it was like. I'd turned myself into a hawk – taken all the traits of goshawks in the books and made them my own. I was nervous, highly strung, paranoid, prone to fits of terror and rage; I ate greedily or didn't eat at all; I fled from society, hid from everything; found myself drifting into strange states where I wasn't certain who or what I was. In hunting with Mabel, day after day, I had assumed – in my imagination, of course, but that was all it could ever be – her alien perspective, her inhuman understanding of the world. It brought something akin to madness, and I did not understand what I had done. When I was small I'd thought turning into a hawk would be a magical thing. What I'd read in *The Sword in the Stone* encouraged me to think it, too, as a good and instructive thing; a lesson in life for the child who would be king. But now the lesson was killing me. It was not at all the same.

Two days before the service something very strange happened on the hill. We'd been walking up a hedgerow running down the edge of a field of undersown stubble. There was a pheasant in the hedge; I'd heard it cluck and run, rat-wise, along the damp and nettly ditch, and Mabel had heard it too. She'd crashed over the hedge and perched out of sight at the top, facing away from me. Her blood was up and mine too. I shouldered my way into the hedge, knowing that any second now the pheasant would rocket out in front of me in a burnished clatter of feathers. I pushed my head through the hedge. Heard a whoosh of air and felt a staggering blow. I reeled. Coshed by a goshawk! First only blackness, then a field of stars. Then a weird proprioceptive sense that I was wearing a crown of thorns; a complicated halo of pain around my head. She'd bounced off me, left eight talon incisions behind, and was back at the top of the tree, craning to see the pheasant, which had done what all pheasants do best: escape. I shook my head dully. *She thought I was the pheasant. She didn't know it was me.* A strange buzzing in my ears, and then a muffled calm as the endorphins kicked in. I held my hand out and whistled her down to my fist, then mechanically started working the rest of the hedge-line. We were walking into the sun at this point, and I started taking a warm, distinct pleasure in the fuzzy gold aura that bathed us. Light-headed, slightly unsure of my footing, I finally wondered, *Why is my vision strange, and why do my eyes sting?* Then, *Why is the goshawk bating at my face?*

It took me a while to work out why both. I rubbed my eyes and my hand came away soaked, dramatically and Shakespearianly, in blood. I pulled off my glasses. They were covered in it. Blood was running in streams down my forehead, into my left eye, and was now attracting the attention of a hungry goshawk.

Christ, I thought, *this is a bit Edgar Allan Poe.*

I used my sleeve and some wet grass to get the worst off. Luckily this was sufficient to make the goshawk uninterested in eating me. I felt for the talon incision: a half-inch long, deep slash right between my eyes. Ah, yes, the sixth chakra, the seat of concealed wisdom, now rouged with an austringer's bindi. I pressed the place hard with my fingers until it stopped bleeding.

And then I kept on hawking, stumbling across the fields in a haze of pained euphoria. The sun had descended behind sheets of cinereal stratus to become a luminous disc glowing through talc-filled air, and it was exactly the same colour as Mabel's eye. I held her up, comparing sun with goshawk eye and marvelled at their correspondence. By the time we'd reached the top of the hill my legs rebelled. *Enough*, they said. *Enough walking. Sit down. Have a nap.*

So I sat in the stubble, woozily glorying at the beauty of it all. The mist rising in the hollows. Flocks of golden plover pouring over in sheaves. The way the bluish new rapeseed leaves contrasted with the vertical straw of the stubble at my feet. The glow of the lost sun beneath the ridge. Crickets beginning to sing. Rooks on their way to roost passing over us in moving constellations of small black stars. And perhaps that cosh to the head had knocked some human sense back into me, because when I got home I sat on the sofa and wrote my father's eulogy, straight out, in twenty minutes, with a small round plaster stuck on my injured forehead.

23

Memorial

I sat on the train clutching the folder with the speech inside, ankles burning from the heater on the floor. Outside, winter breathed in. Papery skies. Glittering trees. A wash of backlit fields that folded and shrank as the city grew. Then I was at the church, folder in hand, staring at hundreds of feet on the black and white floor, hundreds of shoulders and ties and points of collars, hems of skirts, clicks and echoes of tiny black heels. I worried I hadn't dressed smartly enough. I was wearing a black cotton dress from Debenhams. Maybe it was the wrong thing? Why hadn't I gone and bought a *proper* outfit? Something expensive, and smart, and sharp around the edges? It took a few seconds before it struck me that my panic might not be about clothes at all. I sat down in the stalls between my mother and my brother, took their hands, light-headed with love and sorrow. My aunt was here, my brother's partner and her parents too. We were a family. We were. I looked around for the other speakers: Ron Morgans and Alastair Campbell, who'd worked with Dad for years, and Jeremy Selwyn, another photographer, biting his lip and watching the crowds pour in.

I walked up to the lectern with the paper in my hand. I had given so many lectures, so many talks, that I'd thought this would be easy. But it was not. I was terrified. I grabbed the lectern's wooden edges to stop me from swaying. *How can I do this? Don't look at the audience,* said a voice inside me. *Pretend they're not there.*

And then another voice inside said: *Look at the audience.*

I looked. Hundreds of faces. Dad's colleagues, Dad's friends. The fear vanished in an instant. I couldn't be scared any more. And I started speaking. I told them about my father. I told them a little about his early life. I told them he had been a wonderful father. I reminded them, too, of his ridiculous inability to wear anything other than a suit – although he did make concessions on holiday, and occasionally removed his tie. I told them that on our trip to Cornwall to photograph the total eclipse we'd been standing on the beach before the skies darkened when a man who said he was the reincarnation of King Arthur, a man wearing a silver diadem and long white robes, came up to Dad, and said, bewildered, *Why are you wearing that suit?*

Well, said Dad. *You never know who you're going to meet.*

And then I told the story I hoped they would understand.

He's a boy, standing by a fence and staring up at the sky. He's at an aerodrome, Biggin Hill, spotting RAF planes. He is nine? Ten? He's been photographing each aircraft that takes off or lands with the Box Brownie camera that hangs on a string around his neck, and putting their numbers down in a spiral-bound notebook. It is getting late. He ought to leave. Then he hears a sound he cannot place, an unfamiliar engine note, and yes, *there*, this is it, this is the moment he has dreamed of. He stares into the sky. He sees the landing lights of . . . he doesn't know what it is. *He doesn't know what it is.* It is not in any of the books. He takes its picture. He copies its registration number onto the page. It is a visitation from the future: a new American Air Force plane. To the boy plane-spotter of the 1950s, it is like seeing the Holy Grail.

* * *

When I was writing the speech, still a little concussed, I reached for the phone to call my father and ask what type of plane it was, and for a moment the world went very black.

A hand fell on his shoulder, and a voice said, 'Come with me, laddie.' They frogmarched him to the guardhouse, pushed him through the door, and there, behind a desk, a sergeant-major type with a moustache and a frown stood up, barked at him, ripped the page out of his notebook, screwed it into a ball and threw it in the bin, shouted some more, took the back off the camera, exposed the roll of film, pulled it out in loops of falling acetate and dumped that in the bin too. *I was crying my eyes out*, Dad said. *They said, 'Go home. You didn't see anything. Forget you were here.' And they dumped me back at the perimeter and I stood there with my notebook and the Brownie, sobbing away. But then I stopped crying, because I'd thought of something. Something out of* Dick Barton *or the* Eagle. *Maybe I'd written hard enough.* Using his pencil, he shaded the page of his notebook with graphite, and there, white on grey, impressed on the paper from the missing page above, was the registration number of the secret plane. He stopped crying, he said, and cycled home in triumph.

I sat down, dazed. Sun through windows. Things, one after another. The achingly beautiful singing of the choir. The canon's prayers. Eulogies praising my father's photographic skills. When Alastair Campbell walked to the lectern he read Wordsworth's 'Composed upon Westminster Bridge' and prefaced it with a short speech in which he said, with decided emphasis, that my father was a Good Man. This broke me. I hadn't expected this. Or not *this* much this. Everyone sang 'Jerusalem' and I forced my mouth to move, but nothing came out but whispered fragments. And after-wards, out in the shaded churchyard under the trees, a young guy with misted glasses and a purple knitted cardigan walked up, shying nervously, and said, 'You don't know me. I don't know anyone in there. They're all the big guns. But I wanted to say that . . . well. I'm a photographer now. I'm making a living out of it. I moved to London to try and make it, and I didn't know what I was doing. And I met your dad out on a job once and he talked to me. He gave me lots of advice. He helped me. He didn't have to, but he did. He saved my life. He was amazing . . .' And he tailed off, and looked embarrassed, and I stepped forward and gave him a hug, because I didn't know what to say. And more and more people came up and talked about Dad; and all the old guard were there, snappers from back in the 1960s, and I finally got to put names to the bylines I'd seen so many times. They told me they liked the story. They said it was nice to know that my father was a born journalist. That the boy in short trousers was already the man they'd known, the man who had always got the picture, had always pulled the story from the jaws of defeat.

Down in the Press Club after the service the drinks were poured. And poured. And poured some more. Everyone became increasingly expansive, rushed up to tell me stories about my father. The stories got more slurred as the drinking went on, and the hugs and cheek-kisses increasingly off-target. 'Another drink?' said one pressman. 'Just a soft drink,' I said, and back he came with a vast glass of wine. 'Um, is there any soft drink?' I said, embarrassed. He frowned. 'That's what I brought you. This is a soft drink.'

I left with a song in my heart. I felt my family had expanded by about two hundred people, and everything was going to be fine. *Bless you, Dad*, I thought. *I always thought you were a legend, and it turns out you really, really were.*

All the way home on the train I thought of Dad and the terrible mistake I had made. I'd thought that to heal my great hurt, I should flee to the wild. It was what people did. The nature books I'd read told me so. So many of them had been quests inspired by grief or sadness. Some had fixed themselves to the stars of elusive animals. Some sought snow geese. Others snow leopards. Others cleaved to the earth, walked trails, mountains, coasts and glens. Some sought wildness at a distance, others closer to home. 'Nature in her green, tranquil woods heals and soothes all afflictions,' wrote John Muir. 'Earth hath no sorrows that earth cannot heal.'

Now I knew this for what it was: a beguiling but dangerous lie. I was furious with myself and my own unconscious certainty that this was the cure I needed. Hands are for other human hands to hold. They should not be reserved exclusively as perches for hawks. And the wild is not a panacea for the human soul; too much in the air can corrode it to nothing.

And by the time I got home I'd worked out, too, why Mabel had been behaving so strangely. She'd grown heavy with muscle over our weeks on the hill, and though she was flying at a higher weight than before, over this last week she'd got too low. She was *hungry*. Hunger had made her aggressive.

I was furious with myself when I realised that first great error on the train. But this second realisation brought self-hatred. I'd been so blind, so miserable, I'd not seen my hawk was miserable too. I'd not seen her at all. I remembered the man I'd fallen for after my father died. I'd hardly known him, but it didn't matter. I'd recruited him to serve my loss, made him everything I needed. No wonder he had run away. And now I'd made the same mistake again. I'd fled to become a hawk, but in my misery all I had done was turn the hawk into a mirror of me.

The next evening, weak with relief and the sense that something huge, something tectonic, had shifted in my world, I gave Mabel a whole dead pigeon to eat in the grey, cool evening. We sat on a chair under the apple tree, listening to blackbirds chinking in the hedge. The house didn't seem unfriendly any more. The kitchen window threw a soft square of light into the garden. Huge frosty piles of pigeon feathers accumulated on the lawn. And then she ate. Every last scrap. When it was finished her crop was so full she could hardly stand.

With the plucking of the pigeon came more revelations, as if with its uncovering other things were uncovered. I thought of the dreams I'd had that spring of the hawk slipping away into air. I'd wanted to follow it, fly with it, and disappear. I had thought for a long while that I was the hawk – one of those sulky goshawks able to vanish into another world, sitting high in the winter trees. But I was not the hawk, no matter how much I pared myself away, no matter how many times I lost myself in blood and leaves and fields. I was the figure standing underneath the tree at nightfall, collar upturned against the damp, waiting patiently for the hawk to return.

Mabel was cutting through the crisp ribcage of the pigeon now. She was pulling at the thin intercostal membrane. *Snap*. I thought of my father shading a pencil over ghostly impressions on the page. *Snap*. I thought of White and the reasons why his book had haunted me all this time. *Snap*. Another breaking rib. It wasn't just that I saw in his book, reflected backwards and dimly, my own retreat into wildness. It was this: of all the books I read as a child, his was the only one I remembered where the animal didn't die.

Gos never died. He was only lost. For all White's certainty that his hawk was dead, there was always a chance, even to the very end of the book, even further, that the hawk might return. In the childish depths of my mind the hawk was out there, still in the wood, his yellow toes clutching rough bark and his pale eyes watching me from a dark tangle of branches somewhere in the multitudinous sea of a hundred thousand trees.

Melanie Klein wrote that children go through states of mind comparable to mourning, and that this early mourning is revived whenever grief is experienced in later life. She thought that adults try to manage newer losses the way they managed older ones. I thought of that drawing of a kestrel, its carefully worked jesses pencilled over and over again by my six-year-old hand with all its desperate insistence on the safety of knots and lines.

Gos was still out there in the forest, the dark forest to which all things lost must go. I'd wanted to slip across the borders of this world into that wood and bring back the hawk White lost. Some part of me that was very small and old had known this, some part of me that didn't work according to the everyday rules of the world but with the logic of myths and dreams. And that part of me had hoped, too, that somewhere in that other world was my father. His death had been so sudden. There had been no time to prepare for it, no sense in it happening at all. He could only be lost. He was out there, still, somewhere out there in that tangled wood with all the rest of the lost and dead. I know now what those dreams in spring had meant, the ones of a hawk slipping through a rent in the air into another world. I'd wanted to fly with the hawk to find my father; find him and bring him home.

24

Drugs

Sometimes when light dawns it simply illuminates how dismal circumstances have become. Every morning I wake at five and have thirty seconds' lead-time before despair crashes in. I don't dream of my father any more; I don't dream of people at all. I walk over winter sandflats, past storm-pools of fog-reflecting water packed with migrant birds stranded by the weather, unable to fly south for winter. Sometimes I dream I'm climbing trees that crack and fall, or sailing tiny boats that overturn in frozen seas. They are pathetic dreams. I don't need an analyst to explain them. I know now that I'm not trusting anyone or anything any more. And that it is hard to live for long periods without trusting anyone or anything. It's like living without sleep; eventually it will kill you.

I have spent my evenings playing with Mabel. I've made her toys out of paper and tissue and card. She turns her head upside down, puffs out her chin-feathers, squeaks, picks up the toys in her beak, drops them, and preens. When I throw her balls of scrunched-up paper she catches them in her beak and tosses them back to me with a flick of her head. Then she crouches, waiting for me to throw them to her again. It is as good as it gets. When I told Stuart I played catch with her for a while he didn't believe me. You don't play with goshawks. It's not what people do. But I have had to, to somehow leaven the chill. Because other people with goshawks have people too. For them their goshawks are their little splinter of wildness, their balance to domesticity; out in the woods with the hawk, other falconers get in touch with their solitudinous, bloody souls. But then they come home and have dinner, watch TV, play with their kids, sleep with their partner, wake, make tea, go to work. You need both sides, as they say.

I don't have both sides. I only have wildness. And I don't need wildness any more. I'm not stifled by domesticity. I have none. There is no need, right now, to feel close to a fetch of dark northern woods, a creature with baleful eyes and death in her foot. Human hands are for holding other hands. Human arms are for holding other humans close. They're not for breaking the necks of rabbits, pulling loops of viscera out onto leaf-litter while the hawk dips her head to drink blood from her quarry's chest cavity. I watch all these things going on and my heart is salt. Everything is stuck in an eternal present. The rabbit stops breathing; the hawk eats; leaves fall; clouds pass overhead. A car drives past the field, and there are people in it, held securely on their way somewhere, wrapped in life like a warm coat. Tyre sounds recede. A heron bows overhead. I watch the goshawk snip, tear and wrench flesh from the rabbit's foreleg. I feel sorry for the rabbit. Rabbit was born, grew up in the field, ate dandelions and grass, scratched his jaw with his feet, hopped about. Had baby rabbits of his own. Rabbit didn't know what lonely was; he lived in a warren. And rabbit is now just a carefully packed assemblage of different kinds of food for a hawk who spends her evenings watching television on the living-room floor. Everything is so damn mysterious. Another car passes. Faces turn to watch me crouched with rabbit and hawk. I feel like a tableau at a roadside shrine. But I'm not sure what the shrine is for. I'm a roadside phenomenon. I am death to community. I am missing the point.

There is a point? White said that training a hawk was

like psychoanalysis. He said that training a goshawk was like training a person that was not a human, but a hawk. Now I see that I am more of a rabbit than a hawk. Living with a goshawk is like worshipping an iceberg, or an expanse of sliprock chilled by a January wind. The slow spread of that splinter of ice in your eye. I love Mabel, but what passes between us is not human. There is a kind of coldness that allows interrogators to put cloth over the mouths of men and pour water into their lungs, and lets them believe this is not torture. What you do to your heart. You stand apart from yourself, as if your soul could be a migrant beast too, standing some way away from the horror, and looking fixedly at the sky. The goshawk catches a rabbit. I kill the rabbit. There is no lust for blood in my heart. I have no heart at all. I watch it all as if I was an executioner after a thousand deaths, as if all this was just the inescapable way of the world. *I don't think it is. I pray it isn't.*

I have scared myself. I go to the doctor. I drive to the surgery with no hope of rescue, but I can't think of anything else to do. The doctor is a man I have not seen before; small, dark-haired, with a neat beard, red braces and a crumpled cotton shirt. He sits behind a wooden desk. 'Hello,' he says. 'Take a seat.' I sit on a chair. I look at the desk. It is oak. I think of winter trees. 'What seems to be the trouble?' he asks. I say I think I might be depressed. That some things have happened over the last few months. My father died.

'I'm so sorry,' he says.

Then I tell him I have no job any more and no money coming in. And no house either. It doesn't sound convincing. So I tell him more. And more. Now it's hard to stop talking. But when I do, he says some words. I can't hear them clearly. I am watching his eyebrows. Sometimes they are frowning, sometimes very high. He hands me a multiple-choice questionnaire. This strikes me as grimly funny. I sit in front of it for a very long while, fiddling with the pen, worrying that

I'm not getting the answers right. When it is finished it is hard to give it back: I'm convinced I've done it wrong. I don't cry. I hand him the piece of paper and he takes it, turns it over and regards it for a while. He puts it down. He moves a pen from one side of the sheet to the other. He leans across the table. I see his face. I turn away. It is too unbearably kind. 'Helen, we can help you,' he says, in a low voice. 'We really can.' There's a kind of tingling astonishment when I hear his words. It's something like hope. I start to sob.

I sob right through twenty minutes of delicate discussion, and agree to try a course of antidepressants. He is a good doctor. He tells me all about SSRIs, talks me through their side-effects, their history, their mode of operation. He draws little diagrams of neurons, adds dots and wavy lines for serotonin molecules and the action of re-uptake inhibitors. I peer at the pictures, fascinated.

An hour later I'm walking down the street with a white paper bag in my hand. It weighs almost nothing. He says it will make things better. Which is ridiculous. How can this grey and mortified world be washed away by little dots and lines? Then I start to worry that the drugs will make me ill. Even more absurdly, I panic that they'll stop me thinking clearly. That they'll stop me flying Mabel. That whoever I'll become under their chemical influence will be so strange and alien she won't fly to me any more. The worries are a tedious avalanche but I put them to one side for long enough to swallow the drugs with water. There is an almost immediate effect: a tiredness so vast I can hardly walk, and my skull is empty, tight and painful. I don't sleep that night. I lie in bed. The next morning I drink coffee. I drink more coffee. I keep on flying the hawk.

Those books about people running to the wild to escape their grief and sorrow were part of a much older story, so old its shape is as unconscious and invisible as breathing.

When I was a student slogging through the first years of my degree, I read a long and beautiful thirteenth-century poem called *Sir Orfeo*. No one knows who wrote it, and I had forgotten it existed. But one morning while pulling a handful of chicks out of the freezer the poem came to mind, turned out of the ground in one of those strange excavations of the disordered mind.

Sir Orfeo is a retelling of the Greek myth of Orpheus and the underworld by way of traditional Celtic songs about the otherworld, the Land of Faery. In Celtic myth that otherworld is not deep underground; it is just one step aside from our own. Things can exist in both places at once – and things can be pulled from one to the other. In the poem, Heridice sleeps in an orchard under a grafted fruit tree – an *imptree* – and dreams that the next day she will be stolen away by the King of Faery. Terrified, she tells her husband the King. Orfeo surrounds her with armed knights, but they cannot protect her from this otherworldly threat: she slips through the air and vanishes.

Stricken with grief, Orfeo gives up his crown and runs to the forest. For ten years he lives a solitary, feral existence, digging for roots, eating leaves and berries, playing his harp to charm the beasts around him. His beard grows long and matted. He watches the grand hunting parties of the Faery King pass through the forest. He cannot follow them. But one day sixty ladies with falcons on their fists ride by, hunting for cormorants, mallards, herons. As he watches the falcons strike down their prey the world changes. He laughs with delight, remembering his love for the sport – '*Parfay!*' *quath he, 'ther is fair game*' – and he walks towards the women, and sees among them his wife. He has entered that otherworld, and now he can follow them back to the castle of the Faery King, a palace full of people that were thought to be dead but are not. And it is there he plays his harp to the King and persuades him to release his wife. But it was the hawks' flight and the deaths they brought that ushered him into that other world, let him find his wife that was lost. And this ability of hawks to cross borders that humans cannot is a thing far older than Celtic myth, older than Orpheus – for in ancient shamanic traditions right across Eurasia, hawks and falcons were seen as messengers between this world and the next.

There's another poem in Latin about a grief-stricken flight to the forest. It was written by Geoffrey of Monmouth, a twelfth-century cleric best known for his *Historia Regum Britanniae*, The History of the Kings of Britain. The *Historia* was a hugely influential chronicle, but the other poem, also in Latin, is much less well known. It starts with a great battle in which a Welsh king loses many of his friends. For three long days he weeps, strews dust on his hair, refusing food: grief consumes him. Then a 'strange madness' or 'new fury' comes upon him.

> He departed secretly, and fled to the wood and rejoiced to lie hidden under the ash trees; he marvelled at wild beasts feeding on the grass of the glades; now he chased after them and again he flew past them; he lived on the roots of grasses and on the grass, on the fruit of the trees and on the mulberries of the thicket. He became a silvan man just as though devoted to the woods. For a whole summer after this, hidden like a wild animal, he remained buried in the woods, found by no one and forgetful of himself and of his kindred.

Geoffrey's poem is the *Vita Merlini* – the Life of Merlin – and the feral figure who in forgetting himself flew with the birds is Merlin Sylvestris, the Merlin of the Woods, the prophet and seer who in later tales would be recast as the greatest magician of all, and who as Merlyn in *The Sword in the Stone* would educate the King.

It's tempting to imagine an originary moment, one perfect opening scene. An autumn evening in 1937, when

White takes down a book from the shelves that he does not want to read. It is a small blue book with a cloth cover; the first volume of *Le Morte D'Arthur*, Sir Thomas Malory's fifteenth-century retelling of stories about the legendary king. White had written his dissertation on it at Cambridge, and he is disinclined to return to it now. But he's finished all the other books in the house, so he sits in his armchair and begins to read. It is plodding, slow work, like wading through treacle. He nearly puts it down. But suddenly it catches on him, grips him like Gos had his shoulder with eight fierce talons, and he is stricken with amazement. This is a proper story. *A proper tragedy*, he thinks. The people in it are real. They had not been real before. Over two days he reads the whole thing 'with the passion of an Edgar Wallace fiend, then put it down and took up a pen'.

It is easy to say – there. That is how *The Sword in the Stone* began. But I do not think that is the story at all. The book had been started months before, when a round thing that was something like a clothes-basket was set down before his door.

White thought it a warm-hearted book, quite unlike his previous efforts. 'It seems impossible to determine whether it is for grown-ups or children,' he wrote to Potts. 'It is a preface to Mallory.' The boy in the book is called the Wart. He is a kindly soul, loyal and slightly stupid. He is an orphan and does not know he will become king. Sir Ector has raised him along with his natural son. The Wart will never become a knight because he is not a gentleman. But in the book he is given a magical teacher – Merlyn – and a magical education, too. Eschewing schooldesks and lessons learned by rote, Merlyn turns the Wart into animals and sends him off on quests. As a fish the boy learns about the dictator's passion for power by meeting the pike in the castle moat. As a snake he learns of history. He hears the trees speak, and sees the birth of the world through the eyes and ears of an owl. He discusses mankind's role in God's plan with a donnish badger in a comfortably furnished sett. And at the end, his education complete, the Wart pulls the sword from the stone, learns he is the son of Uther Pendragon and is crowned King Arthur.

It is a glorious dream of wish-fulfilment for White. He writes himself into the character of the Wart, the boy of unacknowledged royal blood who runs wild around the castle just as he had raced about West Hill House in St Leonards-on-Sea, wild, and happy, and free. White had been torn from safety and sent away to school, but he saves the Wart from such a fate. There would be no beatings in his education. But even so, his lessons are full of cruelty. I did not understand quite how cruel a book it was when I was young. But I responded to that cruelty all the same. Because my favourite part of the book was the Wart's ordeal as a hawk. It was truly terrifying. I'd read it and squirm, and curl my toes, then read it all over again.

Merlyn turns the Wart into his namesake, a merlin, and looses him in the castle mews at night. And as a new officer in the cadre of the castle's trained hawks, the Wart must undergo the customary ordeal. He is ordered to stand next to Colonel Cully the goshawk until the rest of the hawks ring their bells three times. It is an exquisitely dangerous initiation, for the colonel is insane. As the ordeal begins the goshawk glowers and mutters. He quotes broken snatches of Shakespeare and Webster, run all together in a fugue of rising horror. After the bells ring once the goshawk begs for the test to end, cries, 'I can't hold off much longer.' The bells ring twice. He moves towards the Wart, stamping the perch convulsively: 'He was terrified of the Wart, not triumphing, and he must slay.'

In that awful ordeal, White is the Wart, the boy who must be brave. But he is not just the Wart, and the boy is not the only one imperilled. There's a sad passage in Olivia Laing's book *The Trip to Echo Spring* that reminds me of this desperate scene. She quotes the writer John Cheever, whose alcoholism was intimately bound up with his erotic desires for men. He hated his homosexuality and felt himself in constant danger. 'Every comely man, every bank clerk and delivery boy,' he wrote in his journals, 'was aimed at my life like a loaded pistol.'

Despite several affairs with women, White's fantasies were sadistic and directed mostly at pubescent boys. He was certain that these fantasies had been shaped by his early abuse, and they shamed and horrified him, for in them he played the role of the abuser, just like his father and the masters who had beaten him. Therapy with Bennet had not taken these urges away. They never left him. Late in his life he wrote a pornographic novel about spanking schoolboys: it was a prolonged and awful confession. But he locked it away and never showed it to anyone. All his life he suppressed his desires. But sometimes, just sometimes, he could speak of them through other selves. Colonel Cully is one of them: a hawk wracked with desire to hurt a boy who is also a bird – a boy who is also himself. You can see the whole of his life's tragedy there in one small scene.

Though White had fled from the world of school, he never escaped the models it had given him on how to conduct his life. At school you had to pass tests and ordeals to prove you were brave. You tested your bravery in the playing fields, and through the beatings by masters and prefects. And there were the ceremonies of cruelty of the boys themselves: the initiations and ordeals that were the price of entrance into the school, and later into boys' secret societies. White had put his hand between the cocked hammer of an unloaded revolver and its frame before the trigger was pulled. The pain was a triumph; in bearing the agony, he proved he could belong.

But White was not always the victim in these rituals. School taught him that as he suffered at the hands of older boys, so he should punish the younger. He joined gangs and terrorised those weaker than himself, testing them as he had been tested. One term the test was to jump from a window in Big School fourteen feet to the ground. Puppy Mason was too scared to do it, so White assisted in pushing him out. When the fall broke his leg in three places, they were impressed by his silence. He told the masters that he had tripped over a twig on the headmaster's garden path. Puppy had been tested, had behaved heroically, and his membership of the fraternity was approved.

I knew nothing of such things. I knew about being hurt: the impossibly clumsy child that was me scraped her knees, tripped, grazed herself, hit her head on open windows and bled terribly. But I did not understand the logic behind ordeals of belonging. I did not see pain and bravery as steps toward gaining self-reliance, as necessary parts of growing up. But still I noticed, when I read *The Sword in the Stone*, that whenever the Wart became an animal, he seemed to be in danger. I puzzled over this. *Merlyn is teaching him to be brave*, I thought, eventually. *Because he will need to be brave to be King.*

I read Colonel Cully's ordeal with the Wart over and over again. It mesmerised me because when you are small you don't have to worry about the child heroes in books. They might suffer peril, but they are human: they never, ever die. But there was always a flicker of worry as I read *The Sword in the Stone*, for it was not quite clear if the Wart was human any more. He had been turned into a bird. Was he still the Wart? He was an animal now. Could he die? He might die. He might. And it was that possibility that held me spellbound every time I read the scene; I felt an apprehensive terror that was just big enough to master. I'd read on, desperate to reach the end, for that moment when the Wart

springs up from the perch, the goshawk's great foot clutching at his wing, before he wrenches himself free and survives.
I knew nothing of ordeals, but reading it felt like one. Every
time I finished reading it, part of me was relieved that I'd
survived to read it again.

White had escaped the school by running to the woods,
but he'd rented a cottage on the old road to its door. He'd
gained freedom by changing his life, but he'd not escaped
the concept of freedom that school had given him. At school
you move up from year to year, gaining more power and
privilege until finally you leave. It was this notion of freedom – as the natural end to an ordeal-filled education – that
never left White, and it was working within him when he
lengthened Gos's leash with breakable twine. As a schoolboy
he knew that the boys over whom he'd had authority would
one day have authority themselves. As a schoolmaster, too.
And a falconer. Deep down he knew he was always training
his charges for a time when they would be free.

25

Magical places

Ten days have passed. Last night the forecast was bad. A storm surge threatened to inundate East Anglia. All night I kept waking, listening to the rain, fearing for the caravans along the coast, their frail silver backs against the rain and rising seas. But the storm surge held back at the brink, and the morning dawned blue and shiny as a puddle.

After lunch I take Mabel up to the hill. Fractious gusts of wind rattle the hedgerows, blowing voluminous shoals of leaves over us as we walk up the track. There's sticky mud, and pheasant prints in it. Flocks of fieldfares *chak chak* and dodge in the hawthorns by the cow field, breaking low when we get too near, bouncing over the hedge and away in thrushy strobes of black and white. It's nice to see them. Proper winter is here. And Mabel is fizzing with happiness, wagging her tail in barely suppressed excitement, tummy feathers fluffed over her grippy toes, eyes gleaming silver in the sun. If this hawk could speak, she'd be singing under her breath. Something has changed inside me. Today it's hard to slip into the exquisite, wordless sharpness of being a hawk. Or rather, the hawk seems more human today. A rabbit lopes across the path twenty yards away and she chases it; swings up into a poplar, clutching onto a thin, near-vertical branch and leaning into the wind, narrow as a stoat. She looks about. Sees something. Goes to the next tree, looks down. Then flies back to the first one. I proffer my fist. She comes down immediately, and off we go again. *Raah*, she says. *More*.

By the hayrolls we sneak through the side of the wood, and then make our way to the corner of the top field. I'm a little blurry. I've combated the drug-induced tiredness with two double espressos at breakfast and a caffeinated soda after lunch. I'm hoping that the drugs will prevent the rampant paranoia that this excess of caffeine will inevitably provoke. Mabel clocks a pile of woodpigeons on plough a quarter of a mile away and makes as if to bate at them. 'Don't be daft, Mabes,' I say, but she bates anyway. *Pah*. She looks me directly in the face. *Give me something to chase!*

I do. We walk through chest-high thistles at the corner of the next field, hawk held high as I negotiate the thorns. She's gripping hard with all eight talons, bracing herself against the oncoming gusts of wind. And then out of nowhere, coming out of the ground right from where the tip of my shadow ends, a cock pheasant in bronze and bottle green, all rackety tail and sharp primaries, clatters up from the dry grass, gos already close behind. He turns downwind. She's gaining on him. No more than six inches behind the tip of his tail. But she hasn't flown much in winds like this, and mistimes her attack; is pushed by the wind a little askew, and the pheasant pulls away, climbs up over the wood. She follows, and both are lost to view. I'm just about to start running, but she's already on her way back to me, coming in at treetop height over the wood like a Mustang in a war movie. One vast, stylish arc, carving right through the barricade of oncoming air, like, *Here I come!*, and she's back on the fist, grinning like an idiot, and her whole attitude is, like, *Well! What did you think of that?*

As the days drive deeper into winter, a small and fugitive gleam begins to touch the edges of things. It happens without much fuss. I catch myself watching the sky in the morning and liking simply how it looks. Gone is the austringer's cal-culating eye, concerned only with wind-speed, bearing, likely precipitation. I call on old friends, make plans for the future. I look for a house to rent. My mother comes to visit. I go back to the doctor to discuss my progress. He tells me the deep blurry tiredness is a side-effect of the drugs, and that it will soon pass.

The American writer and ecologist Aldo Leopold once wrote that falconry was a balancing act between wild and tame – not just in the hawk, but inside the heart and mind of the falconer. That is why he considered it the perfect hobby. I am starting to see the balance is righting, now, and the dis-tance between Mabel and me increasing. I see, too, that her world and my world are not the same, and some part of me is amazed that I ever thought they were.

Then I find myself doing something surprising. I raise Mabel's weight even more and let her range more widely when she flies. This is terrible falconry. 'Never let a goshawk self-hunt,' say the books. 'Such independence is the fastest way to lose your hawk.' I know I shouldn't slip her unless there's quarry, right there, in front of her. But how can I resist this method of hawking? Today I walked up to the crest of a hill on a freezing, smoky afternoon, the whole Cambridgeshire countryside laid out in front in woods and fields and copses beneath us, all bosky and bright with golden sunshine, and I can see that what Mabel wants to do is launch a prospecting attack on the hedgerow over the rise. I let her go. Her tactical sense is magnificent. She drops from the fist, and sets off, no higher than a hand's width above the ground, using every inch of the undulating relief as cover, gathering speed until the frosty stubble winks and flashes under her, and she curves over the top of the hill. Then she sets her wings and glides, using gravity and momentum to race downhill, flash up over the top of the hedge in a sudden flowering of cream and white, a good hundred yards away, and then continue down the hedge's far side, invisible to me. I'm running, all this time, my feet caked with mud, feeling earthbound but transported at the same time.

I find her in the hedge bottom, holding onto a rabbit. 'Mabel,' I say, 'you are behaving like a wild hawk. Shocking.' This is nerve-racking falconry, but a wonderful thing. I am testing the lines between us that the old falconers would have called love. They have not broken; they do not look likely to break. Maybe they will. I raise her weight even more, and slowly the world widens. But I'm pushing my luck, and I know it.

She's not in condition, I tell myself all the way there in the car. *You'll lose her*. It is two days later, and I can hear the voice of reason telling me to go back home. I keep driving. Rain spots the windscreen and spines the nearside windows. Will the rabbits be lying out, in this weather? Maybe. I park on the muddy verge against the wet fence at the far side of the field. She's not in yarak, but she's looking about. *Whatever*, I think; I change her jesses and let her go. She chases a rabbit to its hole and swings up into an oak tree. I whistle. She doesn't seem to hear me. The rain starts falling in earnest. At this point, I realise something has changed about the space between the goshawk and me. Usually it's taut with attention. When she flies into a tree all my attention is turned to the hawk, and the hawk turns all her attention to me. Not any more. She ignores me.

There is something religious about the activity of looking up at a hawk in a tall tree. Sir Thomas Sherley wrote in the seventeenth century that flying falcons turns one's eyes to the heavens, which is why falconry is a moral activity. This seems more akin to falling to my knees begging redemption from an indifferent deity. Mabel flies on, deeper into the trees. I follow her. She's still ignoring me. *Look at me, hawk,* I'm willing up at the treetops – and she doesn't. I find myself on someone's lawn; I've trailed dark footfalls across the blue grass. The hawk is thirty feet above me and I'm shouting and whistling like a madwoman. Rain blows everywhere. I caper about. I chuck chick corpses high in the air. They fall with a thump to the grass and she doesn't even turn her head to track their sad parabolae. I whistle some more. Wave my arms. 'Mabel!' I shout. 'Come on!'

A sash window grates – an upstairs window of the huge Georgian house I've been pretending isn't there. A maid leans out. Black dress, white pinafore, white hat. Nothing about this strikes me as strange. I have followed my hawk and walked backwards in time. It's 1923. Any minute now Poirot will wander towards me across the lawn. Only later do I realise I had probably interrupted some erotic afternoon adventure.

'Are you all right?' she calls.

'I'm really sorry!' I shout back. 'I've lost my hawk.' I point vaguely up at the tree. 'I'm trying to get her back. I'm *so* sorry to trespass on your lawn; I'll be gone soon. Just desperate to get her back.'

'Oh?'

She thinks about it for a second, looks up at the tree. Then she looks down at me. 'That's . . . fine,' she says. 'I only wanted to see if you were all right.' She slams the window. The window slams *hard*, and the hawk moves. She flies from tree to tree, taking me away from the lawn towards the edge of the wood. The trees here are taller: now my hawk is the size of a thumbnail. Light shines dully from her spangled front. And out of nowhere, her half-size copy, a miniature doppelgänger, appears. The female sparrowhawk stoops at her, turns, and stoops again. It's like Peter Pan being mobbed by his own shadow. My hawk flies to the next tree. By now I've no discernible thoughts. I know she won't come down. I must just follow her, stumbling through bushes in a quixotic delirium.

Snowberries, I think, as the white nubs brush against my hawking waistcoat. *Didn't Victorian gamekeepers plant them as cover for pheasants? Oh. Oh no.* As soon as the thought is made, I see her twist out of the treetop, swerve to avoid a branch, and then stoop at a fifty-degree angle, wings almost entirely closed. It's exciting enough to make me hold my breath, but I haven't time: I'm already running. I duck under an electric fence, and my heart sinks. She's stooped into a city of pheasants. They are *everywhere. We shouldn't be here. We shouldn't be here.* I can hear her bell ringing. Where is she? Over the muddy ditch, and I'm in the wood. It is silent with leaves and fear. Then I hear pheasants running. I see one, two, three crouching in mortal terror. And then a blue-rumped cock pheasant burning copper against the leaves kicked up behind him, running hell for leather along the ground thirty feet away. Mabel comes up behind him like a gust of wind carrying the angel of death. I can't stop this. Nothing can. She's moving faster than seems plausible, powering down on a glide-slope that ends abruptly: she binds to the pheasant with both feet just as he sticks his head into a pile of brush-wood. And then all hell breaks loose. Leaves fly, feathers fly, pheasant wings batter, and I'm running.

I'm nearly passing out with stress, crouching, dirty, covered in mud and sweat, pulsing with adrenalin. The goshawk is full of adrenalin too. She's killing the pheasant more, even though it's dead. *Stamp stamp, gripe, stamp, foot, clutch, stamp.* Leaves continue to fly as she dances about on it. Her eyes burn with an unholy light, her beak is open. She looks terrifying. Slowly she calms down. I keep looking back behind me. No one is in sight. I feed her all the food in my waistcoat, and give her the whole head and neck of the pheasant. I sneak the pheasant itself into the capacious back pocket of the waistcoat, breaking its long tail feathers in half so no tell-tale ends poke out of the zip, and guiltily heap leaves all over the scene of the crime. And then we sneak back to the car.

I am undone. From the four corners of the field I'm cross-ing, from all sides, every single cock pheasant in the neighbourhood begins to crow simultaneously. It's a terrible, echoing, barrelling sound, like an echo-effects pedal on long sustain, rolling backwards and forwards through the air. It swells into the most terrifying, sustained cacophony, more like an artillery bombardment than calling birds. It is a vast alarum of accusation. I am guilty. I've poached a pheasant from someone's shoot. *I didn't mean to,* I almost say out loud. *It was an accident.* I'm relieved when the calls die away. And then, as I round the corner to the car, the barrage starts again. Chastened and slightly unnerved, I drive away, the pheasants gone but conscience ringing in my ears.

The landscape is changing before my eyes. What I see is not just winter moving onwards to spring; it is a land filling slowly with spots and lines of beauty. There's brittle sun out on the hill this lunchtime, and a fresh westerly wind. Mabel's pupils shrink to opiated pinpricks as I unhood her, both of her eyes narrow with happiness. It is exceptionally clear. The red flag over the range cracks with the wind and the sound of distant rifles; the radio mast on the horizon looks like an ink-drawing over a wash of shadows and lines and bolts of land rippling up to the chalk hills before me. We walk up the track. From the top I can look down and see the whole of Cambridge. The light today is beguiling. The rooftops and spires seem within a hand's grasp; a chess-set town glittering among bare trees, as if I could pick up the brute tower of the university library and move it six places north, set it down somewhere else.

From here, the city is mild and small, and looks all of a piece with the landscape around it. The beauty of a vantage like this is that it obscures the roads and walls with trees, makes Cambridge a miniature playset of forest-set blocks and spires. These days, when I go into town, I'm increasingly finding excuses to park my car in the multi-storey car park, because from the open-air fourth floor I can stare at these fields. They run like a backbone across the horizon, scratched with copse-lines and damped with cloud-shadow. A strange complication arises when I look at them. Something of a doubling. Leaning out over the car-park rail, I feel myself standing on the distant hill. There's a terrible strength to this intuition. It's almost as if my soul really is up there, several miles away, standing on thistly clay watching my soul-less self standing in the car park, with diesel and concrete in her nose and anti-skid asphalt under her feet. With the car-park self thinking if she looked very, very hard, perhaps through binoculars, she might see herself up there.

I feel I might be up there, because now the hill is home. I know it intimately. Every hedgerow, every track through dry grass where the hares cut across field-boundaries, each discarded piece of rusted machinery, every earth and warren and tree. By the road, half an acre of fenced-off mud, scaled with tyre-tracks and water reflecting pieces of sky. Wagtails, pallets, tractors, a broken silo on its side like a fallen rocket stage. Here is the sheep-field, there is the clover ley, now mown and turned to earth. Further up the track are tracts of mugwort: dead now from frost, seeds clinging to stems and branches like a billion musty beads on ragged Christmas trees. Piles of bricks and rubble run along the left-hand side of the track, and the earth between them is soft and full of rabbits. Further up the hill the hedges are higher, and by the time I get to the top the track has narrowed into grass. Cow parsley. Knapweed. Wild burdock. The argillaceous shimmer of tinder-fine clay. Drifts of chalk beneath. Yellowhammers chipping in the hedges. Cumulus rubble. The maritime light of this island, set as it is under a sky mirrored and uplit by sea.

I don't own this land. I've only got permission to fly here. But in walking it over and over again and paying it the greatest attention I've made it mine. I know where its animals live, and how they move about it. Know that the larks sleep on the top of the hill, but on sunny mornings they move to warm themselves on eastward slopes. That when the weather is wet but the rain has stopped, the rabbits in the warrens near the ditches move eastward onto the drier fields to graze. This sense of where the animals are is the coincidence of long experience with unconsciously noted clues. The incidence of sunlight on a stubblefield, and the pressure of wind on the same. The precise colour of the ground. I move towards the larks as if I could see them.

But the biggest field – one planted with oilseed rape – is not like the others. It is a mystery. Walking it with Mabel is like playing natural-historical battleships. Anything could be living in those thick-packed bluish leaves. Pheasants, partridges, hares – even a jack snipe, whirring up with snappy wingbeats from a muddy patch near the hedge. It seems ludicrous that anything could be invisible in a bare two inches of herbage. But everything is. There is a sense of creation about it: when the hare leapt up from our feet today it was as if it had been made by the field *ex nihilo*. The hare had an ally: a strong north-easterly. Mabel tried twice to grab it, and both times it jinked across the wind and she missed. It is very strange watching a hawk chase a land animal in a high wind. The hare has purchase: its claws and furry pads dig into leaves and mud, and it uses the ground to propel itself against. But the hawk moves in air alone. It is like watching one element against another. One world versus another, like a gannet diving into the sea for fish. I am glad she did not catch the hare.

There is the tree Mabel dived from to cosh me on the head. There's the invisible line in the air along which for the very first time she followed a cock pheasant to cover. There's the hedge where she clung, tail fanned wide, wings pressed against twigs, looking for a pigeon already gone. There is the bramble bush that tripped me and pitched me into a flooded ditch. The hawk and I have a shared history of these fields. There are ghosts here, but they are not long-dead falconers. They are ghosts of things that happened.

It's a child's world, full of separate places. Give me a paper and pencil now and ask me to draw a map of the fields I roamed about when I was small, and I cannot do it. But change the question, and ask me to list what was there and I can fill pages. The wood ants' nest. The newt pond. The oak covered in marble galls. The birches by the motorway fence with fly agarics at their feet. These things were the waypoints of my world. And other places became magic through happenstance. When I found a huge red underwing moth behind the electricity junction box at the end of my road, that box became a magic place. I needed to check behind it every time I walked past, though nothing was ever there. I'd run to check the place where once I'd caught a grass snake, look up at the tree that one afternoon had held a roosting owl. These places had a magical importance, a pull on me that other places did not, however devoid of life they were in all the visits since.

And now I'm giving Mabel her head, and letting her fly where she wants, I've discovered something rather wonderful. She is building a landscape of magical places too. She makes detours to check particular spots in case the rabbit or the pheasant that was there last week might be there again. It is wild superstition, it is an instinctive heuristic of the hunting mind, and it works. She is learning a particular way of navigating the world, and her map is coincident with mine. Memory and love and magic. What happened over the years of my expeditions as a child was a slow transformation of my landscape over time into what naturalists call a local patch, glowing with memory and meaning. Mabel is doing the same. She is making the hill her own. Mine. Ours.

26

The flight of time

It's turned cold: cold so that saucers of ice lie in the mud, blank and crazed as antique porcelain. Cold so the hedges are alive with Baltic blackbirds; so cold that each breath hangs like parcelled seafog in the air. The blue sky rings with it, and the bell on Mabel's tail leg is dimmed with condensation. Cold, cold, cold. My feet crack the ice in the mud as I trudge uphill. And because the squeaks and grinding harmonics of fracturing ice sound to Mabel like a wounded animal, every step I take is met with a convulsive clench of her toes. Where the world isn't white with frost, it's striped green and brown in strong sunlight, so the land is particoloured and snapping backwards to dawn and forwards to dusk. The days, now, are a bare six hours long.

It's my first day out with Mabel for a week. I've been interviewing students for my old college. For four days I've sat in front of frightened faces, asking them searching questions while trying to put them at ease. It was hard work. It felt like those first days with Mabel all over again. Now the interviews are over, and today I've been seduced by the weather. It is such a beautiful, fiery day, burning with ice and fine prospects, that I cannot imagine not being on the hill. I know my hawk is too high. I also know that after four days of enforced rest, she will be wanting to hunt very much indeed. What's more, I've run out of chicks; Mabel has been eating nothing but quail for a week, and it's made her a hot-tempered, choleric, Hotspur-on-coke, revenge-tragedy-protagonist gos-hawk. She is full of giddy nowhere-to-go desire. She foots her perch. She gets cross. She jumps in the bath and out again, and then in again. She glares. 'Feed bloody food but three times a week,' say the old books. Too much rich food and this is what happens.

Already I can see the mood she's in, and I suspect if I let her go here, she'll fly straight to the nearest tree and ignore me. So I take her to the top field. There are no trees up there. If she leaves the fist there'll be no close perch to fly to – she'll swing about in mid-air and come back to me. And she does, for a while, but then she starts eyeing the far hedge. I can't see beyond it. Mabel knows there are pheasants in there; woodpigeons, too, and rabbit-holes along the ditch. She starts that curious autocue parallax-bobbing of her head and makes as if to go. And I let her go. It is stupid of me, but I do.

She flips her wings, glides away and disappears behind the hedge. I am strangely calm. I don't even run. I amble in a leisurely manner towards it then realise, heart thumping, that I have no idea where she is. The hedge before me is an eight-foot wall of blackthorn needles. It's impassable. I run up and down looking for passage. *There*. A gap the size of a porthole between two sturdy branches. I squirm through it, pretending I'm an eel. I'm not. There's blood on my hands from the thorns on the ground, and the shoulder-strap of my hawking waistcoat hooks around a stubby branch. I'm caught. I try with all my might to keep going. There's no time to turn and see where it's snagged. Just brute force to try to release me. The branch snaps, and I ping forwards through the gap to land on my knees and the heels of my hands deep in a wet field of sprouting wheat. Mabel is nowhere to be seen.

I run into the middle of the field and look about. The wheat is pale and rich in the spectacular glare of the winter sun. Downhill is another hedge, and behind that another, and beyond that half an acre of pasture and a pale horse. No Mabel. I stand and listen, hard. No bells. Nothing. I whistle and call. Nothing. I get out the telemetry receiver for the first time. *Blip, blip, blip.* The signal is strong in all directions. Radiowaves propagate and bounce and confuse. I run around for ages with the aerial trying to get a fix, and eventually conclude that she's sort of in that direction. I run. Down by the horse field, the ground is still frosted. White dust on hard black earth. Mabel is lost. I feel giddily, terribly alone. It's not that I am worried about her. She'll be fine. She'll rocket around this landscape in high spirits, could live here for years. And just as I think this, a shotgun retort echoes from not far away. *Oh Christ*, I think. *She wouldn't live long at all. Please don't let her be shot. Don't let that noise be someone shooting her.* I stand, stricken, and it is then, in the silence that follows the shot, that I hear crows. Angry crows. Thank God. And I follow the noise, and of course, there is Mabel. She's sitting sun-washed on top of a hedge at the crest of the next hill. She's blazing with intent. She's chased something into cover; had seen a pheasant on the next rise and followed it here. I run across the field towards her and peer through the hedge to see where she's looking. My heart sinks. It's a jungle of saplings as tall as my shoulders woven together with briars and brambles. Thorns, thorns, thorns. There is no way I can flush the pheasant out of that. She makes little prospecting flights out over the brush, sallies that are slow to the point of stalling, before she returns to her branch, craning her neck behind her. *It's in there*, she's thinking. *I can find it.* I stand, panting, watching her for a while. We have to leave. This field, and the one beyond it, are not on our land. Even if I could flush that pheasant for her it would be poaching. And we've done enough inadvertent poaching to last a lifetime.

I call her. She ignores me. So I wait. And slowly, as the

minutes pass, her predatory fire cools. Now she has returned
to the world I am in. She can see me again. *There*, she thinks.
And she has a whole quail in her fist. From her sunlit perch
she descends to the hand I hold out in the shade of a hedge
and I feel a surge of indescribable relief. I start shivering,
cold and hot all at once.

The day-book that records White's long, lost battle with Gos
is not simply about his hawk. Underneath it all is history,
and sexuality, and childhood, and landscape, and mastery,
and medievalism, and war, and teaching and learning and
love. All those things were going to be in the book he was
writing about the hawk. When the hawk was lost he aban-
doned the attempt. But not entirely, because the book, in a
different form, was still being finished, and the hawk would
not be lost for ever.

At the beginning of *The Sword in the Stone* Sir Ector's
son Kay takes the Wart out hawking. He picks up Cully the
goshawk from the castle mews – an unwise thing to do, for
the hawk is deep in the moult and wildly out of condition.
After a half-hearted sally at a rabbit the hawk takes stand
on a high branch and ignores their calls. They follow it
from tree to tree, whistling and luring, but the hawk is in
no mood to return. Kay flies into a temper and storms
home, but the Wart stays with the hawk, because he cannot
bear it to be lost. He follows it into the deep wildwood,
and there he is afraid.

Reading *The Sword in the Stone* after reading *The Goshawk* is a deeply curious thing. You start to confuse which
forest is which. One is the tangled wildwood of Arthur's
Britain, a refuge for outlaws, hawks and wicked men. The
other is the tangled forest around Stowe. It too is a refuge
for outlaws, hawks and wicked men, the place White hoped
would give him the freedom to be who he was. Like the forest in *Sir Orfeo*, the forests of White's imagination exist in

two worlds at once, and it is into these strange, doubled woods that the lost hawk leads the Wart. In following it, the boy is drawn to his destiny, just as White had been drawn to his own by looking for Gos.

Night falls. The Wart sleeps under a tree, and the next morning he comes across a high-gabled stone cottage in a clearing in the wood. Outside it, drawing water from a well, is a tall elderly man with spectacles and a long white beard, wearing a gown splashed with mutes and embroidered with stars and leaves and mystical signs. It is his teacher, Merlyn the magician, and when the Wart walks into his cottage he finds it is a treasury of wonderful things: thousands of books, stuffed birds, live grass snakes in an aquarium, baby badgers, an owl called Archimedes. There is Venetian glass, a set of the *Encyclopaedia Britannica*, paint-boxes, fossils, a bottle of Mastic varnish, purse-nets and rabbit-wires, a rod-box, salmon flies, and a fox's mask mounted on the wall. Nearly all of these things were in White's cottage as he wrote. The book was White's 'Kingdom of Grammerie', wrote Sylvia Townsend Warner, 'where there was room and redress for anything he liked to put in it'. But there is another way of reading this scene, one far less mundane than a writer's amusement at putting in his book the things around him as he writes: it is that Merlyn's cottage in the woods is his own.

On White's shelves were a whole clutch of books on human psychology. He'd read them, underlined passages, made notes in the margins on the pathology of sexual deviance. In Alfred Adler's *Individual Psychology* he'd found a whole chapter on homosexuality. It held that the attitude of homosexuals was 'that of people desirous of interfering with the flight of time'. Adler thought homosexuals were irresponsible because they refused to develop into heterosexual adulthood. But interfering with the flight of time? Words once read run deep.

For White was certainly interfering with time. He was turning it backwards. In that green mound of a grave he had achieved invisibility, and after he emerged he felt he 'had turned St Lucie's day', the shortest, darkest day of the year from which the earth rolls back toward spring. He spoke of that time as a rebirth: wrote that life 'seemed to be creating itself, seemed in the blank walls of chaos to be discovering an opening, or speck of light'. In his imagination, the grave was his dissolution. He had lost the war with Gos, and it had killed the man he was. But now, with his apocalyptic, child's vision of redemption, he saw himself reborn into the world with wisdom. And reborn, too, as a man living backwards in time. I used to think Merlyn was a magnificent literary creation, but now I think of him as a much stranger invention – White's imagined future self. Merlyn was 'born at the wrong end of Time'. He must 'live backwards from in front, while surrounded by a lot of people living forwards from behind'. This backwards life is what gives Merlyn his ability to predict the future – for him, it is always his past. In White's 1941 conclusion to *The Once and Future King*, published much later as *The Book of Merlyn*, Arthur awaits his final battle. He is elderly now, tired and despairing, and when Merlyn appears he wonders if the wizard is a dream. Merlyn rebukes him. 'When I was a third-rate schoolmaster in the twentieth century,' he snaps, 'every single boy I ever met wrote essays for me which ended: Then he woke up.'

Being Merlyn was White's dream, and it makes *The Sword in the Stone* not just a work of fiction, but a prophecy. All White must do is stay put, wait four hundred years and the Wart will appear at his door. Merlyn's cottage, and all the things inside it, are souvenirs of the distant future. 'I have always been afraid of things,' White had written. 'Of being hurt and death.' But now he was recreating himself as someone who would become – who was already – immortalised in legend.

In the imagination, everything can be restored, everything mended, wounds healed, stories ended. White could not trap his lost hawk, but as Merlyn he does, with a ring of upturned feathers and a fishing line, and brings it in triumph back to the castle with the Wart. And thus White gives himself a new pupil to train: not a hawk, but the boy who will be king. He will educate him in the morality of power, inspire him to found the Round Table, to fight, always, for Right over Might. 'A good man's example always does instruct the ignorant and lessens their rage, little by little through the ages, until the spirit of the waters is content,' says the grass snake to the king at the end of *The Book of Merlyn*. For a little boy who stood in front of a toy castle convinced he would be killed, being Merlyn is the best dream of all. He will wait, he will endure, and one day he will be able to stop the awful violence before it ever started.

27

The new world

It is Christmas Eve. Outside my window is an icy tidal river. Everything not fringed with silver and limned lamp-black is white or Prussian blue. Those moving dots are wintering ducks and a loon slides past them on a low, submarine-profile cruise to the sea. Everything is heavy with snow. I'm stuffed to the gills with pancakes and maple bacon and I'm feeling quiet inside, quieter now than at any time since my father died. It is a deep and simple hush. My mother is asleep in the room next door, my brother is home with his in-laws, and Mabel is at Stuart and Mandy's, three thousand miles away.

Mum and I are spending Christmas in America through the kindness of my friend Erin and his parents Harriet and Jim, who run a bed-and-breakfast inn on the coast of southern Maine. I met Erin years ago when I worked breeding falcons in Wales; a young surfer and falconer, he'd turned up at Carmarthen station looking wildly out of place, like a clean-shaven Cary Elwes in *The Princess Bride*. He'd been drawn to Britain by dreams of flying falcons, only to be put to work jetwashing aviaries in driving rain. But he survived the gloom, and we became friends. Proper friends. The kind people say you only make once, twice in a life. I've visited him many times over the years, and through him I've met a crowd of wonderful Mainers. They're not much like my Cambridge friends. They're fishermen, hunters, artisans, teachers, innkeepers, guides. They make furniture, decoys, exquisite ceramic pots. They cook, they teach, they fish for lobster, take tourists out to catch striped bass. And most of them hunt.

Hunting in Maine is not obviously riven with centuries of class and privilege. There are no vast pheasant shoots here where bankers vie for the largest bags, no elite grouse moors or exclusive salmon rivers. All the land can be hunted over by virtue of common law, and locals are very proud of this egalitarian tradition. Years ago I read an article in a 1942 edition of *Outdoor Life* that stirred wartime sentiment by appealing to it. 'One of my grandfathers came from northern Europe for the single reason that he wanted to live in a country where he could try to catch a fish without sneaking onto some nobleman's property where the common people were excluded,' one hunter explained. In fascist Italy and Germany, the article went on, hunting is limited to 'the owners of estates, their guests, and the high and mighty'. It had to backpedal slightly, of course, for the same was true in Britain. 'This is no slap at our courageous ally,' it explained. 'But we do not need her system of land management.' What's more, hunting is far more acceptable here than it is in Britain. One of my friends in Maine is Scott McNeff, a wiry and energetic firebrand who runs an ice-cream emporium in summer and spends the winter flying his hawks. He told me that few households in the whole state aren't touched by the November deer hunt. Even if people don't hunt deer themselves, everyone knows someone who does, and freezers across Maine are full of home-shot venison packaged and parcelled out for friends and families. People swap hunting stories here the way people swap drinking stories at home.

Scott took us hawking yesterday with his male redtailed hawk, a first-year bird called Yoder. He's a handsome beast: his crown and back are chestnut brown, his underparts milk-glass white, sparsely marked with a gorget of spots and dashes. He's not as well-armed as a gos; his toes are shorter, thicker, more like fists than Mabel's armoured pianist's fingers. He has nothing of a goshawk's rangy, leopard-like hunch or conta-gious apprehension. His eyes are dark, his face mild and open. A thick-set, amiable hawk. An unflappable kind of hawk. And he has been borrowed from the wild. Yoder is a passage hawk, one who already knows how to hunt, who has in the weeks since leaving his nest had to learn a hundred different ways of encountering air and rain and wind and quarry, and learn them fast to survive. American falconers are permitted to trap and fly a bird like this over its first winter, and then release it in the spring to return to the wild and breed. Falconers here can do this because they are tested and licensed by the state. It's a good system. I wish we had it at home.

Scott has the kind of fluid physicality that makes everything he does beautiful to watch. He changes the hawk's jesses, checks there's food in the pocket of his battered jacket, and we set out. The ground has a deep crust of snow. Everything is poised as if it might shake itself. There are woods here: thou-sands upon thousands of acres of white pine, of hemlock, spruce and oak. But that is not where we are going. We walk across what looks like a school playground. Yoder leaves Scott's fist, flies up onto a children's playframe. We clamber down a slope behind timber-lapped houses. The hawk follows. The air swallows sound, so that speaking into it your voice stops a foot in front of your face in a cloud of white breath. *What are we doing here?* I think dully. *This is a town.*

Skittering flakes of dislodged bark fall through thirty feet of air. A family waves from an upstairs window. We wave back. The hawk is laddering up a pine tree behind their backyard fence, hoisting itself skyward with leaps and hawkish flour-ishes. 'Squirrel!' shouts Scott, and I am knee-deep in snow, coughing, my jetlagged ears singing in the hush, attempting to follow what is happening above me. The brightness above is blank behind knots and spars of twigs and needles. The flight is the workings out of two creatures above me. Height, vantage, escape, evasion. The squirrel knows about redtails. They live in these woods. The redtail knows about squirrels, too, has hunted them in the wild before Scott trapped him earlier that fall. A thin branch bends and springs back as the squirrel leaps into the next tree, the hawk after it. We crane our necks up at the war above, playing out like a wildscreen *The Enemy Below*. The hawk twists, the squirrel makes another leap, is silhouetted black against the sky, legs outstretched, and then a blunt, black form hits it. It is the hawk. I hear the impact, see the awkward, parachuting fall through thirty feet of snowy, splintered air and they land heavily on the ground, and Scott is running in slow motion through deep snow, and when I get there the squirrel is dead, and the hawk is mantling over his prey, wings out, beak open. A thin stream of smoke climbs from his mouth. Blood has already melted a thin line through the snow and the hawk's feet and feathers are powdered with a crumbly paste of snow and blood that resembles decorative sugar. The hawk looks up and about at his surroundings. A back yard, garages, a low fence. A barbecue heaped deep with snow. An inflatable Santa riding an inflatable Harley David-son. Icicles hanging from Christmas eaves. Somewhere I can hear a television, and beyond that someone is singing 'Happy Birthday'. I have never seen anything so fiercely wild and so familiar. How can it be here? How can the wild be here in this back-lot in the middle of a town, in the midst of home and community? These are the things I had flown from.

It was the wildest hunt I had ever seen. Sitting by the window staring out at the sliding river, I begin to wonder if home can be anywhere, just as the wild can be at its fiercest in a run of suburban back-lots, and a hawk might find a lookout perch on a children's play-frame more useful than one on the remotest pine. Maine has given me a family for Christmas and shown me a hawk can be part of it too. It's shown me that you can reconcile the wild. You can bring it home with you.

* * *

It's our last morning. Erin, Mum and I are walking along Parsons Beach, bracing ourselves against the wind. It is a bitter, salt cold day; we tread on frozen sand. Strings of seaducks fly far offshore, ragged lines over soaked slate baize. The waters under them are full of lobsters; Maine is famous for them; signs for lobster rolls hang everywhere across town. Erin's dad had been a lobsterman once, and I'd gone out fishing with them years ago. Which is to say, I sat on the deck of their boat and watched as they hauled traps, measured, sorted and banded lobsters, rebaited the traps and set them overboard. They worked for hours while I sat there, unable to help, unable to do anything except watch. They were delighted I'd come out with them, and it was a wonderful day, but I felt guilty all the same: I was an English tourist out of her depth. Walking on the beach I remembered that boat-trip and felt uncomfortable as hell. I'd spent months out with Mabel on the hill. I'd seen the harvest come in, tractors harrowing slopes, stockmen turning sheep out to winter in the fields. And I'd not spoken to anyone. No one at all. I thought of the summer tourists here standing in packs to photograph the lobster boats coming in, or angling their cameras to catch the twisted light and shade on stacks of lobster traps on Cape Porpoise quay. Was I like that? I hadn't meant to be a tourist with my hawk. It didn't feel like tourism. But I sure as hell had avoided being part of the working world.

We turn back, walking into the wind now, crunching over ice-crusted rockweed and sending sanderling flocks swirling along the tideline. The off-season streets are deserted, the hotels closed, shutters down, wooden sign-boards swinging in the wind. A Cooper's hawk sits on the overhead stop-light on the intersection of Main Street and Western Avenue, flat-headed and fluffed as Mabel, looking down on the empty town.

Back at the inn, feeling cold and horribly sober, I grab a coffee and pace about by the fire. My face is burning. I suppose it is from the wind. Mum is packing upstairs. Erin and his dad are in the kitchen. I can hear them laughing. *I don't want to go back*, I think. I had fled from community. At my father's memorial I'd remembered it existed. Now I am back in it, in the middle of a community, in the middle of a family home, and I do not want to leave. This place is fixing my broken heart. I can feel it mending, and I'm fearful of what will happen when I'm gone. I'm not sure how I will cope back in England, back in my jobless, hopeless, lonely old town.

The back door slams. Jim is heading off in the truck to his workshop. *I don't want to leave.* I sulk. I fret. I scowl at the fire, hot with self-pity. Then I hear the door open and Erin's tousled head appears round the frame. It wears a vastly conspiratorial expression. I sense a plan is brewing. And a minute later I'm helping him drag their huge Christmas tree out of the room and onto the snowy lawn, tip snaking through the rough trail it makes, branches skittering over and cutting through the crust that glitters in the sparse light. We prop it up in the deep snow as if it had grown there. I have no idea what is going on.

'OK, Macca, let's burn this!' he says.

Puzzlement.

'It's traditional. It's what we do here. In *America*.'

I don't believe him for a second.

'In England we dump them on the street, *traditionally*,' I say. 'Absolutely let's burn it.'

'I'll get the firelighter!' he yells. I can feel the madness to this, its contagious pagan glee. He runs back from the house with a squeezy plastic bottle of firelighting gel and in the snowy hush, fog collecting around us as the thaw turns ice to water that hangs in the warming air, he decorates the tree with gloopy green strings that drip and stick like glutinous tinsel.

'Stand back!' he commands. He strikes a match. A branch catches with a tearing scratch of flame. For a few moments this is pretty: a soft yellow light in the monochromatic gloom.

But then there is an explosive, tearing waterfall of rearing flame that bursts into appalling brightness. Erin's eyebrows go up. He steps back a good few paces. And now I am laughing so much I can hardly stand. 'Jesus, Erin,' I shout. It's as if he's set light to the whole of the world: a twenty-foot pyramid of flame lighting the lawn, the house, the river, the far side of the river, sending black shadows out from trees that a moment ago were lost in darkness, and our faces are gilded with fierce, orange fire. *What the hell have we done?* The smoke mixes with the fog so that everything, everywhere is on fire. The incandescent tree, black twigs sintering, clicking, crumbling, and smoke, and Erin and I now wearing the faces of people who are going to be in serious trouble. 'I think we might be seeing the fire truck any moment now,' Erin shouts, and we're both of us children again, delighted at what we have made and fearful of disaster.

And then the fire is out. The skeleton stands in the snow, all its complexity gone. Just a thin trunk with a few charcoal branches, already damp in the steaming air. And I stare at the remains of the tree and breathe the smoke and fog from the air and Erin makes a face at me and I make one back.

'That,' he says, 'was excellent.'

It was. A ritual burn, a ceremony of strange, protective magic. Bad things had fled from that burning tree. We laugh all the way back to the house, leaving the skeleton upright in the snow. And later that day Mum and I fly back to London. I drive her home, promise to see her soon, then make my way to Cambridge, and Stuart and Mandy's house. I run to their door. I cannot wait to see my hawk. There she is, perched in their garden, fat and happy in a crowd of pointers with wagging tails. I thank Stuart for looking after her while I was gone. He stands by the patio doors, strangely drawn and tired. 'No worries,' he says. 'I've not done much with her, to be honest. I've had flu. It's been terrible. I've been in bed all Christmas. Just thrown her food.'

'Poor Stu,' Mandy says, coming towards the table with three cups of coffee and a packet of open biscuits. 'He's really been in the wars.' I look at my friends and my heart crumples. They have spent so many hours helping me, have shown me so much love. And I had taken it all for granted.

'Thank you. Thank you so much,' I say. 'I love you guys. I really do.' I say it with as much feeling as I can. I am not just thanking them for looking after my hawk. I get up to give Stuart a hug. 'Don't catch it,' he says, backing away. I hug him anyway.

On this breezy August day in 1939 White is in Ireland hiding from the war. He knows he ought to enlist, but he's persuaded himself his flight here is not mere cowardice. He'd be wasted as a soldier, he thinks. He has a more important thing to do – finishing his epic about the Matter of Britain that will solve the problem of why humans fight at all. And that is why he has come here to County Mayo, and rented Sheskin Lodge to write in, a crumbling aristocratic bungalow with a glassed-in winter garden set amid acres of feral rhododendron and pine.

He sits in the torn-leather armchair in the room with the peeling walls. The plangent sound of hawk-bells drifts through the open window each time the falcons bate from their blocks on the lawn. Cully is dead: she tangled herself in strawberry netting in the cottage barn and hung herself, but he has trained two merlins since, and now he has two peregrines: a bad-tempered falcon called Cressida, and a nervous young tiercel as yet unnamed. For the last half-hour he has been recording the delicate steps of their training in a vellum-bound journal. He pauses. A thought has struck him, borne in with the sound of bells. Perhaps he might write the book about hawks after all. He had tried once, and failed. Perhaps he would try again. It would not be the usual naturalist's book about hawks. That would be bogus, he thinks.

This would be *real* literature. He begins to sketch out why:

> The initiation ceremonies, the voodoo hut of the falconer, the noises in the magic dark, the necromantic knots. Knots were probably the earliest spells. The two hawks consider themselves spell-bound to their blocks by my arts . . . I am convinced that if nobody had ever invented knots, nobody would ever have imagined magicians.

As a falconer he would be in the book, along with all the other parts he would play in the hawk's education. First he will be Torquemada, the inquisitor. Then the 'witch doctor of the ceremonies of puberty' – and the terrifying presence that will test them, their 'devil-god of the cave'. And then he will be Prospero, of course, the masterly magician who has led them through all the ceremonies and ordeals of their hawkish adolescence, for White thinks he knows what freedom is now, and what growing up means. He is party to the magic that is the binding of the hawk to the magician's will, and knows that at the end of the book must come the deepest mystery of all. The hawk must escape. Of course it must; for the hawk would have to 'unwind the charm, to escape, to cock his snook at the nigromant – only to find that there was a charm within the charm, that the wizard was a holy man after all, quite happy about the escape himself'. He finishes the paragraph and finds himself greatly moved.

> There he would stand, small and inverted, looking up from the scorned earth, his planetarium of a cloak blowing in the wind, his wand outwitted, his white beard streaming. And Falco ? A triumph, a hatred and a gratitude. No logic or moral. Only the magic for its own sake, weaving and unwoven.

28

Winter histories

There's a complicated sky of cold-front ragged cloud under swathes of high cirrostratus, and a headwind that sends larks up like chaff as we walk through the fields. Clouds of linnets bounce, half-midges, half musical notation, along the hedges surrounding my old home, and all is out of sorts as far as that notion of home lies because my father isn't here. It is late winter and I'm back at my mother's house. Things are better now, I know, and I've been coming here more often, but each time I forget how hard it will be.

The winter fields are shorn, yellowed into stalky, rabbit-grazed sward spotted with foraging rooks. I can hawk with Mabel all the way across this land until it ends in a slumpy hedge so wide it's almost a wood, furrily iced with old-man's-beard. Beyond it is someone else's land; a *terra incognita*, holding the suppressed fascination we all have for places just beyond where we know, or are supposed to be. I stand at the top of the field, change her jesses, remove her leash, thread the swivel onto it, double back the leash, and stuff it deep into my pocket. I hold my arm high, wait for her to look about, and cast her off my fist into the gusty wind. She glides down to the far hedge and swings up into a small ash, shaking her tail. I follow her down and we start hawking proper, looking for rabbits in a tangle of broken, open woodland. This line of trees is not designed for human thoroughfare. There are elder bushes, green twigs and branches starred with lichen. There are fallen oaks, clumps of vicious brambles, screens of hazel, and ivy clambering and covering stumps and extending a hand up to the trees above to scramble into the light, so the whole place is umbrous and decorated with shiny scales of ivy leaves. The air tastes of humus and decay. Each footfall breaks twigs and has that slightly uncertain, oddly hollow quality of walking on thick woodland soil.

Mabel is being extraordinary. I've mostly flown her in open country before. She has grasped how woodland hawking works, and is hugely attentive. More than attentive. Flying a goshawk in a scape of obstacles and broken sightlines makes the connection between us hugely manifest. She breaks through twigs to come down to my fist when I whistle, and she follows me as I walk, moving above me like a personal angel whenever I'm out of sight. I look up and see her crouching, staring at me with round eyes, pupils dilated with excitement and attention, crayon-yellow toes gripping dead ash branches. Or floating above me, above the branches, flickering through, sending submarine ripples behind her.

There's no narrative to be spoken of. There is the moment when I turn and see the calm, haunting face of a young rabbit looking out of a hole ten feet away, ears up, nose twitching. A little grey doe. I can't call attention to it. The world triangulates and halts dead. The rabbit and I look at each other. It realizes this stare is an involvement in death, and disappears. Mabel doesn't see it until the moment where the rabbit becomes air as it pops back down the hole, but she has to fly anyway, to the after-image, just in case; and tears off at low level and brushes the hole with one foot before swinging up high in a tree and shaking her tail, looking down. There is the moment where I'm running blindly after the hawk, and see her footing at a branch forty foot up a sweet chestnut: a failed attack at a grey squirrel, which skitters up the helically coiled saglines of the trunk and away to the safety of a high branch, and bark shards fall around me like delicate, waxen snow as Mabel returns, on call, to my fist, and I'm relieved as hell, because squirrels bite. They can take the toe off a hawk's foot. Not that I can blame them, given the circumstances. Then the moment where she comes towards me at ground level, because that's the only way through a big bank of elder twigs, and as she comes, I am watching the way the feathers on her back lift just a little as she stalls to slam into the glove – *blam* – all eight toes and talons gripping hard, then relaxing; and she looks right at me, in a blaze of expectation. And then, quite suddenly, she sees something through the trees, out there on the other side of the hedge. Her pupils grow wide. She snakes her neck and flattens her crown, and the tiny grey hair-feathers around her beak and eyes crinkle into a frown that I've learned means *there's something there*.

I decide to investigate, even though I don't have permission to fly her over there. Carefully, so as not to put it anywhere near my trousers – so far I have torn three pairs to shreds, out hawking – I high-step over the rusty fence-wire, turn about, and find myself calf-deep in dead game-cover crop the colour of wet tobacco. We are looking out across a wide downland valley. It's beautiful. I take one deep breath and exhale, full of the ballooning light-headedness of standing on chalk.

Chalk landscapes do this to me; bring an exhilarating, on-tiptoe sense that some deep revelation is at hand. This makes me feel guilty. There's a long vein of chalk-mysticism buried in English nature-culture, and I know that what I'm feeling, standing here, partakes of it. I'm guilty because I know that loving landscapes like this involves a kind of history that concerns itself with purity, a sense of deep time and blood-belonging, and assumes that these solitudinous windswept landscapes are finer, better, than the landscapes below. 'The frequenter of downland is occupied with essentials; with structure, with forms and with textures,' wrote chalk-cult ruralist H. J. Massingham in the 1930s. 'Aloft, he breathes an air that tunes him to the grand, archaic, naked forms of things.' It's a landscape that is a parable of the aviator's eye.

I grew up in the lowland pine-forests and heaths of sandy Surrey. But there's a photograph of me, wrapped in a tartan duffel coat, laying a five-year-old hand on one of the stones at Stonehenge, where my childish brain first grasped at intimations of history. And when I was a little older, corn buntings jangling from high-ground fence posts out near Wantage, I remember my father telling me that the track we walked upon, the Ridgeway, was an ancient, ancient path. This impressed me greatly. It was the 1970s, which had seen another great burst of the cult of chalk and history: there were experimental Iron Age re-enactment villages at Butser; scary children's TV dramas about the stone circles at Avebury; great bustard reintroductions on top-secret military establishments on Salisbury Plain. Now, I wonder why. Was it some response to the oil crisis? To economic depression? I don't know. But up on the Ridgeway path, aged nine or ten, was where for the first time I realised the power a person might feel by aligning themselves to deep history. Only much later did I understand these intimations of history had their own, darker, history. That the chalk-cult rested on a presumption of organic connections to a landscape, a sense of belonging sanctified through an appeal to your own imagined lineage. That chalk downlands held their national, as well as natural, histories. And it was much later, too, that I realised these myths hurt. That they work to wipe away other cultures, other histories, other ways of loving, working and being in a landscape. How they tiptoe towards darkness.

I'm standing on the far side of my familiar hedge, looking at this *terra incognita* that is the grand twentieth-century conjuration of our mythical English past. I walk out of the cover crop to where the thin, stony soil is exposed, so thick with chalk it's like white paste; hair roots and flints, spotted with rain; tiny buttons of stone in impasto. The land falls away at my feet into a dry valley; a basin the size of a village, one beech copse hanging grey from its left-hand slope. It is a field of a million tiny tillers – little shoots of wheat. They give the chalky earth a furry tint, like algae on a cliff-face. Even in this dark, watery light, the valley shines palely. And I see what Mabel had seen. About a hundred yards in front of us, crouched in its form, is a big brown hare, black-tipped ears laid to its ginger back. But there's more, much more here: down at the bottom of the valley, where the river would be were there water, is a herd of thirty fallow deer. They are the colour of moleskin on their backs, shading to pale grey underneath. They're tight-clustered, quivering with indecision. They're watching me. Thirty upraised heads. The herd is delicate and powerful, and it is waiting to see what I will do.

I can't resist the urge that takes hold of me then. I hold on to Mabel, who is watching them too, and like a woman possessed, walk towards them, with that strange disconnect between head and feet you feel when walking downhill. I'm technically trespassing, but I can't help it. I want to interact with them in some way. I want to get closer. And as I do, the pressure of my impending arrival pushes single deer off to the right, and they walk, then canter, in a long line, along the bottom of the valley and up to the wood at the far edge of the field, a good half-mile away. They are bewitching. Mabel watches them. She is ignoring the hare. The deer in procession resemble charcoal cave paintings rendered manifest. Art's magic working backwards. The chalk behind them, bone. And now the hare runs, too. The hare runs in the opposite direction to the deer. The animals run, and the landscape seems then to be parting in front of me. Deer one way, hare the other. And now they are quite gone: the hare to the field-margin at the top of the hill to my left, the deer into the wood at the top of the hill to my right. There is nothing before me now but wind and chalk and wheat.

Nothing. The hawk rouses again and begins to preen her covert feathers. The running deer and the running hare. Legacies of trade and invasion, farming, hunting, settlement. Hares were introduced, it is thought, by the Romans. Fallow deer certainly were. Pheasants, too, brought in their burnished hordes from Asia Minor. The partridges possessing this ground were originally from France, and the ones I see here were hatched in game-farm forced-air incubators. The squirrel on the sweet chestnut? North America. Rabbits? Medieval introductions. Felt, meat, fur, feather, from all corners. But possessing the ground, all the same.

We set off, again, homeward this time. But now the rain in the air is harder, and the rabbits are so close to their holes that Mabel's not able to get a foot to them before they disappear. After one hair's-breadth miss in a rocky quarryhole by a bank of wild rose stems, I call her back and feed her up. She is tired. Beads of water spot her head and tiny eyelash feathers. We stroll back to the car park. I'm tired too, and glad to see people walking towards us. I've met them before: a retired couple from my mother's village, walking their white-muzzled terrier on a long lead. They're all wrapped up with scarves and snap-fastened country jackets and their shoulders are set a little against the cold and wet. I meet them here quite often. I've always been delighted to see them. I don't know their names, and they don't know mine, though they know my hawk's called Mabel. I wave, and they stop and wave back.

'Hello', I say.

'Hello! How's the hawk?' they ask.

'She's good,' I say happily. 'But tired. She's been flying all over the place. It's beautiful out here today. I saw the deer!' I went on, glad to have someone to tell. 'A big herd of them, dark-coated, down in the bottom of the valley.'

'Yes,' he says. 'The deer. Special, aren't they, those ones. Rare. We see them quite often.' He is smiling; we're all enjoying our shared secrets of a place. She's nodding too. 'Aren't they beautiful?' she says. 'We counted them once, didn't we?'

He nods. 'There're usually between twenty-five and thirty.'

'Thirty exactly!' I say.

'They're a lovely sight.'

I agree. She tucks her scarf more tightly around her as a squall begins. Her husband nods vigorously, rain darkening his shoulders. 'A herd of deer,' he says, beaming, then his expression folds into something I don't recognise.

'Doesn't it gives you hope?' he says suddenly.

'Hope?'

'Yes,' he says. 'Isn't it a relief that there're things still like that, a real bit of Old England still left, despite all these immigrants coming in?'

I don't know what to say. His words hang and all the awkwardness is silence. The leaves rattle in the hazel stems. And I nod a goodbye, sad as hell, and my hawk and I trudge home through the rain.

It is a miserable walk. I should have said something. But embarrassment had stopped my tongue. Stomping along, I start pulling on the thread of darkness they'd handed me. I think of the chalk-cult countryside and all its myths of blood-belonging, and that hateful bronze falcon, of Göring's plans to exclude Jews from German forests. I think of the Finnish goshawks that made the Brecklands home, and of my grandfather, born on the Western Isles, who spoke nothing but Gaelic until he was ten. And the Lithuanian builder I'd met collecting mushrooms in a wood who asked me, bewildered, why no one he'd met in England knew which were edible, and which were not. I think of all the complicated histories that landscapes have, and how easy it is to wipe them away, put easier, safer histories in their place.

They are only safe for us. The fields where I fly Mabel back in Cambridge are farmed organically, and they are teeming with life. These are not. The big animals are here, it is true: the deer, the foxes, the rabbits; the fields look the same, and the trees, too, but look more carefully and this land is empty. There are few plants other than crops, and few bees, or butterflies, for the soil is dressed and sprayed with chemicals that kill. Ten years ago there were turtle doves on this land. Thirty years ago there were corn buntings and enormous flocks of lapwings. Seventy years ago there were red-backed shrikes, wrynecks and snipe. Two hundred years ago, ravens and black grouse. All of them are gone.

Old England is an imaginary place, a landscape built from words, woodcuts, films, paintings, picturesque engravings. It is a place imagined by people, and people do not live very long or look very hard. We are very bad at scale. The things that live in the soil are too small to care about; climate change too large to imagine. We are bad at time, too. We cannot remember what lived here before we did; we cannot love what is not. Nor can we imagine what will be different when we are dead. We live out our three score and ten, and tie our knots and lines only to ourselves. We take solace in pictures, and we wipe the hills of history.

History, and life too. It might resemble Old England here but it is not anything like the country of four hundred years ago, of one hundred years ago. I am nearly home, now, and I'm sad, and angry, and fired up as hell. I wish that we would not fight for landscapes that remind us of who we think we are. I wish we would fight, instead, for landscapes buzzing and glowing with life in all its variousness. And I am guilty too. I'd wanted to escape history by running to the hawk. Forget the darkness, forget Göring's hawks, forget death, forget all the things that had been before. But my flight was wrong. Worse than wrong. It was dangerous. *I must fight, always, against forgetting*, I thought. And I wish I had run after that couple and explained about the deer. I wish I had stood there in the mud in the rain, waving one hand with a hawk on the other, shouting about history and blood.

Later that night I find my father's plane-spotting diaries at the bottom of his bookshelves: six hardbacked, cloth-spined exercise books. I pull one out at random. 1956. He was sixteen. The pages are divided into columns, headed with careful, inked capitals: *TIME. NUMBER OF PLANES. TYPE OF PLANE. REMARKS. REGISTRATION NUMBER*. I look at the first column. On the twenty-fifth of April he starts watching at 9.40 a.m. and leaves at 7 p.m. On the twenty-sixth he starts at 9 and ends at 9 p.m. *Twelve hours of looking up at the sky. Good God*. There are hundreds of pages and thousands upon thousands of aircraft here. Vickers V70 Viscounts, F-86 Sabres, Airspeed Ambassadors, Lockheed Super Constellations, Gloster Meteors.

Here's his report of a visit to Croydon Airport at the end of May. 'Eight de Havilland Tiger Moths. Two Auster Aiglet trainers. Two Taylorcraft Plus Ds. One Auster 5. Three De Havilland 104 Doves.' I have no idea what these planes are. I find a glued-in snapshot of a Tupolev Tu 104. He has written a few lines underneath: 'This aircraft is undoubtedly a civil conversion of the Type 39 Badger but the Russians said it was a completely new aircraft.' It has all the burning pedantry I remember from my childhood obsession with hawks. Suddenly my father seems very close. Another photograph falls out. I pick it up. *De Havilland 104 Dove, Croydon Airport, 2–4–56*. I cross-check the registration number against the list. *G–AMYO. Morton Air Services*. The edge of the runway is lost in mist. I can see a tiny profile inside the cockpit, the suggestion of a man leaning forward to wipe the canopy before the plane climbs into the grey April sky.

It is then that the knowledge of why my father watched planes drops into my head. When he and his friends had been small boys running feral across London bombsites, he'd told me, they collected things. Collected anything: shrapnel, cigarette packets, coins; mostly things that came in series. Things that could be matched and swapped; sets that could be completed. Collecting things like this, I realised, must have stitched together their broken world of rubble, made sense of a world disordered by war. And my father's aeroplanes were just as much of a set to collect: a series of beautiful, moving things with names and numbers, all deeply concerned with danger and survival. But there was more. Aeroplanes had wings. They took flight, and if you knew them, watched them, understood their movements, you could somehow take flight too; you could watch that Tupolev 104 take off and know it will cross borders you cannot cross except in your imagination. In a few hours it will be on a snowy Soviet airfield. Or any one of a thousand else. In watching the planes, you fly with them and escape. They enlarge your little world and spread it across the seas.

The notebooks are full of a fierce attention to things I do not know. But now I know what they are for. These are records of ordered transcendence. A watcher's diary. My father's talk of patience had held within it all the magic that is waiting and looking up at the moving sky.

I put the notebook back and as I do I see there's a piece of brown cardboard between the next two notebooks on the shelves. Puzzled, I pull it out. It is a blank piece of thick card cut roughly along one edge. I turn it over. My heart misses a beat, because stuck to the other side is a silver doorkey under three inches of clear tape. And five words written in pencil.

Key to flat.
Love, Dad

Dad had posted it to me last year so I could stay at his flat in London when he was away. I'd lost it, of course. 'My daughter the absent-minded professor,' he'd said, rolling his eyes.

'Don't worry. I'll get another one cut.' But he'd never got round to it, and I'd not thought of it since. I don't know what it is doing here. I read the words again and think of his hand writing them. And I think of Dad holding my own tiny hand as I put the other one flat against the sarsens at Stonehenge, back when I was very small and there were no fences to stop you walking among the stones. I looked up at the thing that was like a door but had no walls behind it.

'Is it a house, Daddy?' I asked him.

'No one knows,' he said. 'It's very, very old.'

I held the cardboard and felt its scissor-cut edge. And for the first time I understood the shape of my grief. I could feel exactly how big it was. It was the strangest feeling, like holding something the size of a mountain in my arms. *You have to be patient*, he had said. If you want to see something very much, you just have to be patient and wait. There was no patience in my waiting, but time had passed all the same, and worked its careful magic. And now, holding the card in my hands and feeling its edges, all the grief had turned into something different. It was simply love. I tucked the card back into the bookshelf. 'Love you too, Dad,' I whispered.

29

Enter spring

Mandy opens her door, takes one look at my face, and mirrors it with a horrified expression of her own. 'What's happened, Helen?'

'Mabel!' I say weakly.

'Did you lose her?'

'No!' shaking my head. 'She's in the car.' And then three requests: 'Mandy, can you help? I cut my thumb. Can I use your phone? I need a cigarette.'

Bless her for ever. I collapse into a kitchen chair. My knees hurt. Brambles? I have no idea. My thumb is still bleeding. Mandy hands me iodine wash, fixes the tear with steri-strips and bandages, makes me a coffee, pushes a packet of tobacco and cigarette papers across the table. Then she waits while I call the College where I should, right now, be teaching, and stammer out apologies. Then I tell my sorry story.

I'd seen signs over the last week or so. The season was turning. A bluebottle in the garden; torpid purple crocuses on the lawn. Dots of cherry blossom falling outside the walls of St John's. And one evening last week, a host of blackbirds carrolling into the deepening sky from perches all over the city's gable ends and Gothic spires. Spring was coming. And usually I'd rejoice at the curious bluish tint to the air and the lengthening days. But spring will mean no more Mabel. She'll be moulting in an aviary. I shan't see her for months.

My heart hurts thinking of it. So I wasn't thinking of it; I'd ignored the flowers and the flies. And that was part of the problem. For something was stirring in Mabel's accipitrine heart, and perhaps it was spring.

I had an hour to fly her today. I'd some freelance teaching in town that afternoon, and I knew I was cutting it fine. So I decided to head back to the old field where the rabbits are. *We'll catch a rabbit*, I thought, *then I'll drop her back at the house, pick up the teaching material, and run down the road to teach it.* What could possibly go wrong?

Everything. She flies a rabbit half-heartedly, lights upon a hedge-line and looks about. When I call her back she takes a while to return. The warning signs are there already, but I'm ignoring them. *One more flight*, I tell myself. But what Mabel is doing is revelling in the weight of the sun on her back, and in the little intimations that warm air is rising into this steady, grey-blue sky. She courses another rabbit, and sails onward, away from me, pitching high up in chestnut trees, and now I realise she's losing all interest in me. I kick myself. After the last debacle here, I swore I'd be more careful. The trees are above a road; there's an unsettling proximity of moving cars and trucks and tractors: she doesn't want to be here any more. She crosses the road into a belt of trees and gravelled drives. I follow her. Rabbits break all around me and the PRIVATE: KEEP OUT signs. She ignores them. And me. She's taken stand in a tree a good twenty-five feet above me, and looks out at the prospect all around. I'm waving my glove and whistling, but this is a lost cause. She fluffs her tummy and shakes her tail: a goshawk's signs of happiness and contentment. But on an inaccessible branch, with the seconds ticking past, these lovely signs of relaxation and calm bring a sinking feeling. And I realise I failed to bring my telephone. Or my cigarettes. And the radiotracking receiver is in the car.

After a minute or so, she slips away, out the back of the wood and away into land I know nothing about. It turns out there's a lovely, soft field of burnt-butter coloured grasses here, and a thick grey wood about three hundred yards distant. And no goshawk anywhere. Back to the car I go, unpack the radio telemetry and spend ages tracking her down. The signal is all over the place. *Beep. Beep. Beep.* In this direction, the signal strength is 5. Here, 7.5. But then – 2? *What? Triangulate! Triangulate!* I angle the antenna and spin in circles. Is she moving? She must be. And over the distant wood I see her on the soar. She's letting the rising air carry her, spilling over the wood in rich circles of sun-warmed flight. Another hawk comes up, and the two slip and rival each other for a while. I run, of course. By the time I reach the wood, there's no sign of either of them, though I hear a buzzard mewing some way off. Then, suddenly, bells. Somewhere in there. I dive into the wood. The signs aren't good. It's not a thick wood. It's not a wild wood. It's a habited wood. It's a pheasant release wood, to be sure. Oh lord, this goshawk is making me a criminal again.

I spot her. She's poised on a low branch of an ivy-covered oak, staring fascinated into a tangle of old feed sacks and bins in an inch of water. I walk closer. She's making those snaky-necked prospecting parallax movements of her head that mean she's locked onto something. She's going to ignore me until she's established to her satisfaction that it's gone. Perhaps it has. I edge my way to where she's looking, and before I know what is happening, a wet cock pheasant breaks from my feet, showering me with water. In slow motion, I see the sun through his primaries, splintering into bars and abrupt shadows, and watch Mabel do a smart wingover and her left foot flash out, but its two-and-a-half-inch back talons and crayon-yellow hand just miss him. He rises over – oh horror, I hadn't seen it – a ten-foot chicken-wire fence – and buries himself in a huge stand of laurel and yew on the other side. She dives in after him. I can't get to them. They're in a bloody pheasant release pen! *Shit!* This is like taking a ferret into a fancy rabbit show. Not good. Not good. I can hear wings beating, bells ringing, the sounds of a struggle. I run like a rat around the perimeter of the pen, trying to find a way in. This is not what I had wanted to happen. *Oh God. Oh God.*

There's a door. It's open. I dump the receiver on a blue feeder bin and run in. She's no longer in the laurel. She's on top of it. She turns away from me, and before I can take another breath, she is off again through the sun-filtered branches, fast and determined. *Shit! Shit!* I start running, over branches, past little corrugated shelters, over earth compacted by hundreds of pheasanty toes. Any minute now, I think, I am going to hear the 'Oi!' of an incredibly angry keeper. *Perhaps he will have a shotgun*, I think, as I watch Mabel pile into a hen pheasant at the far corner of the pen in a leafy explosion of buff and cappuccino feathers and beating wings. When I get to her she is sitting in a black puddle of acid woodland water, mantling over the body of a hen pheasant. And as I walk up, another hen pheasant emerges from under her wing, and she grabs that too. She has a pheasant in each foot. *Oh my God. Carnage.* Her tail is spread into the puddle, her feet are buried in feathers, and her whole being seems to be vibrating at some unlikely, scary frequency.

The pheasants are dead. One is in my waistcoat pocket, and the other is being plumed by my errant goshawk in lifting puffs of soft contour feathers that float and catch in the wire behind her. We need to get out of here fast before I have explaining to do. Shaking with worry, I take Mabel from her quarry. And then I injure myself horribly. Cutting through pheasant sinew, I take a wide, shallow strip of skin from my thumb. And as soon as I get Mabel back on the glove and stow her illicit prize in my waistcoat pocket, I start to worry about the amount of blood I'm losing. It's not just that my hand is completely red; I can hear the drips falling to the woodland floor. I press the wound hard into the fabric of my hawking jacket. It's covered in germs, I know, but I must stop the bleeding. *Must. Stop. The. Blood.* And blood pours from me all the long way back to the car, and all the way to Stuart's house. I can never go back there, I think. Never, ever again.

In March 1949, the publisher Wren Howard of Jonathan Cape travelled to the Channel Islands to stay at White's new home. White had moved to the island of Alderney: it was a perfect refuge from the taxman and the world. He'd bought a white three-storeyed house in St Anne's with magnolia wainscoted walls. He'd filled it with new things: his own surrealist paintings, a boudoir grand piano, silver candlesticks and a statuette of the Emperor Hadrian. There were dark curtains printed with bouquets of ghostly silver roses, jazz records, Jacobean chairs, and a sofa, towards which White ushered Howard to sit. Howard sat. It was wildly uncomfortable. He got up and examined the seat. There was something beneath the cushion. He reached under it and pulled out a thick pile of papers. He asked White what it was. White looked worried. It was the manuscript to a book he had written about hawks, he explained. He did not want it published because after it was written he became a good falconer, an authority on the subject, and there were things in it that were embarrassing to remember. Besides, the hawk had been lost.

Howard leafed through the first few pages and was intrigued. He took it upstairs and read it overnight. In the morning he insisted on taking it back to London, for he was sure it should be published. White balked at the idea, but as the weeks went by, Howard and his friends persuaded him, and he consented to its publication on one condition: that he could write a postscript explaining how he *ought* to have trained the hawk, in the light of his later experience.

When *The Goshawk* was published in 1951 it was not a bestseller, but it brought an extraordinary number of letters from readers. Some were congratulatory, others strange: one offered White an eagle. Some disliked the book greatly. And

one of these letters White never forgot. It touched a very raw
nerve. It was from a man who said that he had for thirty
years lectured on birds and watched them all his life. 'How
you can talk of love for a bird after subjecting our wonderful predatory birds to such torture is beyond a normal mind,'
the letter ran. 'Is there not enough cruelty in the world without adding to it for one's amusement or hobby?'

'This letter put me off food for three days,' White later
confessed, 'though I answered it with several pages of affection, apology and explanation.' He waited for a reply. When
it came, White wrote, the letter-writer 'used the word "normal" five times, concluding with the pronouncement that he
did not wish to hear from me again. It seemed polite to leave
it at that.'

I've moved back to the city, to a little rented house in a
street near the river with a small sunny garden that ends in
a tangle of briars. Cats stalk the pavement outside, there
are pigeons all over the roof, and it's good to be in a house
that I can call my own for a while. Today I'm unpacking
boxes and stacking books on shelves. Three boxes down,
five to go. I open the next box. Inside, on top of the other
books, is *The Goshawk*.

Oh, I think, as I pick it up. It is strange to see it again,
because I've not thought of White for a while. As I grew happier his presence receded, his world more and more distant
from mine. I look at the scuffed spine, open it, and flip to the
very end. I want to read the very last page, where White lists
all the things Gos was: a Prussian officer, Attila, an Egyptian
hieroglyph, a winged Assyrian bull, 'one of the lunatic dukes
or cardinals in the Elizabethan plays of Webster'. A litany
of human things in stone and armour, in marks on pages
and dints in sun-baked clay. I peer out of the dusty window
at Mabel in the garden. She has bathed and preened and
now she's leaning backwards to the oil-gland above her tail,

nibbling it gently, then pulling each tail feather through her beak to make it waterproof. I know she is content: the half-closed, happy eye, the rattling of her feathers: these are signs of raw good humour. I cannot know what she is thinking, but she is very alive.

I think of White's list of things and what a strange, sad ending it is. I swear to myself, standing there with the book open in my hand, that I will not ever reduce my hawk to a hieroglyph, an historical figure or a misremembered villain. Of course I won't. I can't. Because she is not human. Of all the lessons I've learned in my months with Mabel this is the greatest of all: that there is a world of things out there – rocks and trees and stones and grass and all the things that crawl and run and fly. They are all things in themselves, but we make them sensible to us by giving them meanings that shore up our own views of the world. In my time with Mabel I've learned how you feel more human once you have known, even in your imagination, what it is like to be not. And I have learned, too, the danger that comes in mistaking the wildness we give a thing for the wildness that animates it. Goshawks are things of death and blood and gore, but they are not excuses for atrocities. Their inhumanity is to be treasured because what they do has nothing to do with us at all.

I put White's book on the shelves, make myself a cup of tea. I'm in a contemplative mood. I'd brought the hawk into my world and then I pretended I lived in hers. Now it feels different: we share our lives happily in all their separation. I look down at my hands. There are scars on them now. Thin white lines. One is from her talons when she'd been fractious with hunger; it feels like a warning made flesh. Another is a blackthorn rip from the time I'd pushed through a hedge to find the hawk I'd thought I'd lost. And there were other scars, too, but they were not visible. They were the ones she'd helped mend, not make.

30

The moving earth

It is 27 February, and I'm feeling distinctly wobbly. Tomorrow I'll be driving Mabel to my friend Tony's house. He's a very old friend of mine, a gifted falconer and a deeply generous man. He lives with his family in a little lemon-coloured house in the flat lands of south Suffolk half an hour from the sea. I'm looking forward to seeing him but am wobbly all the same, because this will not be a flying visit for Mabel. Tony's giving Mabel a spare aviary for the moulting season. Tomorrow I'll be driving back here and leaving her behind.

I have to do it. It's time for her to drop all her feathers, one by one, and grow new ones. She needs to be fat and full of food to grow her new plumage, so all week I've been giving her as much quail and pheasant as she can eat. She's round as a turkey now, and part of me has been waiting for her to get wild. *A fat goshawk is a wild goshawk*, say the books. They are wrong. Of course they are. Mabel's less willing to tolerate strangers in this fed-up state, but she's still as tame as a kitten with me. This morning we played throw and catch with paper balls, and for the last hour she's been snoozing on my fist while I watch bad TV. 'Right, Mabel,' I say. 'Bedtime.' I put her on her perch in the other room, switch off the light and go upstairs to bed.

Some things are too terrifying to comprehend. Seconds can pass in disbelief as the world you live in turns into a lie. At just past one in the morning I'm having one of the worst nightmares of my life. My dreams lately have been small and full of light, but in this one, someone – something, for it cannot be human – has taken hold of the end of my bed and is shaking it, shaking it hard, trying to pitch me to the floor. It is the feeling in the dream that terrifies me most of all. It is not like a nightmare. It is worse. I wake with a start.

Something is still shaking my bed. I can see it move, hear it creaking. There is no one in the room.

Every inch of my skin crawls with terror. I am shaking and unable to move. The wrongness is indescribable. The fear is falling through a thousand feet of air. The bed is still shaking, senselessly, violently, horribly, impossibly.

Then it stops.

For a few seconds I lie there, stricken. I have not been breathing, I realise. I take a vast gulp of shuddering air. The lampshade above me is swinging in circles still.

Then a flash of understanding.

An earthquake. It was an earthquake. Here, in England. They hardly ever happen here, do they? Was it definitely an earthquake? It must have been. *Yes.* I still can't quite believe it. I jump out of bed and peer through the curtains. Lights are on in all the houses. People in the street are wandering fearfully in pyjamas. The phone rings, and I pick it up, and it is Christina.

'Earthquake!' she yells. 'Did you feel it?'

I swear. She curses. Ordinary words fail us: we mouth obscenities in the cause of reassurance. But they are not enough. When I put the phone down I cannot calm myself. I put my hands out flat in front of me, palms down. They are still shaking. *Stop freaking out, Helen,* I tell myself. *It's OK. Nothing is broken. Everything is fine.* But it is not. The earthquake has brought back all those childhood fears of apocalypse: all the expectation that the world would burn and boil. It is a very old, deep terror and it feels now that it has never gone away. The fabric of the world has torn. I cannot stitch it back together. And then I remember Mabel. I've heard all the stories about animals fleeing from earthquakes. *Oh God. She must be terrified.* I race downstairs, three steps at a time, burst through the door and turn on the light in her room. She is asleep. She wakes, pulls her head from her mantle-feathers and looks at me with clear eyes. She's surprised to see me. She yawns, showing her pink mouth like a cat's and its arrowhead tongue with its black tip. Her creamy underparts are draped right down over her feet, so only one lemony toe and one carbon-black talon are exposed. Her other foot is drawn high up at her chest. She felt the tremors. And then she went back to sleep, entirely unmoved by the moving earth. The quake brought no panic, no fear, no sense of wrongness to her at all. She's at home in the world. She's here. She ducks her head upside down, pleased to see me, shakes her feathers into a fluffy mop of contentment, and then, as I sit with her, she slowly closes her eyes, tucks her head back into her feathers, and sleeps. She is not a duke, a cardinal, a hieroglyph or a mythological beast, but right now Mabel is more than a hawk. She feels like a protecting spirit. My little household god. Some things happen only once, twice in a lifetime. The world is full of signs and wonders that come, and go, and if you are lucky you might be alive to see them. I had thought the world was ending, but my hawk had saved me again, and all the terror was gone.

She sleeps all the way to Suffolk in my car. Tony's house is tucked behind trees on a road between two fields and lines of hedgerow elms. I pull into the drive, take Mabel onto my glove and walk across the lawn. He comes out to greet me. We walk together to the high, white-walled aviary behind his mews. He unlocks the door and I step through. Her new home is huge. There are bark-covered branches, and perches upholstered in astroturf to massage her feet. There is a bath, a chute through which Tony will drop her food; weedy undergrowth, gravel, a nest-ledge to lie on, a patch of warming sun. Above the wire-mesh roof the Suffolk sky. 'Well, Mabes,' I say, unhooding her, 'This is your home for the next few months.' She looks down at my hand as it pulls each jess free from her anklets: now she stands on my fist wearing none at all. She cocks an eye up to the moving clouds, then examines her surroundings. She follows the line of the roof to the corners, peers at the cinderblock foundation walls. For a moment we are back in the darkened room on that first day of our meeting. I remember that moment when the hawk first forgot me and flinch inwardly at the knowledge that now she will forget me again.

'I'll see you after the summer's over,' I say. Forgetting. Remembering. I put my hand out, drag the tips of my fingers down her teardrop-splashed front. The new feathers she will grow will be barred stone-grey and white. The tones of earth and ochre will disappear. Her eyes, when I see her next, will be the deep orange of glowing coals. Everything changes. Everything moves. I lift my hand, cast her towards the nearest perch. She flies, lands, shakes her tail, sees a branch above her and leaps upon it. She's facing away from me. 'I'll miss you,' I say. No answer can come, and there is nothing to explain. I turn and walk out of the door, leaving the hawk behind. Tony is waiting outside, his eyes crinkled into a smile. 'Come inside the house,' he says. He knows what I am feeling. And in I go, where the dogs lie flat on the kitchen floor, tails wagging, and the kettle is whistling, and the house is very warm.

Postscript

I needed to find out more about White to write this book. So I spent a week in the Harry Ransom Center, the Texas archive where T. H. White's papers and journals are kept. Reading about muddy English winters while sitting in an air-conditioned library was a very strange experience; outside, vultures soared on tilted wings through ninety-degree heat and grackles hopped on the burning sidewalks. I turned pages, sifted through manuscripts, read through the books he had owned, returned home with stacks of notes and thoughts. But they did not seem enough. There was something else to be done. So one hot July day I drove across England to Stowe. It's still a school, but its grounds are open to the public. I parked my car in the National Trust car park, paid my entrance fee, clutched a map, and walked up the long lane to the gate. 'Turn left for the best views,' the man at the sentry box said. I turned right out of sheer contrariness and set off on my quest, the vast Palladian palace bright on the horizon, everything under metallic sunlight that made the lime-leaves black and the lake-water a deep, painful blue. Water lilies glowed on it in thick constellations. Ink-black shadows underpinned the parkland trees. Swifts pushed through air so thick they hardly beat their wings against the breeze. These were the grounds of the school where White had taught, landscape gardens that had drawn tourists for hundreds of years.

After an hour of walking past temples with fluted columns and painted doors, cupolas, obelisks, porticoes and follies, I started to freak out. Nothing made any sense. Greek Temples, Roman Temples, Saxon gods on runic plinths starred with orange lichen. A vast Gothic Temple in rouged ironstone. Palladian bridges, tufa grottoes and Doric arches. Nothing here seemed solid or understandable but the trees. The buildings littered the landscape as if they had been dropped by some crazed time machine, and all of them, I realised, were there to teach me a lesson. This was a landscape of aristocratic moral certainty, designed and built to lecture visitors of the dangers of modern vice and the ways of ancient virtue. It might have been the sun, it might have been incipient heatstroke, but I started to hate it. Here is the temple of British Worthies. Look at them all. *Ugh*. I turned round and began to walk back to the car. I was feeling extremely sorry for White. This was a very beautiful place, and a marvellous lesson in the exercise of power, but I would have felt unreal here, yes; I would have fled from it too. And I did. I fled from the school grounds. I got back in my car and drove, and parked, and then walked to the place where I had to go.

There it was, White's cottage, Merlyn's cottage, quiet on the Ridings over the hill. It looked so ordinary; not a magical place at all. Black leaf-shadows moved on its high gables. A grey horse grazed outside. Electric wires chased fenceposts down the grassy slopes. The forest behind the house was still there. But not all of it: the dark wood where the hobbies had been had gone; now it was Silverstone racing circuit, and the chapel where White had walked with Gos was long demolished; as Chapel Corner it is just a curve on the track under which the long-dead sleep. But as I stood there in the hot sunlight there was a buzzing in my ears. It was the strangest sound, as if on that windless day I could hear the marine roar of wind in all the oaks. It was winter history. Time's receding. Or possibly heatstroke. I wished I had brought some water.

I stood for a long while and looked at the house. It was a private place. I did not want to get closer; I didn't want to intrude on the person who lived there. But I saw that the trees had grown, that the barn was now a garage. The well would still be there. And then I heard a chipping, scraping noise, and froze. Behind a bush in the garden was a flash of white; a shirt. There was a man kneeling in the garden, bowed over the ground. Was he planting something? Weeding? Praying? I was far away. I could see his shoulders, but not his face, nor anything of him but his concentration. I shivered, because for a moment the man had been White, planting out his beloved geraniums. The feeling that White was haunting me had returned. I wondered if I should go and speak to this man. I could. I could talk to him. He wasn't White, I knew, but there were people here who had known him still, and I could talk to them. The farmhouse was still there, and behind it the ponds where Gos had bathed and White had fished. Perhaps the same carp swam in them. I could find out more about him, make him alive again, chase down the memories here. For a moment that old desire to cross over and bring someone back flared up as bright as flame.

But then I put that thought aside. I put it down, and the relief was immense, as if I had dragged a half-tonne weight from myself and cast it by the grassy road. White is gone. The hawk has flown. Respect the living, honour the dead. Leave them be. I saluted the man, though he could not see me. It was a silly, wobbly salute, and even as I did it I felt foolish. And then I turned and walked away. I left the man who was not a ghost, and I walked south. Over the bright horizon the sky swam like water.

Notes

Place of publication London unless otherwise stated.

1: Patience

7 *Travelling Sands* – John Evelyn, *Memoirs of John Evelyn*, ed. William Bray, Henry Colburn, 1827, vol. 2, p. 433.
7 *There are divers Sorts* – Richard Blome, *Hawking or Faulconry*, The Cresset Press, 1929 (originally published as part of *The Gentlemen's Recreation*, 1686), pp. 28–9.

3: Small worlds

21 *No matter how tame and loveable* – Frank Illingworth, *Falcons and Falconry*, Blandford Press Ltd, p. 76.
22 *She is noble in her nature* – Gilbert Blaine, *Falconry*, Philip Allan, 1936, pp. 229–30.
22 *Among the cultured peoples – ibid*, p. 11.
23 *Do not house your graceless austringers* – Gace de la Bigne, quoted in John Cummins, *The Hound and the Hawk*, Weidenfeld & Nicolson, 1988, p. 221.
23 *One cannot feel for a goshawk* – Gilbert Blaine, *Falconry*, Philip Allan, 1936, p. 182.

23 *Bloodthirsty ... Vile* – Major Charles Hawkins Fisher, *Reminiscences of a Falconer*, John Nimmo, 1901, p. 17.

27 *When I first saw him* – T. H. White, *The Goshawk*, Jonathan Cape, 1951, p. 11 (hereafter *The Goshawk*).

29 *The Goshawk is the story* – Back cover text, T. H. White, *The Goshawk*, Penguin Classics, 1979.

31 *For those with an interest* – Anonymous, review of *The Goshawk*, *The Falconer*, Vol. II, No. 5, 1952, p. 30.

33 *would be about the efforts* – *The Goshawk*, p. 27.

4: Mr White

35 *1) Necessity of excelling* – T. H. White, unpublished manuscript notebook 'ETC', Harry Ransom Humanities Research Center, University of Texas at Austin.

35 *Bennet is the name ... like a wagtail in the streets* – Letter from T. H. White to L. Potts, 18 January 1936, in *T. H. White, Letters to a Friend: The Correspondence between T. H. White and L. J. Potts,* ed. François Gallix, Alan Sutton, 1984, pp. 62–3.

36 *Because I am afraid of things* – T. H. White, *England Have My Bones*, Collins, 1936, p. 80 (hereafter *England Have My Bones*).

37 *I am told that my father* – T. H. White, quoted in Sylvia Townsend Warner, *T. H. White: A Biography*, Jonathan Cape 1967, p. 27.

37 *I pounce upon a bird* – T. H. White, unpublished manuscript notebook 'ETC', Harry Ransom Humanities Research Center, University of Texas at Austin.

38 *You will be sympathetic* – Sylvia Townsend Warner, unpublished manuscript of interview by François Gallix, 28 March 1974, Harry Ransom Humanities Research Center, University of Texas at Austin, p. 1.

38 *His sewing basket* – Sylvia Townsend Warner to William

Maxwell, 22 July 1967, in *The Elements of Lavishness: Letters of Sylvia Townsend Warner and William Maxwell 1938–1978*, ed. Michael Steinmann, Counterpoint, New York, 2001, p. 179.

39 *A magpie flies like a frying pan* – T. H. White, entry for 7 April 1939 in unpublished manuscript 'Journal 1938–1939', Harry Ransom Humanities Research Center, University of Texas at Austin.

39 *There is a sense of creation* – T. H. White, *England Have My Bones*, p. 59.

39 *Falling in love* – *ibid*, p. 31.

39 *He was an extremely tender-hearted* – David Garnett, *The White/Garnett Letters*, ed. David Garnett, The Viking Press, New York, 1968, p. 8.

39 *The safest way to avoid trouble* – Henry Green, *Pack My Bag: A Self-Portrait*, Vintage, 2000 (first published 1940), p. 58.

40 *is one of the best parlour games* – T. H. White, letter to Leonard Potts, 2 February 1931, in *T. H. White: Letters to a Friend*, p. 15.

40 *Can one wear topper* – T. H. White, unpublished letter to Ronald McNair Scott, 2 November 1931, Harry Ransom Humanities Research Center, University of Texas at Austin.

40 *I believe I did not misbehave* – T. H. White, unpublished manuscript 'Hunting Journal 1931–1933', Harry Ransom Humanities Research Center, University of Texas at Austin.

40 *concealed its individuality* – *England Have My Bones*, p. 15.

41 *almost always fatal . . . choke them like ivy* – *England Have My Bones*, p. 120.

41 *Independence – a state* – *England Have My Bones*, p. 105.

42 *train them to place no reliance . . . more food* – *ibid,* p. 121.

42 *it was impossible to impose* – *ibid*, p. 107.

42 *All through his life* – T. H. White, *The Once and Future King*, G.P. Putnam's Sons, New York, 1958, p. 327.

43 *tense, self-conscious . . . that of the human* – T. H. White, unpublished manuscript 'Hunting Journal 1931–1933',

Harry Ransom Humanities Research Center, University of Texas at Austin.

43 *boiling with a strange unrest* – T. H. White, unpublished manuscript 'A Sort of Mania', Harry Ransom Humanities Research Center, University of Texas at Austin.

43 *This party has no racial* – Harriet Hall, *Bill and Patience: An Eccentric Marriage at Stowe and Beyond*, Book Guild Ltd., 2000, p. 53.

43 *I was like that unfortunate man* – T. H. White, unpublished manuscript 'A Sort of Mania', Harry Ransom Humanities Research Center, University of Texas at Austin.

44 *It needed courage . . . a complete write-off* – T. H. White, letter to Leonard Potts, 16 May 1936, in *Letters to a Friend*, p. 70.

44 *We all stand in the shadow* – Denis Brogan, 'Omens of 1936', *Fortnightly Review,* 139 (Jan–June 1936), pp. 1–2.

44 *masters of men, everywhere* – T. H. White, unpublished manuscript 'A Sort of Mania', Harry Ransom Humanities Research Center, University of Texas at Austin.

44 *From being on the day* – Gilbert Blaine, *Falconry,* Philip Allan, 1936, p. 181.

45 *The sentence was: 'She reverted* – T. H. White, unpublished manuscript 'A Sort of Mania', Harry Ransom Humanities Research Center, University of Texas at Austin.

6: The box of stars

56 *Of all Hawks, she is doubtless* – Richard Blome, *Hawking or Faulconry*, The Cresset Press, 1929, p. 28.

57 *You're a good watcher* – John Le Carré, *Tinker Tailor Soldier Spy*, Hodder and Stoughton, 2001, (first published 1974) p. 16.

60 *It must have been like death* – *The Goshawk*, pp. 11–12.

61 *All that time was too beautiful . . . sent us to schools* – T. H. White, unpublished manuscript fragment 'A Valentine', Harry

Ransom Humanities Research Center, University of Texas at Austin.

61 *Please God, don't let me be beaten tonight . . . that charge* – T. H. White, unpublished manuscript 'Journals, Volume 6', entry dated 28 November 1957, T. H. White collection, Queens' College Library, Queens' College, Cambridge.

7: Invisibility

65 *A headlong dive of rage* – *The Goshawk*, p. 15.
72 *Your eye must see a composition* – Henri Cartier Bresson, 1957, in Adam Bernstein, 'The Acknowledged Master of the Moment', *The Washington Post*, Thursday 5 August, 2004, p. A01.

8: The Rembrandt interior

75 *Days of attack* – *The Goshawk*, p. 36.
75 *I had only just escaped* – T. H. White, in Sylvia Townsend Warner, *T. H. White: A Biography*, p. 90.
76 *I had been a schoolmaster* – T. H. White, unpublished manuscript 'A Sort of Mania', Harry Ransom Humanities Research Center, University of Texas at Austin.
76 *patient excursion into the fields* – *The Goshawk*, p. 27.
76 *dropped out of the curious . . . monastic boy* – T. H. White, entry for 20 January 1938 in unpublished manuscript notebook 'Horse', Harry Ransom Humanities Research Center, University of Texas at Austin.
77 *a velvet stoole* – Edmund Bert, *An Approved Treatise of Hawkes and Hawking.* 1619, repr. Thames Valley Press, Maidenhead, 1972, p. 22.
78 *I had a sort of schoolgirlish 'pash'* – T. H. White, unpublished manuscript 'A Sort of Mania', Harry Ransom Humanities Research Center, University of Texas at Austin.

78 *The old hawk masters had invented a means* – *The Goshawk*, p. 16.
78 *Man against bird* – *ibid*, p. 28.
78 *but the tragedy had to be kept out* – *ibid*, p. 64.

9: The rite of passage

86 *tolerate a loss of self* – A. D. Hutter, 'Poetry in psychoanalysis: Hopkins, Rossetti, Winnicott', *International Review of Psycho-Analysis*, vol. 9, 1982, pp. 303–16, p. 305. See: John Keats, letter to Richard Woodhouse, 27 October 1818, in John Keats, *Selected Letters*, Oxford University Press, Oxford, 2002, pp. 147–9.

10: Darkness

90 *6.15–6.45 walked round + round Gos* – T. H. White, unpublished manuscript notebook 'Flying Supplement', Harry Ransom Humanities Research Center, University of Texas at Austin.
92 *It was not that one drank enough* – *The Goshawk*, p. 68.
97 *The key to her management* – Gilbert Blaine, *Falconry*, Philip Allan, 1936, p. 181.
97 *the grand secret of discipline* – Edward Michell, *The Art and Practice of Hawking*, Methuen, 1900, p. 83.
97 *her eye doth still behold ... acquainted with any thing* – Edmund Bert, *An Approved Treatise of Hawkes and Hawking*, p. 16.

11: Leaving home

102 *For the goshawk, the necessity* – *The Goshawk*, p. 52.

102 *all the family. . . He bates repeatedly on these trips* – T. H. White, entry for Thursday 30 July, unpublished manuscript notebook 'Flying Supplement', Harry Ransom Humanities Research Center, University of Texas at Austin.

103 He had to learn to stand that bustle – *The Goshawk*, p. 101.

103 *the red moon . . . had seen to sink as a yellow one at dawn* – *ibid*, p. 53.

104 On the pastoral craze as cultural salvage, see Jed Esty, *A Shrinking Island: Modernism and National Culture in England*, Princeton University Press, 2003.

105 *I thought of the small race* – *The Goshawk*, p. 81.

12: Outlaws

111 *She purrs and chirps* – Humphrey ap Evans, *Falconry For You*, John Gifford, 1960, p. 36.

111 *peculiar and somewhat sulky* – Gilbert Blaine, *Falconry*, Philip Allan, 1936, p. 179.

111 *Never was there a more contrary* – Frank Illingworth, *Falcons and Falconry*, Blandford Press Ltd., 1948, p. 74.

111 *not like her or her kin* – Charles Hawkins Fisher, *Reminiscences of a Falconer*, John Nimmo, 1901, p. 17.

111 *a thousand pities* – Gage Earl Freeman and Francis Henry Salvin, *Falconry: Its Claims, History and Practice*, Longman, Green, Longman and Robert, 1859, p. 216.

112 *sociable and familiar . . . altogether shye and fearfull . . . stately and brave* – Simon Latham, *Lathams New and Second Booke of Falconry*, Roger Jackson, 1618, p. 3.

112 *joye in her selfe . . . my playfellow* – Edmund Bert, *An Approved Treatise of Hawkes and Hawking*, pp. 41–2.

114 *crazy and suspicious* – *The Goshawk*, pp. 146–7.

114 *man who for two months* – *ibid*, p. 37.

114 *The thing he most hates* – T. H. White, entry for 14 August

1936 in unpublished manuscript notebook 'Flying Supplement', Harry Ransom Humanities Research Center, University of Texas at Austin.

115 *monkish elite . . . small, tenacious sect* – Lord Tweedsmuir, 'Gos and Others', *Spectator Harvest*, ed. Henry Wilson Harris, Ayer Publishing, 1970, pp. 7–9, p. 8.

115 *deeply rooted in the nature . . . born, not made* – Gilbert Blaine, *Falconry*, Philip Allan, 1936, p. 13.

115 *It was not until I had kept some hawks* – T. H. White, unpublished manuscript 'A Sort of Mania', Harry Ransom Humanities Research Center, University of Texas at Austin.

115 *that ancestor's bony hand* – The Goshawk, p. 18.

115 *the wind in your face* – J. Wentworth Day, *Sporting Adventure*, Harrap, 1937, p. 205.

116 *Falconry is certainly of high descent . . . I believe he was mistaken* – Gage Earl Freeman and Francis Henry Salvin, *Falconry: Its Claims, History and Practice*, pp. 3–4.

13: Alice, falling

121 *Skipping and leaping* – The Goshawk, p. 100.

121 *was evidently a matter of exquisite assessment* – ibid, p. 95.

126 *Now, now* – ibid, p. 105.

126 *a hump-backed aviating Richard III* – ibid, p. 106.

127 *I braced the breast muscles* – ibid, p. 107.

127 *grow up a big, brave . . . any of these noble things* – England Have My Bones, pp. 349–50.

127 *I cry* prosit *loudly* – T. H. White, entry for Thursday 27 August, unpublished manuscript notebook 'Horse', Harry Ransom Humanities Reasearch Center, University of Texas at Austin.

131 *the wisdom of certainty* – T. H. White, unpublished manuscript 'You Can't Keep a Good Man Down', pp. 261–2, Harry Ransom Humanities Research Center, University of Texas at Austin.

131 *To anybody who has spent two months – ibid*, p. 271.
131 '*You went back to school voluntarily – ibid*, p. 263.

15: For whom the bell

146 *avoid the kicks which frighten me . . . actually a horrible surprise . . . only a man* – T. H. White, entry for 25 August 1936 in unpublished manuscript notebook 'Horse', Harry Ransom Humanities Research Center, University of Texas at Austin.

16: Rain

154 *insensate El Dorado – The Goshawk*, p. 124.
155 *It had hardly any breaking strain. It had already been broken twice – ibid*, p. 123.
156 *You bloody little sod . . . my fault – ibid*, p. 124.

17: Heat

161 *To him I am still the rarely tolerated enemy, and to me he is always the presence of death* – T. H. White, entry for 2 September 1936 in unpublished manuscript notebook 'Horse', Harry Ransom Humanities Research Center, University of Texas at Austin.
161 *I have lived for this hawk . . . never seen before – ibid*.
161 *growing sensual* – Sylvia Townsend Warner, *T. H. White: A Life*, p. 29.
162 *He has been frightened into insanity . . . and persecution* – T. H. White, entry for 2 September 1936 in unpublished manuscript notebook 'Horse', Harry Ransom Humanities Research Center, University of Texas at Austin.

18: Flying free

171 *Rooks observed to be mobbing* – Gilbert Blaine, *Falconry*, Philip Allan, 1936, p. 199.

173 *I cannot remember that my heart stopped beating* – *The Goshawk*, p. 136.

174 *Love asketh but himself* – William Blake, 'The Clod and the Pebble', misquoted in *The Goshawk*, p. 147.

19: Extinction

180 The exhibition was the excellent *Three Days of the Condor* by Henrik Håkansson, Kettle's Yard, Cambridge.

20: Hiding

188 *Consider this, and in our time . . . look there* – W. H. Auden 'Consider this' (first published 1930) in *The English Auden*, ed. Edward Mendelson, Faber & Faber, 1978, p. 46.

191 *Silver-gold through the blue haze* – T. H. White, unpublished manuscript notebook 'ETC', Harry Ransom Humanities Research Center, University of Texas at Austin.

192 *He was a Hittite* – *The Goshawk*, p. 214.

192 *I now flinch from anything frightful* – Siegfried Sassoon, unpublished letter to T. H. White, 15 October 1952, p. 1, Harry Ransom Humanities Research Center, University of Texas at Austin.

193 *tonic for the less forthright savagery* – *The Goshawk*, p. 212.

193 *At a particular point in the journey* – T. H. White, 'The Hastings Caves', *Time and Tide Magazine*, 8 December 1956, p. 152.

194 *It will be charming to have a rest* – T. H. White, *The Once and Future King*, G. P. Putnam's Sons, New York, 1958, p. 228.

21: Fear

202 *get for you a other passager Gos* – *The Goshawk*, p. 187.
202 *Plan for a Passage Gos . . . turns at this* – T. H. White, annotations to inside cover of Edmund Bert's *Treatise of Hawkes and Hawking*, Harry Ransom Humanities Research Center, University of Texas at Austin.
203 *It made me feel cleaner* – T. H. White, letter to John Moore, in Sylvia Townsend Warner, *T. H. White: A Biography*, p. 92.
204 *Think of Lust . . . like that* – *The Goshawk*, p. 204.

22: Apple Day

211 *humans and animals can turn into each other* – Rane Willerslev, 'Not Animal, Not Not-Animal: Hunting, Imitation and Empathetic Knowledge among the Siberian Yukaghirs', *The Journal of the Royal Anthropological Institute*, Vol. 10, No. 3 (Sept. 2004), pp. 629–52, p. 659.

23: Memorial

218 *Nature in her green, tranquil woods* – John Muir, *John of the Mountains: The Unpublished Journals of John Muir*, ed. Linnie Marsh Wolfe, 1938, repr. University of Wisconsin Press, Madison, Wisconsin, 1979, p. 208.
218 *Earth hath no sorrows that earth cannot heal* – *ibid*, p. 99.
220 On mourning in children and adults, see Melanie Klein, 'Mourning and its relation to manic depressive states', in *The*

Writings of Melanie Klein, Volume 1, Love, Guilt and Repa-ration, The Hogarth Press, 1940, pp. 344–69.

24: Drugs

225 *'Parfay!' quath he – Sir Orfeo and Sir Launfal*, ed. Lesley Johnson and Elizabeth Williams, The University of Leeds School of English, Leeds, 1984, p. 11.

226 *He departed secretly* – Geoffrey of Monmouth, *Vita Mer-lini*, ed. and trans. John J. Parry, *Illinois Studies in Language and Literature 10*, 1925, pp. 243–380.

227 *With the passion of an Edgar Wallace* – T. H. White, 'King Arthur in the Cottage', *Readers' News*, Volume 2, Number 3, August 1939, pp. 26–7, p. 26.

227 *It seems impossible to determine* – Letter to L. J. Potts, 14 January 1938, in *T. H. White, Letters to a Friend*, pp. 86–7.

229 *Every comely man* – John Cheever, *The Journals*, Jonathan Cape, 1990, p. 219.

230 The story of Puppy Mason is in T. H. White, unpublished manuscript fragment 'A Valentine', Harry Ransom Human-ities Research Center, University of Texas at Austin.

26: The flight of time

246 *Kingdom of Grammerie* – Sylvia Townsend Warner, *T. H. White: A Life*, p. 99.

246 *that of people desirous* – Alfred Adler, *The Practice and Theory of Individual Psychology*, Kegan Paul, Trench, Trubner & Co., 1924, p. 196.

247 *seemed to be creating itself* – *The Goshawk*, p. 186.

247 *born at the wrong end of Time* – T. H. White, *The Sword in the Stone*, Collins, 1938, p. 46.

247 *When I was a third-rate schoolmaster* – T. H. White, *The*

Book of Merlyn: The Unpublished Conclusion to The Once and Future King, University of Texas Press, Austin, 1977, p. 3.

248 *A good man's example – ibid*, p.128.

27: The new world

250 *One of my grandfathers . . . land management* – Logan J. Bennett, 'This is Ours to Fight For', *Outdoor Life*, November 1942, Volume 90, No. 3, pp. 32–3, p. 52.

257 *The initiation ceremonies . . . weaving and unwoven* – T. H. White, entry dated 22 August 1939 in unpublished manuscript 'Journal 1938–1939', Harry Ransom Humanities Research Center, University of Texas at Austin.

28: Winter histories

260 *The frequenter of downland* – H. J. Massingham, *English Downland*, B.T. Batsford, 1936, p. 5.

260–1 On the chalk-cults of interwar England, see Patrick Wright's excellent *The Village that Died for England*, Faber & Faber, 1995.

29: Enter spring

274 *How you can talk of love for a bird* – T. H. White, unpublished manuscript 'The Merlins', p. 20, Harry Ransom Humanities Research Center, University of Texas at Austin.

274 *one of the lunatic dukes – The Goshawk*, p. 215.

Acknowledgements

My thanks go first to those people who made this book possible, and two in particular: to my wonderful agent Jessica Woollard, for her friendship, expertise and long-standing support, and to my inspiring and extraordinary editor Dan Franklin at Jonathan Cape. I'd also like to thank everyone at the Marsh Agency, and Clare Bullock, Ruth Waldram, Joe Pickering and everyone else at Jonathan Cape who worked on this book behind the scenes.

For their patience, warmth and expertise during my research visit to the Harry Ransom Research Center at the University of Texas, Austin, I'd like to thank Jean M. Cannon, Pat Fox, Margi Tenney, and Richard Workman. And in Buckinghamshire, particular thanks to William Goldsmith, who showed me around Stowe School.

The greatest of love and thanks to my mother, brother, Cheryl, Aimee, Bea, and the rest of my family, of course, for letting me tell this story without even a flicker of worry about what I might say. And love and gratitude also to Christina McLeish, the best of friends and superb underfalconer, who was a fount of support after my father's death and during the writing of this book, and Olivia Laing, whose own books are a constant inspiration and whose wise counsel and good humour kept me writing; and to Stuart Fall and Amanda Lingham, who helped me through very dark times, and my surrogate American family: Erin Gott,

Paige Parkhill, Jim and Harriet Gott, Wyatt and Curran Gott, who always make me feel at home.

So many people helped me with friendship, love, inspiration, encouragement, or in other ways while I wrote this book. Thanks are due to them all: Pat Baylis, Steve Bodio, Lee Brindley, Tim Button, Tracy Carmichael, Jake Daum, Tim Dee, Steve Delaney, John Gallagher, Andrew Hunter, Tony James, Polly Appleby and Archie James, Conor Jameson, Boris Jardine, Nick Jardine, Bill Jones, Lauren Kassell, Tim Lewens and Emma Gilby, Josh Lida, Greg Liebenhals, John Loft, Robert Macfarlane and Julia Lovell, Robert and Margaret Mair, Scott McNeff, Gordon Mellor, Toby Metcalf, Patricia Monk, Adam Norrie, Rebecca O'Connor, Ian Patterson, Robert Penney, John Pittman, Marzena Pogorzaly, Joanna Rabiger, Mike Rampey, Joe Ryan for his chaffinches, Katharine Stubbs, and Lydia Wilson. Special thanks to Andrew Metcalf and to Fiona Mozley. And to Chris Wormell for his exquisite cover image.

And last of all, and most of all, I would like to thank my father, who taught me how to love the moving world, and to my beautiful hawk who taught me how to fly in it after he was gone. Mabel flew for many more seasons before a sudden, untreatable infection with Aspergillosis – an awful airborne fungus – carried her from her aviary to the dark woods where dwell the lost and dead. She is much missed.